Disability and the Life Course: Global Perspectives

Disability and the Life Course explores the global experience of disability using a novel life course approach. The book explores how disabling societies impact on disabled people's life experiences, and highlights the ways in which disabled people have acted to take more control over their own lives. It provides a unique combination of analysis, policy issues and autobiography, offering the reader a rare opportunity to make links between the theoretical, the political and the personal in a single volume. The material is set in a truly international context, with contributions from thirteen different countries bringing together established and emerging writers, both disabled and non-disabled. The book bridges some important gaps in the existing disability literature by including issues relevant to disabled people of all ages and with different kinds of impairments and also by offering a unique analysis of the relationship between disability and generation in a changing world.

MARK PRIESTLEY is Senior ESRC Research Fellow at the Disability Research Unit, University of Leeds. He has written on a number of disability-related topics, including theoretical paradigms, social movements, research methodology, multiple oppression, integrated living, community care and quality measurement. He is the author of *Disability Politics and Community Care* (1999), which was shortlisted for the British Sociological Association's Philip Abrams Memorial Prize.

Disability and the Life Course
Global Perspectives

Edited by Mark Priestley

2001

CAMBRIDGE
UNIVERSITY PRESS

CAMBRIDGE UNIVERSITY PRESS
Cambridge, New York, Melbourne, Madrid, Cape Town, Singapore,
São Paulo, Delhi, Dubai, Tokyo, Mexico City

Cambridge University Press
The Edinburgh Building, Cambridge CB2 8RU, UK

Published in the United States of America by Cambridge University Press, New York

www.cambridge.org
Information on this title: www.cambridge.org/9780521797344

© Cambridge University Press 2001

First published 2001

A catalogue record for this publication is available from the British Library

Library of Congress Cataloguing in Publication data
Disability and the Life Course: Global Perspectives / edited by Mark Priestley.
  p. cm.
Includes bibliographical references and index.
ISBN 0 521 79340 8 (hardback) – ISBN 0 521 79734 9 (paperback)
1. Handicapped.   2. Handicapped – Social conditions.
3. Handicapped – Cross-cultural studies.   I. Priestley, Mark, 1963–
HV1568.D5673   2001
305.9′0816–dc21   00–065156

ISBN 978-0-521-79340-7 Hardback
ISBN 978-0-521-79734-4 Paperback

'International Solidarity'
by Micheline Mason, England.

Our people can be found
In every class and race
Of every age and nation
Our people are awakening.
We will not beg
We will not hide
We'll come together
To regain our pride.

(extract from a song, performed by Frankie Armstrong)

Contents

List of figures   *page* ix
List of tables   x
Notes on contributors   xi
Preface   xv
Acknowledgements   xvi
A brief note on terminology   xvii

I   Concepts

1   Introduction: the global context of disability   3
     MARK PRIESTLEY

2   Repositioning disability and the life course: a social claiming
     perspective   15
     SARAH IRWIN

3   Marginalisation and disability: experiences from the
     Third World   26
     ANITA GHAI

4   Where do we draw the line?: surviving eugenics in a
     technological world   38
     GREGOR WOLBRING

5   A complicated struggle: disability, survival and social change
     in the majority world   50
     EMMA STONE

II   Methods and stories

6   Life event histories and the US independent living movement   67
     DEVVA KASNITZ

7   A journey of discovery   79
     SWAPNA MCNEIL

8   Using life story narratives to understand disability and
    identity in South Africa   RUTH MORGAN   89

9   Social change and self-empowerment: stories of disabled
    people in Russia   101
    ELENA IARSKIA-SMIRNOVA

10 Lifting the Iron Curtain   KAIDO KIKKAS   113

11 Revisiting deaf transitions   123
    MAIRIAN CORKER

12 The hidden injuries of 'a slight limp'   136
    DEVORAH KALEKIN-FISHMAN

III   The politics of transition

13 Disabled children: an emergency submerged   151
    SUE PHILPOTT and WASHEILA SAIT

14 Failing to make the transition? Theorising the 'transition to
    adulthood' for young disabled people   167
    KAY TISDALL

15 Breaking my head in the prime of my life: acquired
    disability in young adulthood   179
    ALLISON ROWLANDS

16 Work and adulthood: economic survival in the majority
    world   MAJID TURMUSANI   192

17 The possibility of choice: women with intellectual
    disabilities talk about having children   206
    KELLEY JOHNSON, RANNVEIG TRAUSTADÓTTIR,
    LYN HARRISON, LYNNE HILLIER and
    HANNA BJÖRG SIGURJÓNSDÓTTIR

18 Ageing with disability in Japan   219
    MIHO IWAKUMA

19 Ageing with intellectual disabilities; discovering disability
    with old age: same or different?   231
    NANCY BREITENBACH

20 Epilogue   MARK PRIESTLEY   240

Index   249

Figures

5.1 Revised version of the 'deprivation trap' *page* 53
6.1 Life course event history model 69
6.2 Multiple linear life course model 70
6.3 Model Key 72
6.4 Barbara's life event history 72
6.5 Annette's life event history 73
6.6 John's life event history 73
13.1 Significant factors to be addressed if the rights of disabled
  children are to be protected, and their full potential realised 159
13.2 Felicity's picture 162
13.3 Langalihle's picture 163
15.1 Competing discourses of human services 187

Tables

14.1 Extended transition to adulthood   *page* 172
19.1 Evolution of average life expectancy   231
19.2 The parallel myths of disability and old age   235

Notes on contributors

NANCY BREITENBACH is Chief Executive Officer of Inclusion International, the worldwide federation of societies for persons with intellectual disability. She was previously Head of Programmes for disabled people at the Fondation de France in Paris. Her area of interest is in increased life expectancy and its effects on disabled people.

MAIRIAN CORKER is Senior Research Fellow in the School of Education and Social Science, University of Central Lancashire, England, and Visiting Senior Research Fellow in the School of Education, Kings College, London. She is an executive editor of the international journal *Disability & Society*. Her research interests are in Deaf and disability studies.

ANITA GHAI is a disabled woman and an academic. She is currently a reader in the Department of Psychology, Jesus and Mary College, University of Delhi, India. Her research interests include developmental psychology, disabled women, children, and understanding motherhood in the context of disability.

LYN HARRISON is a lecturer in Health and Physical Education at Deakin University, Australia, and was formerly a research fellow at the Australian Research Centre in Sex, Health and Society at La Trobe University. Her interests include gender, identity formation, sexuality education and the social construction of sexualities.

LYNNE HILLIER is a social psychologist and research fellow at the Australian Research Centre in Sex, Health and Society, La Trobe University. Her research over the past five years has focused on cultural constructions of domestic violence, adolescence, marginalisation and sexuality, intellectual disability and sexuality.

ELENA IARSKIA-SMIRNOVA is Professor and Head of the Department of Social Work at Saratov State Technic University, Russia. She is a sociologist with an interest in social inequality, disability and gender studies. She has written specifically about Russian experiences of mothering disabled children.

SARAH IRWIN is Senior Lecturer in the Department of Sociology and Social Policy at the University of Leeds, England and a member of the ESRC Research Group for the Study of Care, Values and the Future of Welfare. Her research interests are in the sociology of the life course, and in contemporary transformations in family, work, welfare and inequality.

MIHO IWAKUMA is a disabled Japanese researcher, currently conducting doctoral research on communication and disability issues at the University of Oklahoma, USA. She is interested in globalisation, changing cultural values towards disabled people in Japan, and cross-cultural representations of disability.

KELLEY JOHNSON teaches and does research at the Australian Research Centre in Sex, Health and Society, La Trobe University, Australia. She has worked with women with learning difficulties for fifteen years as both researcher and advocate.

DEVORAH KALEKIN-FISHMAN grew up in New York in the 1920s and moved to the State of Israel shortly after its foundation. She is Senior Lecturer in the Faculty of Education at the University of Haifa, where her research interests include biographical research in sociology, the sociology of knowledge and the sociology of education.

DEVVA KASNITZ is Research Director for the NIDRR Research and Training Center on Independent Living and Disability Policy, at the World Institute on Disability, Oakland, USA. She has a background in anthropology and disability activism, and is a founding director of the Society for Disability Studies. She currently holds a Mary Switzer Fellowship to study life course approaches to peerage and leadership in the disability rights movement.

KAIDO KIKKAS grew up as a disabled child in the Soviet Union. He now works at the Rehabilitation Technology Laboratory, Tallinn Technical University, Estonia, where his research interests focus on the empowering potential of the Internet for disabled people.

SWAPNA MCNEIL grew up as a disabled young woman in India. She moved to England in the 1970s, where she later became a peer advocate, discovered disability, and established the Association of Blind Asians in Leeds.

RUTH MORGAN teaches at the Graduate School for Translators and Interpreters at the University of the Witwatersrand, South Africa. Her research focuses on the life stories of Deaf people.

SUE PHILPOTT is a member of the Disability Action Research Team, KwaZulu-Natal, South Africa. She has been involved with numerous action research projects in the area of disability, most recently with disabled children.

MARK PRIESTLEY is Senior ESRC Research Fellow in the Centre for Disability Studies at the University of Leeds, England and administrator of the international discussion forum *disability-research@ JISCmail.ac.uk* He is currently working on a three-year programme of research on disability, social policy and the life course.

ALLISON ROWLANDS teaches social work at the University of Newcastle, Australia, and is a community social worker with people with traumatic brain injury and their families. She is particularly interested in supporting friendships and genuine community participation.

WASHEILA SAIT is a staff member of the South African Federal Council on Disability. Prior to this, she was the national co-ordinator of the Disabled Children's Action Group (DICAG) formed in 1993 by parents, with the aim of empowering themselves to develop and educate their disabled children within an inclusive environment.

HANNA BJÖRG SIGURJÓNSDÓTTIR is a doctoral student at the University of Sheffield, England. She has worked as an advocate and researcher with people with learning difficulties for many years. Recently, her work has focused on mothers with learning difficulties.

EMMA STONE is Senior Research Manager for the disability programme of the Joseph Rowntree Foundation, England. Her personal research interests are in the area of disability and development in the majority world, particularly in China.

KAY TISDALL lectures in social policy at the University of Edinburgh and is Policy and Research Manager at Children in Scotland (the national policy development agency for organisations and professionals working with and for children and their families).

RANNVEIG TRAUSTADÓTTIR is Associate Professor at the University of Iceland, where she teaches on research methods, gender, disability and diversity, and does research with disabled and other minority women. She has worked as an advocate with women with learning difficulties for more than two decades.

MAJID TURMUSANI was involved in disability and development work with national and international non-governmental organisations in Jordan during the 1990s. His research interests include participatory and community based rehabilitation, research methods, employment and welfare rights for disabled people, culture and religious issues.

GREGOR WOLBRING is a research scientist at the Department of Biochemistry and Molecular Biology, and Adjunct Assistant Professor at the Department of Community Rehabilitation and Disability Studies, University of Calgary, Canada. He advises disability and equality rights groups on bioethical issues and is administrator of the international discussion group *Bioethics@egroups.com.*

Preface

This book examines how change in modern societies is affecting disabled people's lives, and how disabled people are acting to change the societies in which they live. It asks what we can learn about the nature of disabling societies from the life course experiences of disabled people.

The patterns of our lives, and the life course pathways that we follow, are influenced by many factors (from the global socio-economic context to unique aspects of our personal biography and embodied experience). Within this array, significant moments or turning points punctuate the lives of individuals and their generational cohorts. These moments may be historic events of national significance, local issues or personal encounters. Throughout our lives we also develop, and reproduce, shifting relationships of interdependence with other people – not only as individuals but also collectively, through our communities and states.

This book takes as its starting point the lived experiences of disabled people in a range of cultural contexts. The chapters vary considerably in their scope, from the individual and the personal to the political and the cross-national. The book offers an analysis of disability and generation in a changing world, including issues relevant to disabled people of all ages, in many societies.

The chapters include contributions from thirteen different countries across five continents, bringing together established and emerging writers, both disabled and non-disabled. The content provides a combination of theoretical analysis, policy issues and personal life stories. In this way, it offers opportunities to make links between the theoretical, the political and the personal. My hope is that it will contribute to a better understanding of the expanding field of disability studies and to the development of life course methods within the social sciences.

Acknowledgements

The bulk of the credit for this book is due to the many contributors, for their creativity and diligence in producing such a readable text. Special thanks are due to Emma Stone for widening my horizons, to Sarah Irwin for helping me to make connections, and to Mairian Corker, Alison Sheldon, A.K.M. Momin and Carolyn Baylies for thoughtful comments on some of the initial drafts. My own input has been part of a three-year programme of research on disability, social policy and the life course, funded by a fellowship award from the UK Economic and Social Research Council (award number R000271078). Finally, this book would not have happened at all without the development of inter-national dialogue through the Internet discussion group *disability-research@jiscmail.ac.uk*, funded through the UK Higher Education Funding Council.

A brief note on terminology

Those familiar with the existing disability studies literature will be aware that there has been a great deal of academic and political debate about the choice of appropriate terminology. Since the emergence of the disabled people's movement, there have been moves away from the language of 'handicap' towards a more politicised notion of 'disability'. However, there are variations both within and between national cultures. Within the Anglophone world, the increasing popularity of 'people first' language (Vaughan 1993) led to the frequent use of terms such as 'persons with disabilities' (particularly in North America). Yet, there has also been considerable resistance to such language from within the disabled people's movement (particularly in Britain). Increasingly, the spread of social model thinking has resulted in preference for the term 'disabled people', emphasising the structural or cultural location of disability, as a form of social oppression residing outside the person. However, such debates are considerably complicated in the translation of terms and concepts between languages (*see* for example, Stone 1999).

Disability discourse and language is highly contextual (Corker and French 1999). It is both culturally and historically situated. Bearing in mind these complexities, and the cross-cultural analysis presented in this book, I have encouraged the contributors to exercise their own choice of words in describing the experience and location of disability. However, I have also encouraged them to be reflexive and critical in their choices, especially in responding to the claims of disabled people for self-determination in defining their own experience. Inevitably, this results in some inconsistencies of language within the book, particularly in the use of quotations from other sources. For my own part, I have chosen to adopt the term 'disabled people', as articulated within the British disabled people's movement (*see* Priestley in Corker and French 1999: 7). In this sense, I understand disability to refer to a form of social oppression, experienced by people with perceived impairments and manifested in discriminatory practices. To borrow a much used quote:

In our view, it is society which disables . . . Disability is something imposed on top of our impairments, by the way we are unnecessarily isolated and excluded from full participation in society. Disabled people are therefore an oppressed group in society. (UPIAS/Disability Alliance 1976: 3)

It is from this perspective that I have commissioned the various chapters. However, each individual contribution reflects the authors' own views on the complex and dynamic relationship between social environments and the lived experience of disabled people.

Outline of the book

The aim of the book is to explore the relationship between disability and generation using a life course approach. The method locates the lived experience of disability within contexts of time and place, focusing on different societies and generational cohorts. The book is organised in three parts.

Part one addresses concepts of disability and the life course in a global context. Connections are made between disability and generation, and disability is identified as a global 'life and death' issue. Particular attention is paid to understanding the links between social organisation, social change and the liberation of disabled people. Part two highlights the use of narrative life course methods in disability research. This section includes both research based writing and autobiography. The emphasis here is to demonstrate how a greater knowledge of life course trajectories and generational pathways in different societies can help us to understand both the processes of disablement and the opportunities for self-empowerment in a changing world. Part three provides a number of case studies relating to specific generational issues in particular cultural contexts. These studies help to illustrate the significance of social context in the experience of disability throughout the life course.

The book concludes with an epilogue, in which I have drawn together some core issues and questions. In particular, I have sought to emphasise the research potential of a life course approach in disability studies, and the significance of thinking about disability in relation to generation and the life course.

REFERENCES

Corker, M. and French, S. (eds.) (1999) *Disability Discourse*, Open University Press, Milton Keynes.
Stone, E. (1999a) 'Modern slogan, ancient script: impairment and disability in

the Chinese language', in M. Corker and S. French (eds.) (1999) *Disability Discourse*, Open University Press, Milton Keynes.

UPIAS/Disability Alliance (1976) *Fundamental Principles of Disability*, UPIAS/Disability Alliance, London.

Vaughan, C. (1993) 'People First Language: an unholy crusade', *Braille Monitor*, August 1993: 868–70.

I

Concepts

1   Introduction: the global context of disability

Mark Priestley

Disability is a global issue. More than half a billion disabled people live in the world today – approximately one in ten of the population. This number is set to rise dramatically over the next twenty-five years, both in richer technological societies and in the poorer majority (International Disability Foundation 1998). At the same time, disabled people throughout the world are empowering themselves to claim greater participation, integration and equality. Such claims are not only about greater control over individual lives but also about greater influence over the social structures within which such lives are lived. For this reason, it is impossible to disentangle the lived experience of disability from the context of disabling societies. They are part of the same story. The various contributions in this book demonstrate the complexity of this connection and reveal how disabling barriers and enabling strategies interact in a changing world.

Uneven economic and political development means that impairment and disability affect children, adults and older people differently in different societies. According to United Nations (UN) estimates, around 80 per cent of disabled people live in so-called 'developing' countries. More accurately, we might say that most disabled people spend most of their lives in the 'majority world' (Stone 1999). Yet, the academic literature of disability studies consistently privileges minority world accounts (especially, those from Western Europe and North America). The result is that disability (in both medical and social model senses) has been framed within a minority worldview. Consequently, it is important to think about disability issues in the bigger picture. As Majiet (1998: 1) argues:

If one looks at the [disability] agenda, we can ask who sets the agenda globally for human rights. My impression and humble opinion is that this agenda is very much set by the North and that we need to take issue with that.

Similarly, Montero (1998: 1) observes that, 'When we come to the developed countries from the underdeveloped countries we see differences. We are fighting for different issues.' Such differences can lead to differences in political emphasis between disabled people in different regions. So, for example, while disabled people's organisations in the UK were campaigning against the principle of charitable support from the National Lottery, disabled people in Thailand were protesting to maintain the employment of disabled Lottery ticket sellers. Such differences are not necessarily conflictual but they do illustrate some of the societal influences at work in defining the disability rights agenda.

The issues facing disabled people in rich technological countries, with highly developed welfare provision, are indeed different from those in the majority world. In a global context, most disabled people encounter both disabling barriers *and* barriers to scarce resources (Coleridge 1993). Access to resources is highly gendered, and the life experiences of disabled women require specific attention. Generational issues are also important and the life experiences, or life chances, of disabled children and disabled elders merit particular attention.

Majority world perspectives do exist, particularly within the 'rehabilitation' literature, and within the growing body of knowledge emanating from the international disabled people's movement. However, such contributions are rarely cited within the academic literature of disability studies. In order to address this, a number of contributions in this book relate directly to majority world experiences. In particular, Anita Ghai (chapter three) and Emma Stone (chapter five) seek to re-conceptualise disability and personhood within a majority world context, while Majid Turmusani (chapter sixteen) considers the particular significance of paid employment for disabled adults in the majority world.

The international policy agenda

Over the past twenty-five years, disability has moved from the margins to the mainstream of the international human rights agenda. It was in 1975 that the UN General Assembly made its first Declaration on the Rights of Disabled Persons. Following the Declaration, the UN proclaimed 1981 as the International Year of Disabled Persons (IYDP) and embarked upon the development of a World Programme of Action. In 1985, the Universal Declaration of Human Rights was specifically extended to include disabled people. The focus provided by the UN Action Plan and IYDP gave rise to many debates within the international policy community and the emergent disabled people's movement.

Towards the end of the Decade of Disabled Persons (1983–92) the UN began work to develop a longer-term strategy under the slogan 'towards a society for all' (UN 1983) and 1992 saw the establishment of an International Day of Disabled Persons (marked on 3 December each year). Implementation of the long-term strategy, at national, regional and global levels, also coincided with the development of new *Rules on the Equalization of Opportunities for Disabled Persons* (UN 1993). The UN Rules address participation in eight specific areas of life: accessibility, education, employment, income maintenance and social security, family life and personal integrity, culture, recreation and sports, and religion. Social model definitions of disability also became more mainstream thus, 'society creates a handicap when it fails to accommodate the diversity of all its members', and, 'People with disabilities often encounter attitudinal and environmental barriers that prevent their full, equal and active participation in society . . .' (United Nations 1994, paras 3 and 4).

Within this changing global policy framework there has been a great deal of uneven regional development. In 1995, the Danish Council of Organisations of Disabled People commissioned an index to monitor implementation of the UN Rules (DCODP 1995). The results of this research, in forty-six countries, provided a very patchy picture of progress towards the universalisation of opportunities for disabled people. There was evidence that some states with a relatively long history of addressing disability issues through public policy (such as the Scandinavian countries) still had a long way to go, while others with less disability policy history (such as South Africa and Uganda) had made good progress. However, a further UN survey of eighty-eight governments (Michailakis 1997) suggested that at least 80 per cent of states had reformulated their thinking on disability issues in response to the UN Rules.

Since IYDP and the introduction of the UN Rules, more and more states have introduced anti-discriminatory legislation. However, as Masemene (1992) notes, such legislation does not arise spontaneously within state constitutions, which are generally framed to protect majority interests, and 'This process must be preceded by sensitisation/ politicisation or conscientisation of society or the community'. The self-organisation of disabled people has been the major catalyst in these processes. Ironically (from a Western perspective) progress towards civil rights in developing countries has sometimes proved easier than in richer parts of the world, although implementation has often been difficult (O'Toole and McConkey 1995).

For example, little attention was paid to disability issues during the first twenty-five years of the European Economic Community (EEC). Verney (1996) notes how the founding Treaties on European Union failed even to mention disability (up to and including the much-vaunted Maastricht Treaty). Indeed, it was not until a report published for the 1996 European Day of Disabled Persons that disabled people were overtly recognised as citizens, consumers and workers within the Union (Waddington *et al.* 1996). Under concerted pressure from disability organisations, the EU finally made disability rights 'visible' in the 1997 Amsterdam Treaty (e.g. Article 13). In the majority world, issues of economic survival can easily outweigh the apparent benefits of such legislation on paper (Nkeli 1998).

Disabled people's self-organisation

Mirroring the global context of disability, disabled people have organised on an international scale. The primary mechanism for this has been the development of Disabled Peoples' International (DPI). Officially founded in Singapore in December 1981, the main purpose of DPI is 'to promote the human rights of disabled people through full participation, equalisation of opportunities, and development' (DPI constitution; see also, Driedger 1989). As an international representative forum, DPI now has consultative status with the UN, the ILO and UNESCO. Within DPI, national and regional assemblies represent the interests of disabled people in each member state. DPI includes organisations from some 130 countries, although there are still about thirty countries with no national assembly of disabled people.

Speaking at a seminar in Sweden in 1998, Kalle Könkkölä (then chairperson of DPI) emphasised the significance of DPI's mission as a human rights organisation in the majority world.

As chairperson I have felt that DPI's meaning is more important in the Southern, Eastern and developing countries than in the Western countries especially when we look at the level of commitment. Of course the organisations in Western Europe have a commitment of working together but it appears as if the expectations on DPI are greater outside of Europe than in Europe. (Könkkölä 1998)

In this way, the disabled people's movement has adopted an internationalist perspective from its inception, seeking to draw on the common strengths and diverse experiences of disabled people throughout the world. As Heumann (1998) argues:

We need to focus more on what each country is respectively doing and to look at ways that we can benefit from the different political and philosophical approaches that countries are taking. We need to look at the actual work that is going on within those countries and to learn about strategies that those countries are taking. We have to have some meaningful discussions about where we feel we are being successful, what we believe success is the result of and what we believe needs to occur in order to allow us both in our individual country and across the world to be a more powerful movement. (Heumann 1998)

Although the development of disabled people's organisations in the USA, the UK and parts of mainland Europe has been well documented in the disability studies literature, there has been much less awareness about developments elsewhere. Yet, disabled people's organisations have been very active in the majority world. For example, Jayasooria and Ooi (1994) analyse the development of the disabled people's movement in Malaysia, while Shah (1990) examines some of the issues for self-help organisations in Pakistan. Here, negative cultural attitudes and the problem of communicating with those in rural areas raised many barriers to mobilisation.

The 'African Decade of Disabled People', was launched by DPI in December 2000, organised by the Pan-African Federation of the Disabled (PAFOD), with the aim of effecting 'permanent positive impact for the region's population with disabilities' (Wong-Hernandez 1999). Jogie (undated) describes how the development of self-help groups led to the formation, in 1984, of Disabled People South Africa (DPSA). The issues facing disabled people there included negative stereotyping, lack of access to apartheid services for black disabled people, widespread poverty and violence. Nkeli (1998) provides a specific account of the Self-Help Association of Paraplegics in Soweto (arising from disabled survivors of the government massacre there in 1976) and their subsequent politicisation within the independent living movement. In her chapter for this book, Ruth Morgan (chapter eight) draws directly on the life experiences of three black disabled people during these developments.

War and peace

Armed conflict and political instability have had a dramatic effect on disabled people's lives. Indeed, as Driedger (1987) notes, 'Disabled persons' rights as human beings are violated in wars and armed conflict every day around the globe'. Today, there are millions of disabled refugees and displaced persons in and around war zones such as the Middle East, the Balkans, Central Africa and South East Asia. For earlier generations, war was a significant factor in Western Europe and North America too, yet it may never be an issue for younger disabled people living there today.

In many parts of the world, war is a major cause of impairment. Consequently, world peace has become a disability issue. For example, at least 2,000 people are killed or injured every month by landmines in more than seventy countries around the world, and much attention was focused on this issue at DPI's 1998 World Assembly in Mexico City. Similarly, a visit by the DPI World Council to Hiroshima (site of the first atomic bombing by the United States) resulted in an International Peace Declaration by disabled people's organisations.

War and political upheaval have a variety of impacts on disabled people's lives, not all of them negative. For example, Montero (1998) draws on the Sandinista revolution in Nicaragua to illustrate how political circumstance can influence the life course pathways of disabled people (*see* also, Bruun 1995). As with other conflicts around the world, many Nicaraguans became disabled during the war. However, veterans experienced disability in very different ways to those who were disabled before the revolution. Making comparisons with Vietnam veterans in the USA, Montero notes how, 'These disabled people were practically considered national heroes and were given all the opportunities possible to develop and strengthen their own organisations' (and not only to those on the Sandinista side).

Similarly, the dramatic political changes sweeping through the countries of the former Eastern block since 1989 have not been entirely negative for disabled people. Thus, Brichtová (1998) argues, 'The vision of democracy has affected also the lives of people with disabilities. Maybe for the first time in our history, their views and desires for real civil involvement and participation have been heard in public'. Those who have lived through these changes are witness to such impact in their lives. Thus, in chapter nine Elena Iarskia-Smirnova reviews her research into the life course events surrounding the self-empowerment of disabled people in post-Soviet Russia, while in chapter ten Kaido Kikkas tells his own story, of life as a disabled person in both pre- and post-Soviet Estonia.

Work, education and poverty

In the modern world, work and employment are major signifiers of independent adulthood (particularly male adulthood). Yet, disabled men and women throughout the world continue to be disproportionately unemployed, underemployed and underpaid (along with young people and women), resulting in conditions of extreme poverty for many millions of their families. In 1983, the International Labour Organization (ILO) adopted a convention of international standards to ensure equality of opportunity and treatment for disabled persons in relation to employment and social integration. Article 4 notes that:

The said policy shall be based on the principle of equal opportunity between disabled workers and workers generally. Equality of opportunity and treatment for disabled men and women workers shall be respected. Special positive measures aimed at effective equality of opportunity and treatment between disabled workers and other workers shall not be regarded as discriminating against other workers. (ILO 1983, Article 4)

As global markets and technologies develop in new ways, access to education becomes ever more important, particularly for children and young people. Yet, many disabled people have been denied educational opportunities to develop the knowledge and skills required for survival in a changing world (Peters 1993). Many millions have been excluded from formal education altogether. Shah (1990: 51) draws on her own life experience, as a young blind woman in Pakistan, arguing that, ' . . . disabled females, children and girls are not considered fit for education and according to general belief its utility is nil'. These barriers to education leave many young disabled women in poverty and dependent upon their families in many countries. Others have found themselves segregated in socially stigmatised special schools. Negative attitudes and access to resources both play a part here (IDDC 1998). In addressing these issues, the UN seeks to:

Ensure equal educational opportunities at all levels for children, youth and adults with disabilities, in integrated settings, taking full account of individual differences and situations. (World Summit on Social Development 1995, Commitment 6f)

Differential access to the benefits of work and education means that world poverty is a key issue for disabled people (Beresford 1996). Indeed, the first priority in DPI's current action plan (1999–2002) is, 'to eradicate poverty so that people with disabilities enjoy a good quality of life along with their communities'. As Majiet (1998) argues:

In the South's reality we are looking at basic rights, at survival. Many of the rights, and fruits of freedom that you enjoy in the North are well beyond survival. At this stage there is this gap and we would need to close it in our relations to make sense between North and South . . . We are talking about worlds apart . . .

In a global context, poor people are more likely to be affected by impairment and disability, and disabled people are more likely to live in poverty. The causes of such disadvantage are not simply to do with disabling attitudes or prejudice. They are deeply rooted in structural inequalities and conflicts arising from uneven economic, technological and political development (Kisanji 1995). Disabled women are particularly disadvantaged in this way (Boylan 1991). In chapter three,

Anita Ghai graphically illustrates the interaction of poverty and gender in the life experiences of disabled people in India.

In a commitment to eradicate absolute poverty within member states, the UN Copenhagen Declaration on Social Development aimed to, 'Develop and implement policies to ensure that all people have adequate economic and social protection during unemployment, ill health, maternity, child-rearing, widowhood, disability and old age' (World Summit on Social Development 1995, Commitment 2d). To this end the Declaration includes specific pledges on equal educational opportunities for disabled children and young people, access to independent living services and to assistive technology.

Independent living

The concept of independent living (or integrated living) has been a central theme in the development of disabled people's self-organisation, and in disabled people's claims to greater self-determination. As Evans (1993: 63) puts it, 'Life is more than just a house and getting up and going to bed. Independent Living is about the whole of life and it encompasses everything'.

However, a recent review of independent living in forty countries (Doe 1998) shows just how variable the implementation of independent living concepts can be in different socio-economic and cultural contexts. Disabled people in the minority world have claimed independent living resources to maximise individual choice, and to escape from segregated welfare state institutions. For disabled people in the majority world survival often came before issues of equality. In such circumstances, the development of micro-economic enterprises and segregated sheltered employment schemes has been a common user-led response. For example, in Brazil, all of the recently founded centres for independent living are based on employment projects (by comparison, those in North America and Europe have not taken up employment as a major function).

In Western Europe, the concept of independent living has become closely associated with demands for control over the employment of personal assistants. At the first European Independent Living Conference (held in April 1989 at the European Parliament in Strasbourg, France) representatives from fourteen European countries met to discuss personal assistance services. The meeting affirmed disabled people's claims to expertise and self-determination over their own lives, and condemned the provision of segregated services as a violation of human rights. The conference resulted in the founding of the European Network for Independent Living (ENIL 1989).

Writers in the United States frequently lay claim to the birth of the independent living movement there, in the wake of earlier civil rights struggles. For example, the Centre for Independent Living (CIL) at Berkeley, California (founded in 1973) is often regarded as the first of its kind, although parallel developments in Europe were also important around the same time (*see* Klapwijk 1981; Zola 1987 or Davis 1993). In her chapter for this book, Devva Kasnitz (chapter six) examines the life event histories of disabled people who were involved with the early American independent living movement of the 1960s and 1970s. In this way, she examines the utility of a life course approach in explaining some of the choices and social conditions that led disabled individuals to become political activists at that time.

A matter of life and death

In both majority and minority world contexts, disability is a life and death issue. There is a growing body of knowledge about the diverse policies and practices that result in decreased life chances and life expectancy of disabled people around the world. In this sense, the extermination of disabled people at the hands of Nazi doctors (Lifton 1986) the abandonment of disabled children in Russia (Human Rights Watch 1998) the mass sterilisation of disabled people in Scandinavia (Munthe 1996), eugenic social policies in China (Stone 1996), poverty in the Indian sub-continent, physician assisted suicide in the USA (Dworkin *et al.* 1998), and the eugenic possibilities of the Human Genome Project are not unconnected in the continuing threat to disabled people's lives at the beginning of the twenty-first century. Thus, in chapter four, Gregor Wolbring asks whether we can 'draw the line' between disabled and non-disabled lives.

One of the purposes of this book then is to challenge the concept of 'normal' life course progression in the modern world. The various chapters demonstrate how the diversity of life experience and life style in a globalising world sit uncomfortably alongside policies and practices intended to police the boundaries of normal life course progression. The increasing claims of disabled people for self-determination, choice and control over their lives highlight the significance of this paradox. The lived experience of disabled people in different societies offers an important insight towards its resolution.

REFERENCES

Beresford, P. (1996) 'Poverty and disabled people: challenging dominant debates and policies', *Disability & Society*, 11(4): 553–67.

Boylan, E. (1991) *Women and Disability*, Zed Books, London.

Brattgard, S. (1972) 'Sweden: Fokus: a way of life for living', in D. Lancaster-Gaye (ed.) *Personal Relationships, the Handicapped and the Community*, Routledge and Kegan Paul, London.

Brichtová, L. (1998) *Independent Living and Proposed Slovak Social Reforms*, paper presented to the Legislation for Human Rights conference, Stockholm, Sweden, 24 August 1998.

Bruun, F. (1995) 'Hero, beggar, or sports star: negotiating the identity of the disabled person in Nicaragua', in B. Ingstad and S. Whyte (eds.) *Disability and Culture*, University of California Press, Berkeley, CA, USA.

Coleridge, P. (1993) *Disability, Liberation and Development*, Oxfam, Oxford.

Danish Council of Organisations of Disabled People (1995) *Disability Index*, DCODP, Hvidovre, Denmark.

Davis, K. (1981) '28–38 Grove Road: accommodation and care in a community setting', in Brechin, A., Liddiard, P., Swain, J. (eds.) (1981) *Handicap in a Social World*, Hodder and Stoughton, London.

Davis, K. (1993) 'On the movement', in Swain, J., Finkelstein, V., French, S. and Oliver, M. (eds.) (1993) *Disabling Barriers: Enabling Environments*, Open University Press/SAGE, Milton Keynes.

Doe, T. (1998) *Cultural Variations of Independent Living: an international review*, World Institute on Disability, Oakland, CA, USA (unpublished).

Driedger, D. (1987) Disabled Peoples' International, *Rehabilitation Gazette*, 28: 13–14.

Driedger, D. (1989) *The Last Civil Rights Movement: Disabled People's International*, Hurst & Co., London.

Dworkin, G., Frey, R. and Bok, S. (1998) *Euthanasia and Physician-Assisted Suicide (For and Against)*, Cambridge University Press, New York, USA.

European Disability Forum (1998) *Guide to the Amsterdam Treaty*, EDF, Brussels, Belgium.

Evans, J. (1993) 'The role of centres of independent/integrated living', in C. Barnes (ed.) *Making Our Own Choices: Independent Living, Personal Assistance and Disabled People*, British Council of Disabled People, Clay Cross, England.

Hastie, R. (1997) *Disabled Children in a Society at War: A Casebook from Bosnia*, Oxfam, UK and Ireland, Oxford.

Heumann, J. (1998) *Human Rights and Disability*, paper presented to the Seminar on Human Rights for Persons with Disabilities from a North and South Perspective, Stockholm, Sweden, 23 August 1998.

IDDC (International Disability and Development Consortium) (1998) *Inclusive Education: Making A Difference, Report of an International Seminar*, Agra, India, printed by Save the Children Fund, Delhi.

Ingstad, B. (1995) 'Public discourses in rehabilitation; from Norway to Botswana', in B. Ingstad and S. Whyte (eds.) *Disability and Culture*, University of California Press, Berkeley CA, USA.

International Disability Foundation (1998) *World Disability Report*, IDF, Geneva, Switzerland.

International Labour Organisation (1983) *Convention Concerning Vocational Rehabilitation and Employment (Disabled Persons)*, ILO, C159, 20 June 1983, Geneva, Switzerland.

Jagoe, K. (undated) *The Disability Rights Movement: Its Development in South Africa*, Disabled People South Africa, PO Box 662, 5256 Gonuble, Republic of South Africa.

Jayasooria, D. and Ooi, G. (1994) 'Disabled People's Movement in Malaysia', *Disability & Society*, 11(2): 97–100.

Kallehauge, H. (1999) 'Rating the Rules', *Disability International*, 6 (1).

Kalyanpur, M. (1996) 'The Influence of Western special education on community-based services in India', *Disability & Society*, 11(2): 249–70.

Kisanji, J. (1995) 'Growing up disabled', in P. Zinkin and H. McConachie (eds.) *Disabled Children and Developing Countries*, Clinics in Developmental Medicine, No. 136, MacKeith Press, London.

Klapwijk, A. (1981) 'Het Dorp, an adapted part of the City of Arnhem (The Netherlands) for severely disabled people', in Development Trust for the Young Disabled (booklet 5/81), *An International Seminar on the Long-term Care of Disabled People*, DTYD, London.

Könkkölä, K. (1998) *Disabled Peoples International (DPI): Perspective on Human Rights*, paper presented to the Seminar on Human Rights for Persons with Disabilities from a North and South Perspective, Stockholm, Sweden, 23 August 1998.

Lifton, Robert J. (1986) *The Nazi Doctors: Medical Killings and the Psychology of Genocide*, Basic Books, New York, USA.

Lindqvist, B. (1998) *Experience of International Legislation* [in Swedish], paper presented to the 'Conference on Legislation for Human Rights', arranged by Handikappombudsmannen in co-operation with Independent Living Sverige, Stockholm, Sweden, 24 August 1998.

Majiet, S. (1998) *Human Rights from Disabled Peoples' Perspective in Africa*, paper presented to the Seminar on Human Rights for Persons with Disabilities from a North and South Perspective, Stockholm, Sweden, 23 August 1998.

Masemene, M. (1992) *Constitutionalism and Access Legislation*, paper presented to the CIB Expert Seminar on Building Non-Handicapping Environments, Harare, Zimbabwe.

Michailakis, D. (1997) *Government Action on Disability Policy: A Global Survey*, Liber Publishing, Stockholm, Sweden.

Montero, F. (1998) *Human Rights and Organisations of Disabled Persons in Costa Rica*, paper presented to the Seminar on Human Rights for Persons with Disabilities from a North and South Perspective, Stockholm, Sweden, 23 August 1998.

Munthe, C. (1996) *The Moral Roots of Prenatal Diagnosis: Ethical Aspects of the Early Introduction and Presentation of Prenatal Diagnosis in Sweden*, Studies in Research Ethics no. 7, Centre for Research Ethics, Götenborg, Sweden.

Nkeli, J. (1998) *How to Overcome Double Discrimination of Disabled People in South Africa*, paper presented to the Legislation for Human Rights conference, Stockholm, Sweden, 24 August 1998.

O'Toole, B. and McConkey, R. (eds.) (1995) *Innovations in Developing Countries for People with Disabilities*, Lisieux Hall, Chorley.

Peters, S. (ed.) (1993) *Education and Disability in Cross-Cultural Perspective*, Garland, London.

Quinn, G., McDonagh, M. and Kimber, C. (1993) *Disability Discrimination Law in the United States, Australia and Canada*, Oak Tree Press, Dublin, Ireland.

Ratzka, A. (1997) *Independent Living and Our Organisations*, paper presented to 'Our Common World' conference organised by Disability Rights Advocates Hungary in Siofok, Hungary, 9–11 May 1997.

Shah, F. (1990) *Disability, Self Help and Social Change*, Bungalow no. 54, 12th Street, Phase V, Defence Housing Society, Karachi, Pakistan.

Stone, E. (1996) 'A law to protect, a law to prevent: contextualising disability legislation in China', *Disability & Society*, 11(4): 469–83.

Stone, E. (ed.) (1999) *Disability and Development: Learning from Action and Research on Disability in the Majority World*, Disability Press, Leeds.

Thomsen, S. (1996) *A Cross-National Pilot Test of the DSI Index for the Rights and Opportunities for Persons with Disabilities*, paper presented at the international seminar on 'Methods for studying living conditions of persons with disabilities', by the Swedish Council for Social Research, Uppsala, 12–13 November 1996.

United Nations (1975) *Declaration on the Rights of Disabled Persons*, General Assembly resolution 3447, 9 December 1975.

United Nations (1983) *World Programme of Action Concerning Disabled Persons*, United Nations, New York, USA.

United Nations (1994) 'Towards a society for all: long-term strategy to implement the world programme of action concerning disabled persons to the year 2000 and beyond', annex to *Implementation of the World Programme of Action Concerning Disabled Persons*, Report of the Secretary-General, 27 September 1994.

UPIAS and the Disability Alliance (1976) *Fundamental Principles of Disability*, UPIAS/Disability Alliance, London.

Verney, A. (1996) *EU Programmes With Relevance to Persons With Disabilities*, paper presented to the European Network on Independent Living, Stockholm, 10 June 1996.

Waddington, L., Hendriks, A., McCarthy, T. and Wall, J. (1996) *How Can Disabled Persons in the European Union Achieve Equal Rights as Citizens? The Legal and Economic Implications of a Non-discrimination Clause in the Treaty of European Union*, a report by the Legal and Economic Expert Working Group of the European Union, Brussels, Belgium.

Wong-Hernandez, L. (1999) 'African decade of disabled persons', *Disability International*, 6(1).

World Summit for Social Development (1995) *Copenhagen Declaration on Social Development*, Copenhagen, Denmark.

Zola, I. (1987) 'The politicisation of the self-help movement', *Social Policy*, 18: 32–3.

2   Repositioning disability and the life course: a social claiming perspective

Sarah Irwin

A life course orientation sensitises us to various issues and processes and puts these at the heart of analyses of social change. As well as the importance placed on individual trajectories through different life course stages, and on the dynamics and historical aspects of people's lifetimes, a life course perspective can facilitate exploration of change in general social arrangements. This chapter is organised around three sets of issues concerning life course and general social arrangements which all raise interesting questions in respect of theorising aspects of disability.

In the first part of the chapter I will outline what is conventionally thought of as a life course perspective, with its emphasis on the dynamics of individual lifetimes and their articulation with social structures and historical context. There are a range of insights to be gained from exploring the experience of disability from a life course perspective as well as associated insights into the structuring of 'standard' social arrangements which can remain hidden from view and taken as given in non-disabled perspectives.

In the second part of the chapter I shall consider conceptualisations of the modern life course as a tripartite structure shaped in large part through the organisation of work, education and welfare in modern society, and through relations of dependence and independence, issues that are also core to conceptualisations of disability. Discussions of the shaping of the modern life course provide a point of departure for reconceptualising processes shaping patterns of inequality, difference and the nature of interdependence in modern society.

In the third part of the chapter I will consider how we might better interrogate the structuring of social inclusion and marginalisation through a perspective that makes patterns and processes of claiming central to analysis. I will argue that an analytical framework which foregrounds social claiming has valuable insights to offer in respect of conceptualising aspects of disability. I will explore two issues in developing the argument. One is the way in which a conceptual framework of claiming offers a useful 'take' on the articulation of 'material' and 'cultural' processes, a concern of much recent theorising in the area of disability studies. The second issue relates to the structuring of social dependence and independence, the ways in which these statuses are embedded in processes of claiming and their articulation with the claims of disabled people.

Life course perspectives

It is difficult to point to any coherent body of literature of 'life course studies', in sociology or elsewhere, yet life course related issues are increasingly recognised as crucial to understanding people's experiences at a micro level and to understanding general, macro level, patterns and processes. This is true within sociology and in the realm of social policy. The idea of the life course draws attention to the limited value of chronological age, *per se*, as a sociological variable, and offers a framework for interrogating the historically specific nature of different life course stages, and the kinds of social processes and assumptions which shape the experience of people in these life course stages.

Researchers have explored the social and historical shaping of biographies, or lifetime trajectories, and the processes involved in shaping the experience of particular life course stages and in shaping transitions through significant life course events and turning points. Examples include changing inter-relations between groups in different life course stages. So, in recent decades there has been particular concern surrounding the restructuring of transitions between youth and adult status. Research focused on the restructuring of youth transitions, and some drew attention to a prolonging of the partial dependence of youth as young people's claims were increasingly met through parental resources and less through access to independent income (Irwin 1995). Other research has focused on the recent very significant changes in patterns of exit from the labour force and the experience of retirement, and change in the nature of the inter-generational contract. A good deal of social policy research lately has explored trajectories into, and out of, lone parenthood, locating change in the prevalence of this family form as integral to changing norms and changing material bases of demographic behaviour (e.g. Leisering and Walker 1998). Although not usually explicitly designated life course research, we need also consider as relevant research in the area of childhood and later life. Some of the work in these areas has explored historical developments and changes in the contours, and experience, of these life course stages.

A number of writers have stressed the articulation of individual lifetimes and the positioning of different cohorts in respect of broad social circumstances and events. For example, the historical point at which members of a given cohort experience a particular life course transition may impact on their subsequent, lifetime experience in particular ways. Examples of rapid social change may have variable impacts across members of different cohorts or those in different life course stages. The ways in which different cohorts (and generations) are positioned in respect of radical social changes, offer a stark illustration of how the experience of particular life course stages may change. The collapse of the Soviet Union and the shift from communist to market regimes in Eastern Europe provide examples, such as the collapse in employment amongst older workers in former East Germany (Kohli 1994).

A life course perspective can offer a valuable orientation not only to the dynamics of individual lives in historical and social context but can orient us also to elaborating that context. That is, a simultaneous consideration of individual lives and social structure yields insights into that structure (e.g. Bryman *et al.* 1987; Hardy 1997). Life course related claims and obligations are a key component for understanding wider social relations. Structure is not 'bracketed off' as context. For example, patterns of change in individual trajectories through school, paid work and retirement over the last century within Western societies reveal aspects of the reordering of social arrangements generally. Schooling and retirement have become general, encompassing the entire population but also now covering very substantial parts of people's lifetimes. Another example is provided by patterns of change in the timing and social organisation of parenthood as these are embedded in changing gender and family relationships, and change in the organisation of paid employment (e.g. Irwin and Bottero 2000). Life course processes can also be considered to contribute to social change. Some writers emphasise how cohorts, reaching a particular life course stage, may manifest historically new forms of behaviour and modes of action which 'rewrite the script' in respect of expectations and norms regarding what it is to be in a certain life course stage (e.g. White Riley *et al.* 1994). Another example is the way in which changes in life course related claims and obligations contribute to broader changes. Changing claims to employment amongst those in their late teens over recent decades, and changes in patterns of employment amongst women in the family building period have contributed to a restructuring of patterns of inequality across households (Irwin 1995).

Research into life course issues articulates with disability issues in important ways. In particular the lifetime trajectories of disabled people can offer insights into the institutions and assumptions that shape the experiences of disabled people as well as non-disabled people. Many of the chapters in this book deal with the ways in which issues of disability relate to the sorts of life course issues described. A general issue, which is highlighted here, is the way in which non-standard, disabled life course trajectories reflect upon how the category of disability is constructed and then 'managed' in society. Differences with more standard life course trajectories offer a route to interrogating the disabling assumptions, expectations and institutional arrangements as these shape day-to-day lives and livelihoods. A life course dimension also may offer an interesting way to look at the diverse experiences of disability, contributing to a better understanding of why and how disability takes different forms in different contexts, as advocated by Thomas (Thomas 1999).

The life course as a structure of inequality, and a critique

Another general issue relates to how the life course is embedded in the structure of social relations. Here our focus turns to the life course contours of social arrangements. In their broadest outline we can see these in terms of the social organisation of schooling (and childhood), of employment (and independent adulthood) and of retirement (and later life). For a number of writers this tripartite structure both reflects and reinforces an age related structure of social inclusion and marginalisation. Sometimes the life course is described as, roughly, a structure of inequality, which reveals differential access to citizenship rights and to meaningful social participation. This view has informed much of the new sociology of childhood, debates about the transition from youth to adulthood, and many discussions regarding the marginalisation of those in later life (*see* Irwin 1999 for a review of the latter). Childhood and later life are positioned, in cultural representations and in social and institutional constructions, as dependent statuses and as social locations that deny children and those in later life full social participation or a proper measure of dignity. In contrast, independent adulthood is positively valued, carrying social status and prestige (Turner 1989; Hockey and James 1993). There is a clear parallel, in these constructions, with the positioning of disabled experiences in modern society. The latter is seen by some to designate a broadly parallel location of social marginalisation.

Hockey and James (1993) argue that participation in paid employment is fundamental to social identity and prestige, and that those not so engaged are marginalised in a variety of ways. They maintain that a growing ideology of individualism increasingly marginalises those around the perimeters of the productive sphere and stigmatises 'welfare' groups. Independence is highly valued, dependence increasingly problematic. 'Vertical' lines of cleavage, which separate life course stages (and structure access to paid employment), become the markers of social differentiation and inequality. Their argument is that in a work society, where paid employment remains key to social inclusion, children, (unemployed) youth, the elderly and disabled people are marginalised in various ways. Hockey and James treat exclusion from independent (working) adulthood as a form of dependence, or at least a social location that is popularly perceived as such, and consequently a form of disadvantage. In similar vein, Turner maintains that the low status of the young and the old is a function of age varying reciprocity and social exchange over the life course (Turner 1989). The picture parallels that of Hockey and James, with social status and prestige located in people's (popularly perceived) position with regard to reciprocity. Priestley too, has highlighted parallels in the experience of members of 'marginalised' life course groups and disabled people, emphasising in particular the ways in which modern welfare systems have constructed and marginalised these groups in Western, industrialised societies (Priestley 2000).

The model of life course based stratification focuses our attention on how social citizenship rights are biased in respect of age and life course stage. Citizenship claims clearly have an important, and undertheorised, life course dimension. However, perspectives that treat life course divisions as markers of inequality may offer a partial take on social arrangements (Irwin 1999). There is a tendency to treat dependence and independence, and the associated life course stages, as distinctive statuses, and as independent categories. I have argued elsewhere that the model of life course based inclusion and marginalisation has tended to under-theorise the coherence of work and welfare processes and the mutuality of different life course stages (Irwin 1996, 1998; see also Turner 1998). The model understates the importance of continuities across the life course, and underplays the significance of how claims to, and within, paid employment shape patterns of inequality and poverty amongst children and those in later life.

For example, the relative success of claims to a family wage for men in many Western societies is inseparable from the economic vulnerability of women, the widespread poverty of women and children in lone parent households, and the poverty of many women in later life. Further, recent decades have not seen an impoverishment of those in later life. The average situation of retirees relative to the rest of the population has improved. However, the average hides great diversity and a worsening situation of poverty for many. In developing an alternative account of the articulation of life course processes and inequality we need to develop an approach that emphasises the importance of social relations and social claims in developing our understanding of contemporary inequality and its reproduction.

Here, then, I explicitly leave life course issues behind, other than as a springboard to re-conceptualising relations of work and welfare, and of independence and dependence, utilising a framework of social claiming.

Disability and social claiming

A claiming perspective has been of value in locating apparently material differences, such as between dependence and independence, and between welfare and work, on the same conceptual plane. For example, patterns of inequality in access to paid employment and in levels of reward, are constructed not as given by 'economic' or human capital factors but as structured by social claims. The approach is of value since it allows us to locate 'material', economic processes as culturally and socially embedded. This is in contrast to a tendency (in popular understandings and in some social scientific research) to see independence and paid work as given by economic demands, and to see forms of dependence and welfare as 'cultural' issues. In such views independence and work are treated as givens, social 'goods', whilst dependence and welfare are construed as problematic. There is a tendency to treat situations of welfare as being about making claims and situations of paid employment as 'naturally rewarded' – and not about claims at all. The claiming perspective allows us to see the work–welfare divide as itself an outcome of processes of claiming, and similarly to locate patterns of access to and rewards from paid work. In respect of the latter, various welfare claims are embedded in paid employment yet are rarely perceived as such, indeed they may appear quite natural. So for example, gendered wage patterns partly reflect the historical success of male claims to a family wage.

Before elaborating how such an approach could offer some insights for disability studies I will preface the discussion by noting some assumptions embedded in materialist accounts of disability.

In materialist accounts of disability the dominant capitalist mode of production requires social relations to function in particular ways. Disability is partly engendered by capitalist social relations that 'create', marginalise and devalue groups that do not straightforwardly meet the demands of the capitalist labour market. Cultural values and assumptions serve to buttress and legitimate the disablist social relations of modern capitalism. In particular the values of dominant social groups become general and the experience of subordinate groups thereby defined – and met – in specific ways, which often further the disadvantaging, and oppression of these groups. In the recent disability literature writers have pointed to an emergent dichotomy between those who stress the material bases and those who stress cultural constructions of disability (Priestley 1998, Thomas 1999). These writers still maintain the importance of material relations but stress how cultural processes may become embedded within those material relations. The issue of the link between 'the material' and 'the cultural' is an important one, and requires further investigation.

If disablist values and attitudes are both general and serve to buttress and reproduce capitalist relations of production then how can we explain the significance of the voice of disability in recent decades? In the context of an apparent intensification of capitalist social relations and their extension into more corners of human existence, how is it that dissenting voices have achieved acknowledgement and some measure of success in having their claims recognised? To question the success of disabled voices is to ask why – at this particular historical juncture – they have become firmly established and gained some ground in pressing their arguments. To do so is simultaneously to question the comprehensiveness of models of oppression embedded in hegemonic capitalist social relations.

The difficulties which emerge from contemporary materialist accounts of disability and oppression is that they appear to take interests as given and, consequently, seem ill equipped to explain processes of change in the experiences and claims of disabled people. The alternative, claiming, analysis offers another angle on the articulation of material and cultural processes, since it invites us to re-interrogate 'material' relations as simultaneously cultural relations.

Stone (1984), in exploring how the category of disability has emerged and developed historically, locates it in the articulation of two distinct distribution systems in modern society: the work based and needs based distribution systems. The division parallels the work–welfare boundary discussed above. Stone is particularly interested in the social and historical construction – and changeability – of this boundary: 'Instead of seeing disability as a set of objective characteristics that render people needy, we can define it in terms of ideas and values about distribution' (p.172). The argument is of interest here since it offers a perspective on locating the work–welfare divide, and constructions of independence and dependence, as changeable, the outcome of processes of claiming and contestation.

Rather than take interests as given and formally generated by capitalist relations of production, an alternative angle suggests we should see these interests as part of a dynamic process, which needs to be interrogated. Peattie and Rein articulate the value of the concept of claiming as follows:

Both the neo-classical and Marxist views take interests as given in reality, in the first framework by prices, in the second, by position in the structure of production. The claiming framework, rather than focusing on primary interests as the moving parts in the system of thought, focuses on the construction of purposes, which is seen as a social process. Social meaning and justificatory rationales for action which we describe as claims activity shape and reshape the interests which they reflect. (Peattie and Rein 1983: 134–5)

Peattie and Rein stress the conscious articulation of claiming – as a political process, but they point also to the importance of the link between claims and context, that claims may be as much a product as a cause of social change. I would argue also that it is necessary to analyse the ways in which social arrangements have altered the grounds for different claims, and for appeals to certain truths, and which alter the relative power of different groups in making claims.

Recently Honneth has developed an analysis with some shared concerns, developing a (largely social psychological) framework for exploring patterns of social recognition, and emphasising the connection between the emergence of social movements and the moral experience of disrespect. He argues that sociological analyses of protest movements have often constructed them in terms of interests that are seen as 'given' by objective inequalities. These interests are rarely analysed as elements of the 'everyday web of moral feelings'. He argues that moral feelings of indignation should be the starting point for theorising social conflict (Honneth 1995). Clearly we could see these moral feelings as translating into claims, although a claiming perspective would also entail analysis of processes shaping related change in the social topography of diversity, and associated change in subject positions. So, for example, a state of affairs previously accepted as natural or as immutable, comes to be constructed as political and challengeable.

Such a perspective offers a valuable 'take' on conceptualising both current claims by disabled people, but also change in the social location of disability. Oliver and Barnes (1993) have described some of the reasons why the disability movement took off in recent decades, locating it partly in relation to civil rights movements, initially focused around the claims of black people and women, and in relation to dissatisfaction with the dependence constructed through modern welfare systems. Clearly the claiming position of disabled people has altered, a development that must be integral to analysing the position of disabled people in a changing social landscape. In the past the claims of disabled people were constructed in terms of needs and in terms of medical and individual solutions, whereas now claims of disabled people are clearly and explicitly articulated in terms of challenging a disabling social order and disabling social relations. The framework of claiming opens up (and may redefine) some interesting questions.

We can, for example, explore the social structuring and cultural values assigned to independence and dependence through utilising a claiming perspective. As elsewhere (especially in the domain of gender) these categories have been the subject of discussion and critique. Writers have described how both are socially constructed categories, and have stressed the importance of inter-dependence in all social relationships and situations. In the disability literature there has been similar discussion, although more of this has centred on the issue of physical and practical independence. Here writers have criticised the importance placed on *practical independence* in efforts to 'cure' or at least alleviate incapacity in undertaking everyday practical tasks. Their argument is that disabled people's rights would be better established through ensuring *independence in decision-making* and control over their own lives and livelihoods (e.g. Oliver 1993; French 1993). Wendell, in parallel, notes other problems with conventional constructions of 'practical' independence, arguing in particular that it may diminish the dignity of those who cannot aspire to such independence (Wendell 1996). This argument parallels that made by a number of authors on later life (e.g. Featherstone and Hepworth 1995). The objective should be not to secure practical independence for all, but rather to transform the social valuations which privilege independence over dependence (Wendell 1996).

Wendell points to the philosophical arbitrariness of ideas concerning which of us is independent. She argues that independence, like disability, is defined according to societal expectations about what people normally do for themselves and how they do it. We can develop this argument in respect of understandings of social and economic forms of independence and dependence, and argue that whilst expectations may have a philosophical arbitrariness about them, they do not have a social or historical arbitrariness about them. Rather they tend to reflect the power of different groups in pressing various claims, which then become embedded in systems of distribution and recognition. Patterns of social difference are translated into social hierarchies. A claiming framework allows us to explore such hierarchies in relation not to interests given by the requirements of capital or by capitalist social relations but in relation to the differential ability of groups, at different historical junctures, to press claims more or less effectively.

Claims, then, contribute to generating norms which privilege particular groups, or particular activities, and devalue others. Interests are not given by position within capitalist relations of production, although the system is clearly bound up with the privileging of certain claims over others. Rather those interests, and ideas about the nature of social participation, and the ways in which social diversity is valued or devalued, are made and remade. The potential value of a claiming framework for analyses of disability is that it can contribute to an analysis of the marginalisation and disadvantaging of disabled people, but also help explore the ways in which the dis/ability category is reproduced and altered over time.

In summary, there are a number of ways in which analysis of life course issues and processes can enhance our understandings of the nature and meaning of disability in contemporary societies. The life course offers a lens on general social arrangements and on patterns of inter-dependence between various social groups. I have argued that a claiming perspective can offer important insights into the configuring of social inter-dependencies, the translation of social difference into hierarchy and the articulation of cultural and material factors in the social (re-)positioning of disability.

REFERENCES

Bryman, A., Bytheway, B., Allatt, P. and Keil, T. (eds.) (1987) *Rethinking the Life Cycle*, Macmillan, Basingstoke.
Featherstone, M. and Hepworth, M. (1995) 'Images of positive ageing: a case study of Retirement Choice magazine', in Featherstone, M. and Wernick, A. (eds.) *Images of Aging. Cultural Representations of Later Life*, Routledge, London.
French, S. (1993) 'What's so great about independence?', in J. Swain, V. Finkelstein, S. French and M. Oliver (eds.), *Disabling Barriers: Enabling Environments*, Sage, London.
Hardy, M. A. (ed.) (1997) *Studying Aging and Social Change: Conceptual and Methodological Issues*, Sage, London.
Hockey, J. and James, A. (1993) *Growing Up and Growing Older: Ageing and Dependency In The Life Course*, Sage, London.
Honneth, A. (1995) *The Struggle for Recognition: the Moral Grammar of Social Conflicts*, Polity Press, Cambridge.
Irwin, S. (1999) 'Later life, inequality and sociological theory', *Ageing and Society* 19: 91–715.

Irwin, S. (1998) 'Age, generation and inequality' (a reply to Brian Turner), *British Journal of Sociology*, 49(2): 305–10.

Irwin, S. (1996) 'Age related distributive justice and claims on resources', *British Journal of Sociology*, 47(1): 68–92.

Irwin, S. (1995) *Rights of Passage: Social Change and the Transition From Youth to Adulthood*, UCL Press, London.

Irwin, S. and Bottero, W. (2000) 'Market returns? Gender and theories of change in employment relations', *British Journal of Sociology*, 51(2): 261–80.

Kohli, M. (1994) 'Work and retirement: a comparative perspective', in M. White Riley et al. (eds.) *op cit.*

Leisering, L. and Walker, R. (1998) (eds.) *The Dynamics of Modern Society*, Policy Press, Bristol.

Oliver, M. (1993) 'Disability and dependency: a creation of industrial societies?', in J. Swain, V. Finkelstein, S. French and M. Oliver (eds.), *Disabling Barriers: Enabling Environments*, Sage, London.

Oliver, M. and Barnes, C. (1993) 'Discrimination, disability and welfare: from needs to rights', in J. Swain, V. Finkelstein, S. French and M. Oliver (eds.), *Disabling Barriers: Enabling Environments*, Sage, London.

Peattie, L. and Rein, M. (1983) *Women's Claims: A Study in Political Economy*, Oxford University Press.

Priestley, M. (1998) Constructions and creations: idealism, materialism and disability theory, *Disability & Society*, 13(1): 75–94.

Priestley, M. (2000) 'Adults only: disability, social policy and the life course', *Journal of Social Policy*, 29(3): 421–39.

Stone, D. (1984) *The Disabled State*, Temple University Press, Philadelphia PA, USA.

Thomas, C. (1999) *Female Forms: Experiencing and Understanding Disability*, Open University Press, Milton Keynes.

Turner, B. (1998) 'Ageing and generational conflicts: a reply to Sarah Irwin', *British Journal of Sociology*, 49(2): 299 304.

Turner, B. (1989) 'Ageing, politics and sociological theory', *British Journal of Sociology*, 40(4): 588–606.

Wendell, S. (1996) *The Rejected Body: Feminist Philosophical Reflections on Disability*, Routledge, London.

White Riley, M., Kahn, R. and Foner, A. (eds.) (1994) *Age and Structural Lag*, Wiley-Interscience, New York, USA.

3 Marginalisation and disability: experiences from the Third World

Anita Ghai

> Destiny, Fate, God, past sins . . . Call it whatever you will . . . It is not justified . . . It would have been better if I'd been allowed to die one day instead of dying everyday.
>
> (Lakshmi)

This is the voice of a 21-year-old disabled woman living in an urban slum in Delhi, the capital of India. Such voices are more the rule than the exception in my country, where I am existentially located as both an academician and a woman with visible physical impairment. From my vantage point, I have shared the dominant Hindu conceptions but, given the diversity of India, I wish to exercise a note of caution for the reader. Although I outline a common thread in my narrative, one must not discount the discrepancies.

India is perceived as the emerging superpower of the Third World, within the paradigm of globalisation and liberalisation. Globalisation has constructed a world that offers open-ended possibilities and new life patterns, like access to information and technology. However, the paradox is that its emphasis on power and profit has systematically dislodged vulnerable groups from access to even basic resources such as food and livelihood. Consequently this transformation of society has a very different meaning for people who have been oppressed because of their gender, class, race, religion, caste, displacement and disability status.

As disability cuts across all categories, it has been suggested that it is a global issue, thus implying that its meaning and nuances are universal. However, for me there are serious problems with this understanding. Whereas I, who have access to the Internet and a hand driven car, can be considered a privileged disabled person, others in my country are fighting for their very survival. Thus the notion of commonality raises significant questions in a country like India. In the fight for rights, whose ideology and whose agenda are more important? Who will determine the dominant cultural ethos? What kind of social systems will be sanctioned? Answers to such questions in the Third World are extremely complicated, considering the diversities of the various populations. An understanding of disability has therefore to be located within specific contexts. With this background, let me share my experiences within my own country.

The meaning of disability in the Indian context

The comprehension and meaning of disability in India needs to be negotiated as embedded in multiple cultural discourses, with subtle nuances. On the one hand is the assumption that disability implies a 'lack' or 'flaw', leading to significantly diminished capability. This assumption is rooted in the dominant Hindu mythology where, in the epic Mahabharata, King Dhritrashtra is deprived of the throne because of his visual impairment. Another set of images associates disability with deceit, mischief and evil. Within the stories of both the epics Mahabharata and Ramayana, the central twist comes with the interventions of an orthopaedically impaired man and a dwarf woman.

If I shift focus, I find that another theme in the narrative depicts disabled people as suffering the wrath of God, being punished for misdeeds that either they or their families have committed. As one of the mothers was told by a family member, 'All this has happened because I gave you a "Shrap" (curse). If you had been nice to me, I wouldn't have felt the need to curse you'. For the mother, the consequential guilt of responsibility for a child's disability is not difficult to conceptualise. Disability thus is perceived as retribution for the past. Yet another strand conceives of disability as eternal childhood, where survival is contingent upon constant care and protection. Here, the emphasis is on images of dependency, thereby reinforcing the charity/pity model. This list, though not exhaustive, illustrates the underpinnings of a negative cultural identity.

Historically, there are also narratives that indicate instances where disabled people were considered as children of God. This positioning provided spaces, in spheres of religion and knowledge, where the ability to transcend the body was a distinct possibility. Even though the implicit meaning of such possibilities may be disturbing within our present understanding of disability, it does indicate a dignified negotiation of difference. Thus, the renowned scholar Ashtvakra, who had eight deformities and the great poet Surdas who was visually impaired, are illustrations of strength and the ability to fight oppression.

However, owing to a lack of systemic historical research, contemporary constructions portray disabled people as possessing a negative identity, perceived from a predominantly medical angle. That Western medical explanations are predominant is evident from the latest Indian human development report, which states that, 'physical disabilities are genetic, biological and even birth defects and future research must focus on the causes of such disabilities' (Shariff 1999: 148) – thus, reiterating that medical intervention is regarded as a prerequisite, without any contemplation of the social perspective.

Resistance to such notions has come from disabled people, who have struggled for their place in society. The outcome of their efforts saw the first Persons with Disabilities (Equal Opportunities, Protection of Rights and Full Participation) Act 1995. Though notified some years ago, the Act still awaits proper implementation. Notwithstanding this legislation, the state has continued to be apathetic. The physical environment is largely inaccessible and information is restricted (there is one sign-language news bulletin per week for people with hearing impairments). The range of reading materials and technological advancements is extremely limited.

This indifferent attitude is further reflected in a recent decision that the 2001 Census will exclude disabled people (*Hindustan Times*, 23 February 2000). A proper census is vital for policy planning and fund allocation and is more accurate than sample surveys. The reality on the ground is that 60 million disabled people (National Sample Survey Organisation 1991) remain outside the ambit of mainstream Indian society. Their lives remain mired in vicious patterns of helpless cynicism, political inertia and poor social innovations that offer no long-term solution. Inequalities and deficiencies in life experiences tend to affect individuals' expectations and desires, since it is difficult to desire what one cannot imagine as a possibility. The state continues to rely on the voluntary sector for the provision of basic services for disabled people, although this sector can barely cover even a minuscule proportion of those in need.

However, the most dangerous and widespread threat to disabled people comes from a less dramatic source, so pervasive as to be increasingly invisible – poverty.

Disability in the context of poverty

According to Mabub ul Huq (quoted in Shariff 1999: 45) 'Nearly one-third of the total number of absolute poor in the world live in India. What is more distressing is that while 46 per cent of India's people survive in absolute poverty . . . about two thirds are "capability poor" i.e. they do not receive the minimum level of education and health care necessary for functioning human capabilities'.

Poverty de-individualises, and alienates those affected from the mainstream of society. Marked by feelings of helplessness and hopelessness, poverty places limitations on the person, in terms of the personal and environmental resources to improve the quality of his or her life. As the most vulnerable and least vocal members of any society, poor disabled people are often not even perceived. While the unparalleled economic growth of the twentieth century is celebrated, the issues facing disabled people living in the remote villages, urban slums and tribal belts of India escapes notice. The problems of inequality and injustice are so massive as to appear unchangeable, while more shocking categories of violence, torture, war and sexual abuse seem manageable.

For poor families, with a hand to mouth existence, the birth of a disabled child or the onset of a significant impairment in early childhood is a fate worse then death. In developing countries like India, impairment is largely caused by poverty. The prevalence of impairment, particularly polio and blindness, is at least four times higher among those who are below the poverty line than those who are above it (Dalal 1998). This situation becomes bleak in the face of environmental barriers, which are both structural and attitudinal. For the poor there is no allowance for disability, in any area of life. With practically no access to education or training, they are forced to live a life marked by extreme defencelessness on every score. To demand more from themselves, or what is fair and right from others, does not appear possible.

With the loss of economic power comes a drop in social status, a lack of confidence, low self-esteem, and feelings of injustice, powerlessness and increased vulnerability. The misery of bitter poverty is worsened by the enormous cost of disability. For those who cannot allow even a sufficient quantity of foodstuff such as rice, the increased pressure of disability is expressed in a further regression into vulnerability. Between 65 and 80 per cent of our 60 million disabled people live in rural areas, and urban slums, where very few facilities are available. Civic amenities, such as water, electricity and sanitation, are unavailable. These conditions are a breeding ground for the chief causes of ill health and impairment in India. Coupled with a lack of immunisation, malnutrition and difficult birth deliveries, the trauma seems never-ending.

Poverty is most devastating in the case of women, whose survival becomes precarious. It should not be surprising to discover that these women are often permanently in poor health, not from specific problems but from deficiencies caused by too little food. Additionally, women frequently experience too many pregnancies without gaps in between. The journey from girlhood to womanhood has no transitions. Women in very many parts of India are routinely fed last and least. Not only is there overwhelming evidence of differential food intake, there is also evidence to show that girls are given poorer quality medical care. In my own experience girls are admitted to hospitals less often than boys are, and when admitted are often in a dangerous condition.

Under these conditions, the major causes of impairment and disability among children reflect the state of the mother's health. Women with borderline heath status, coupled with poor educational status, eventually have high-risk pregnancies and low birth weight babies, whose chances of acquiring impairment increase considerably. A vicious cycle sets in, as low weight girls become the mothers of low weight babies. These women frequently work twelve to sixteen hours a day, doing the bulk of poorly paid work, after which they remain exclusively responsible for all the domestic chores and the care of children. Under such circumstances disability often comes like the last straw to the camel's back. For those experiencing the triple marginalisation of poverty, gender and disability, death is very close to life – an isolation, degeneration, anguish and pain that are matchless. As one visually impaired girl from a remote village lamented, 'God ought to kill me if this is what life is'.

It is within this context of extreme deprivation and desolation that I situate the experience of the disabled child in India. It is a situation where our theoretical underpinnings lose focus, as we negotiate with the lived reality of a person with the label of disability.

Childhood: a time to reckon with

Family can be both a safe haven for children as well as a risk from which children need protection (Anadalakshmy 1994). Nowhere is this truer than in the case of the disabled child, specifically in families that cope with the miseries of poverty. Within this context, it is useful to know that children are generally conceptualised as 'lineage capital' and economic capital (*see* Emma Stone's chapter in this book). Thus, impairment may undermine the family's capacity for economic survival. In this sense, disabled sons are far more problematic, as the breadwinner is usually male. Much more attention is generally paid to a son's rehabilitation than to a daughter's.

Children become inextricably bound up with their families, as there are no opportunities for early childhood or pre-school education. The Integrated Child Development Scheme (ICDS), launched by the Indian government to provide services for the most vulnerable sections of the population does not cover disabled children. The anguish that this generates is expressed eloquently by Saraswathi, the mother of a disabled child, who said, 'No, they are not for us. Our children are not normal'. Since the ICDS works in the slums, the tribal and rural areas, it is the most appropriate service to include disabled children. However, professionals associated with early childhood care seem to be insensitive and ignorant of the pressing need to include disabled children within the scope of such policy measures. Clearly the policy makers in our country are unaware of 'disabling conditions'. The disability legislation is powerless in the face of non-inclusion and low fiscal support. As one parent exclaimed on being informed about the legislation, 'What Law? If you say it is on our side, you may be right, but who is going to have that money to go to the court?'

In this situation, the search for cure often appears the only alternative. Even when cure is expensive and prolonged, the illusion of a complete recovery remains intact. Poverty does not reduce the drive for cure, since cure is perceived as a way to avoid chronic poverty for the entire family. Unsurprisingly, gender continues to impact on this desire, since the disabled girl child is seen as a liability. Consequently, she is often left in a confined area of the house with few chances for any kind of education. Her marginalisation is complete. If she does attend school at all, she is taken out when extra hands are needed at home – boys rarely are. Thus opportunities for improving the quality of life of a disabled girl child are virtually non-existent. Living a life of subordination without education and employment, caring for a disabled girl child is a burden that poor women can do without: 'wasn't it enough that we are poor and helpless. Why did God have to add to our burden by giving me a daughter and that too, blind?' (mother).

Such views raise questions about the Western assumption that, in cultures like India, families always provide the care for their disabled children. It highlights how caring, especially where it involves girls, can become very demanding and is not considered either a natural or an unquestioned part of family life. As another parent from a remote village in Assam commented, 'What more I can do? Isn't it enough that I work hard throughout the day to get her some food to eat? As it is, my destiny was to suffer, she has added to my plight! Must be a punishment for my past sins'.

However, I would be failing if I were to depict family relationships in India solely in terms of the exigencies involved. Despite the hardships, family is the agency that provides emotional strength, although emotional bonding may be unexpressed, subterranean, unrealised or unarticulated. The specific emotional expression may change. What is important is that, despite the odds, there is a relatedness within the family that sustains the subsistence of a disabled child. Though there may be a temporary loss of agency, the resilience of close family ties makes it possible to generate the necessary resistance to fight ongoing oppression.

Education: an uphill struggle

The family struggle often becomes especially difficult in the attempt to provide education for disabled children. In India, almost half of all children are out of school. Two thirds of these are girls. With such high rates of uneducated children, the chances for disabled children to gain an education are practically non-existent. Any special issue, such as disability provision, is de-prioritised. Consequently, out of roughly 30 million disabled children, a meagre two per cent are currently receiving elementary education. Higher education remains out of reach, except for the very privileged.

Integration is an illusory concept in a country where schools continue to marginalise children for being different. A low caste girl child for example has enormous difficulties in securing education. Children with significant impairments are trapped within a school culture that has no place for them. Inclusion and integration are difficult concepts in a culture embedded in discrimination. The implication that impairment means inability has strong historical and cultural roots (as in the Hindu epic Mahabharata, where the archery teacher Dronacharya tricks the poor boy Aklavya into giving his right thumb as a token, thereby eliminating him as a threat to his own royal pupils).

Policy decisions regarding educational provision have been the responsibility of the Ministry of Social Welfare – it is interesting to note that the latter's name has been changed recently to the Ministry of Social Empowerment and Justice (if only political correctness could make even a small dent in attitudinal barriers!). Constitutionally, there is provision for free and compulsory education up to the age of 18 for disabled children. However, in practice, no concrete steps have been taken to enforce this. The government acknowledges that the, 'General education system is not yet mobilised, to a noticeable extent, for the education of the handicapped . . . The goal of education for this disadvantaged group would remain an unachievable dream unless concerted and urgent measures are taken' (Ministry of Human Resource Development 1992).

In a country like ours, there is simply not enough money to establish ordinary schools. How can we then introduce the option of more expensive special education? While advocating mainstreaming, non-governmental organisations have been encouraged to develop parallel school structures for children with impairments. However, numbers are large and the results are disappointing. As one parent, living in the Delhi slums, comments:

Our children have not been able to get admission into schools, as we could not get medical certificates. Every time, we go for a certificate they tell us to come next month. Now the school says that the children are over age. The teachers also tell us that; 'if we take your children, the quality of school will be affected. Why don't you let her stay at home and teach household work?'

Youth: the unrealised potential

For disabled people, the dizzying euphoria of youth translates into a host of identity issues. Lacking control over political and economic agendas, it is hard to imagine how young disabled people can hope to fight the negative identities imposed by 'disabling' environments. In particular, the need to establish adult autonomy, respect and interdependency through paid employment remains largely unmet. An understanding of the state of employment in India may give the reader an idea of this crisis. Out of the projected figure of 60 million disabled people, 7 million seem to be awaiting employment. Barely 3,500 find jobs anywhere, despite a three per cent quota in the disability legislation. Research conducted by the National Centre for Promotion of Employment for Disabled People (NCPEDP) in collaboration with the National Association of the Blind (NAB) in 1998, indicates that earnings are extremely low, with 47.5 per cent earning less than 1,000 rupees per month.

Those in employment rarely find it smooth sailing. Most are routinely replaced with non-disabled workers, on the assumption that disability hampers their competence. The dream of independence through employment is largely unrealised. The data further reveal that the corporate world too, is not terribly forthcoming in resolving the problem. Within 1,628 private sector companies that were approached for placements by the non-governmental organisations, in the years 1996 to 1998 only 1,157 disabled people found jobs. Only 220 disabled people found jobs in the 804 public sector companies approached in the last two years. Within this data, specific gender estimates are not available, but the best estimate is that only one quarter of total employment opportunities go to women. Given the widespread inaccessibility and lack of facilities, those with career aspirations remain frustrated. Schemes for self-employment exist largely on paper, as vocational training often fails to consider local market demands, resulting in ill-equipped individuals with inadequate skills for the competitive market.

Sexuality and marriage: unattainable goals

Indian society, with its emphasis on perfection, has failed to recognise the universality of fundamental needs for sexual expression and intimacy. Disabled people are constructed as largely asexual, encouraging the repression of their sexuality. Socialisation for sexuality leans clearly towards the restrictive end of the continuum for young people in India. Chastity for girls is considered an essential virtue, with more permissiveness for boys. Anxious parents, who have devotedly cared for their disabled children, are often bewildered when it comes to coping with the difficulties of adolescence. They play safe and try to protect them from ideas and aspirations that they feel can never be fulfilled. This desire leads to a complete de-sexualisation of disabled children, especially girls. Despite these attempts, disabled women from poor families do not escape widespread sexual abuse, which often comes from within the home. The trauma that these experiences generate is difficult to cope with. To quote Kamla, the mother of a 19-year-old disabled daughter, 'I wish, either she or me would die'. Despite an acknowledgement of instances of domestic violence involving disabled women, none of the women's activist or academic groups include disability as a concern.

Such conflicts are often resolved by trying to marry disabled girls off. In India, arranged marriages are still customary. Marriage is clearly a family affair, emphasising partnership for a lifetime, and providing a link to successive progenies. Within poor families, disabled people are severely hampered in their efforts to get married. Indeed, their mere presence affects the marriage chances of other members of family (because disability is regarded as shameful), thereby causing resentment towards the disabled person within the family. Gender and poverty surface again here, as poor disabled women have even lower chances in the marriage market. Consequently the constant worry is, 'To whom will my daughter get married? How will I get her extra dowry?'

Stereotypical notions and negative attitudes are so deeply rooted that marriage arrangements are exceedingly difficult, if not impossible. Even if marriages can be arranged, there may be many compromises. With the belief that marriage is for life, disabled women are fortunate if they find a partner. Escaping the family is next to impossible. The plight and dilemma of Umavati, a disabled teacher from a village, is apparent, 'He married me for the salary that I was getting. Now all he does is beat me and take the salary away'. On being questioned as to why she would not leave him she said, 'My parents arranged this marriage with great difficulty. They are unable to take me back, as my brother will not let me stay in the house'. It is clear that disability for women in an Indian context can bring an extreme loss of agency.

Disability and ageing

The experience of growing old as a disabled person is probably the most traumatic in India. Infirmities common to ageing become all the more serious due to disability, thereby jeopardising any degree of independence that might have been achieved. Shah (1999) mentions the problems of old and disabled parents, and their extreme dependence on children for nursing and care. For children living in chronic poverty there is no scope to provide additional care for a disabled or destitute old father or mother. Even in such circumstances, within the dominant Hindu tradition, moving to live in a daughter's house is unthinkable. The idea behind this behaviour is the notion of 'Kanyadan' (an understanding that a daughter at her marriage is given away as a gift to her husband and family and, therefore, that nothing can be expected from her in return).

The increasing number of elderly disabled people is a challenge to modern India. As in the West, India has deliberated on the building of homes for the aged. Although some castes and sectors have set up homes for their aged in pilgrim centres, such community institutions are not equipped to cater for all the various problems that poverty, gender and disability pose. This reflects societal and cultural attitudes that serve to exclude rather than include, marginalise rather than integrate, disabled people. In fact, this is one reason why carers often hope that their disabled relatives will die before they do.

Conclusion: the possibilities for change

In the midst of such chaotic life conditions, it is indeed difficult to visualise change, especially when one must face the challenge of deeply entrenched negative attitudes towards disability. In a culture where pain and suffering are often accepted as karma (fate) and learned helplessness becomes a life trait, consideration of disability as a social issue is a difficult goal. To fight societal exploitation, one has to contend not only with external impediments but also with the experience of chronic internalised oppression. In deliberating the possibility of qualitative change in the lives of disabled people living with the additional burdens of poverty and gender discrimination, serious attention has been devoted to service provision strategies like Community Based Rehabilitation (CBR).

However, according to disability activists like Dalal (1998), such programmes are highly vulnerable to local influences. Within India, and I am sure the same is true for other developing countries, the notion of community is rather complex. Communities are often faction-ridden, with undercurrents of suspicion, mistrust and personal rivalries. Cultures of dependency have been built up and initiatives to mobilise local resources are often viewed with scepticism. Consequently, when a national calamity, such as a cyclone, hits it is often disabled people who are left behind to die, or have to await the magnanimous gestures of philanthropic intervention. As one woman with physical impairments lamented, 'I kept telling everyone to take me to a safer place, but no one did. They (the village community) left me to die'. Restorative work in such a milieu cannot be detached from the broader realities of socio-economic and political development. The task of creating a cohesive community is formidable and the viability of strategies such as CBR will need to be evaluated in specific cultural contexts.

Finally, although I often despair that the system is creating a category of uneducated, unskilled and marginalised people – particularly women – I have come to realise that although fate is the agency to which eternal order is attributed, the religious doctrine of 'karma' (action) does not allow passive resignation. As indicated by Johri (1998), in a different context, 'traditional notions such as kismet (fate) also suggest an attitude of acceptance and fight against practices such as amniocentesis'. In the context of disability, I have witnesed a slow but definite battle for rights. Whether it is the campaign to implement legislation or for inclusion in the 2001 Census, my fellow disabled people have responded to the challenges. They have gone to court with public interest litigations against the government, for not allowing postal ballots, and organised public protests to register their claim for a rightful place in society.

This ongoing struggle underscores the fact that disabled people in India are in the process of re-constructing their narratives of desolation and dejection. As one of them comments, 'so big deal if I cannot walk. If there is a will there is a way. I will definitely prove it to the world that I am much more than my disability'. I am sure this commitment will be familiar to disability activists all over the world. It is in this sense that disability truly becomes a global issue. The evolution of effective possibilities for change would be greatly enriched by an understanding of the universal issues that confront disabled people. The sharing of experience provides opportunities to learn from one another, and to connect to the common fight from our specific locations. As someone who has always dared to dream, I sense that slowly but surely we will win the battles of poverty, gender and disability. The fight is on . . .

REFERENCES

Anandalakshmy, S. (1994) *The Girl Child and the Family*, Department of Child and Women Development, Government of India.

Dalal, A. (1998) 'CBR in action – some reflections from the Sirathu project', *Asia Pacific Disability Rehabilitation Journal*, 9(1): 29–31.

Johri, R. (1998) *Cultural constructions of Maternal Attachment: The Case of a Girl Child*, Unpublished doctoral thesis, University of Delhi, India.

Ministry of Human Resource Development (1992) *National Education Policy*, Government of India.

National Sample Survey Organisation (1991) *Report of survey of disabled Persons, no. 393*, Department of Statistics, New Delhi, India.

Shah, A. M. (1999) 'Changes in the family and the elderly', *Economic and Political Weekly*, 34(20), 1179–82.

Shariff, A. (1999) *India: Human Development Report: A Profile of Indian States in the 1990s, Oxford University Press*.

4   Where do we draw the line?: surviving eugenics in a technological world

Gregor Wolbring

Throughout history, science and technology have had a profound impact on disabled people's lives, both positive and negative. Prevailing ideology contends that science and technology are value neutral, and that the only problems caused by technologies are either unintended side effects or abuses. In this chapter, I will dispute both these claims. Advances in science and technology are the results of human intervention, imbued with intention and embodying the perspectives, purposes and particular objectives of powerful social groups. Current technologies do not benefit all segments of society equally, and are not meant to do so. To maximise public support for technological developments, and to minimise opposition, technology proponents rarely acknowledge the distributional inequities and ramifications of their proposals.

Technologies are not neutral; they are social and political phenomena, and the field of bio/gene technology research is no different. It has the potential to alter society fundamentally, to divide us into two classes: those whose characteristics are in tune with expectations and those viewed as undesirable. Whenever it is detected that a human being is not measuring up to societal expectations, whether prior to birth or after, the 'offending' person will have his or her right to exist put at risk. Different characteristics will be targeted, depending on the cultural, political, philosophical, economical and spiritual background of any given society. Therefore, our propensity to judge each other, based on attributed characteristics and fuelled by the unravelling of our genetic code, increases our potential for intolerance (Kelves and Hood 1992). With the increase in intolerance comes an increase in eugenic practices.

Today, the main targets for eugenic practices are the characteristics of 'disability' and 'disease', both of which seem to be viewed as a medical problem in need of a medical eugenic solution. Bob Edwards, the world-renowned embryologist, has predicted that the increasing availability of prenatal screening for genetic disease gives parents a moral responsibility not to give birth to disabled children: 'Soon it will be a sin of parents to have a child that carries the heavy burden of genetic disease. We are entering a world where we have to consider the quality of our children' (*Sunday Times*, 4 July 1999).

Eugenics in theory and practice

In theory, eugenics is a philosophy of selection and deselection, based on the genotype/phenotype of a human being and is therefore inherently discriminatory. Eugenic decisions can occur on the individual level (personal eugenics) or on the level of a society or culture (societal cultural eugenics). Eugenic measures may be directed at potential off-spring, identified as containing undesirable characteristics; leading to testing at different stages of development, selective re-implantation, selective abortion and somatic gene therapy. They may also be directed at those parents whose procreation might generate offspring with un-desirable characteristics; leading to prevention of marriage, prevention of conception, sperm and egg banking, germ line gene therapy and adoption. They may be directed at living human beings who exhibit undesired characteristics; leading to infanticide, mercy killing, involuntary, or non-voluntary, euthanasia and somatic gene therapy.

Eugenics is based on the values of individuals or societies (stated or unstated) as to which characteristics should be part of society and which should not. In practice, we need to ask which characteristics are accepted in any given societal setting and which are targeted for eugenic measures. What distinctions are made between characteristics such as Tay-Sachs, beta-Thalassemia, sickle cell anaemia, thalidomide, Alzheimer's, PKU, female male, gay, lesbian, bisexual, mental illness, cystic fibrosis, cerebral palsy, spina bifida, achondroplasia, haemophilia, Down's Syndrome, coronary heart disease, osteoporosis, obesity, suicidal behaviour, infertility and so on? Much impairment at birth does not necessarily have a genetic component (e.g. cerebral palsy) and eugenics decisions are not based solely on genetic composition. There is no legal framework, no real discussion, examining in a differentiated way the deselection of attributed disability or disease through eugenic practices.

A survey of obstetricians in France (Geller *et al.* 1993) reveals that conditions such as haemophilia (41 per cent) or dwarfism (63 per cent) are seen fit for termination through second and third trimester abortion. A related survey (Renaud *et al.* 1993) notes that nearly 30 per cent of practitioners in Quebec and France would favour abortion for a foetus that exhibited the possibility of developing a condition such as schizophrenia later in life and 11 per cent in Quebec and 20 per cent in France would favour termination if the tests revealed a predisposition for Alzheimer's disease. The British Abortion Act allows termination after 24 weeks *only* where a significant impairment has been discovered (*see* Hubbard 1997 for a further discussion on disability and abortion issues).

Williamson (1998) suggests that the key in eugenic decision-making is the social, economic, personal and family circumstances of the parents, rather than the details of impairment. Thus:

. . . most people in my experience have fairly clear views on what level of disability appears to them to be consistent with a worthwhile outcome to themselves. I am actually irritated if people say, everyone thinks that condition X is so bad that we should have prenatal diagnosis and termination of pregnancy but condition Y (e.g. cleft palate) isn't bad enough. The truth is you can't say that in terms of a condition, you can only say it in terms of a woman, of her family, her perceptions, her social context, her economic context and everything else. For some people cleft palate will be something they will be at ease with, but for other people it will not be. The same is true for Down syndrome. We must avoid categorizing diseases as severe or not severe. This can only be seen in the context of the overall holistic situation of a family and individuals.

One of the consequences of this undifferentiated view of disability/ disease is that even a 'disease' such as infertility could become the target for eugenic practices. In many countries being gay is still viewed as a disease. In this model, unwanted characteristics need only be labelled as disease in order to become the justifiable targets of eugenic measures. Furthermore, if we follow Williamson's argument, can than there really be a line between disability, disease and other unwanted characteristics? Is the widespread practice of eugenics based on the characteristic female in some parts of India (Bumiller 1990; Kusum 1993; Miller 1981) not also a reflection of the social context, economic context, and personal and family circumstances of the parents? If so, does that make it justifiable to choose male lives over female ones?

Sex and sexual orientation versus disability

In many countries laws exist that give special protection to the genetic characteristic of sex (*see* for example the UK's Preimplantation diagnostic guidelines; the Pennsylvania abortion law in the USA; the Maharashtra Prenatal Diagnostic Techniques Act, India or the proposed new Canadian Biotechnology law). The prohibition of sex selection also forms part of the World Health Organization's Draft Guidelines for Bioethics and the Council of Europe's Convention on Human Rights and Biomedicine. It is therefore helpful to review some of the main arguments used to justify the special protection of the characteristic sex and to compare that with treatment given to the characteristic of disability.

One argument used to justify the prohibition of choices based on gender selection, while allowing those based on disability selection, is that disabled people are considered a burden while women are not.

Wertz and Fletcher (1989: 484) write, 'The main arguments for selective abortion arises from: 1) the obligation to reduce suffering for the affected family and the fetus when a serious and untreatable genetic disorder has been diagnosed, and 2) the obligation to prevent genetic disease and its impact on present society and future generations, in the absence of effective genetic therapies'. However, this argument clearly fails to fit those communities in which female offspring may also be perceived as burdens. Indeed, the perception of 'burden', whether associated with gender or disability, is based on societal perceptions and familial circumstances. Let us ask ourselves what constitutes a burden? Is it the dependency of a person? Is it the need for emotional adjustments? Each person will define burden differently, and that which is not valued or wanted will seem a burden. The 'burden' is then in the eye of the beholder.

In addition to the burden argument, there are equality arguments. Thus, a Government of Canada paper accompanying the 1997 Biotechnology Bill defends the prohibition of gender selection, saying that it is 'a) contrary to Canadian values of equality and respect for human life and dignity and b) a form of sex discrimination' (Ministry of Supply and Labour 1996). Wertz and Fletcher (1989: 46) argue that:

There are three reasons why it is important to draw a moral line on sex selection and stay behind it. The first is that gender is not a genetic defect . . . Second . . . sex selection violates the principle of equality between females and males and the attitude of unconditional acceptance of a new child by parents, so psychologically crucial to parenting . . . Third, sex selection is an unacceptable precedent for "genetic tinkering" at parental whim with characteristics that are unrelated to any disease.

A third argument is that 'sex selection lowers the status of women in general and perpetuates the situation that gave rise to it' (ibid.).

If valid, these arguments lead to discomforting conclusions: First, they suggest that 'disability' does not allow those who 'have it' to partake of the benefits of equality and respect for human life in society. Put another way, it means that equal protection under the law is not to be accorded to disabled people. Second, it suggests that societal discrimination is not to be equally applied among groups. By targeting 'disability', and not sex, discrimination against disabled people becomes institutionalised. Third, the preoccupation with 'disease' is misleading. Many unwanted characteristics other than gender are unrelated to disease. For example, being born without arms or legs (because one's mother used thalidomide) is not a disease but appears to be a suitable candidate for parental tinkering. Any test for an unwanted characteristic undermines the unconditional acceptance of a child by the parent. Why should we see that only in relation to gender? The rules for discrimination, if that is what we wish to have, must be better drawn than simply putting gender based discrimination into one class and discrimination related to all other perceived-as-negative characteristics into a second class.

There has also been much media debate about genetic deselection on the grounds of sexuality. James Watson, the Nobel prize winner who discovered DNA, provoked outrage by claiming that women should be allowed an abortion if their unborn babies are found to be carrying a gene for homosexuality, 'If you could find the gene which determines sexuality and a woman decides she doesn't want a homosexual child, well, let her' (*Sunday Telegraph*, 16 February 1997). Similarly, Aaron Greenberg, a Chicago lawyer who has published articles about the legal and ethical issues of sexual orientation research, argued that if the so-called gay gene is ever isolated, parents should have the right to abort a gay foetus or manipulate its genetic makeup (*San Francisco Examiner*, 26 August 1998). Many have found such arguments unacceptable and it is useful to consider their arguments in opposing deselection on the grounds of sexuality.

As Tasmanian Gay and Lesbians Rights spokesman Rodney Croome noted, 'It is as morally unacceptable to suggest the abortion of gay babies as it is to say that Nazis were right to propose the sterilisation of so called inferior races' (*Australian Associated Press*, 17 February 1997). Stein (1998: 1) argues that:

. . . the availability of procedures to select the sexual orientation of children would contribute to discrimination and prejudice against lesbians, gay men and bisexuals and, more generally, undermine the maintenance of a just society. These effects carry significant weight in determining whether genetic technologies should be developed and whether their use is, or should be, legally permissible and morally acceptable'.

Stein continues:

The claim that a parent is simply trying to protect a child from the wrath of society's prejudice often is a rationalisation for homophobia and heterosexism . . . The emergence of orientation selection procedures in cultures with negative attitudes towards homosexuals will reinforce the preference for heterosexual children over homosexual ones and, further is likely to encourage the view that homosexuals and bisexuals are diseased, not worthy of living. (pp. 14–15)

This line of argument seems to follow that of Wertz and Fletcher – that such testing leads to a worsening of the social condition of target groups and increases prejudice against them.

Unfortunately Stein then notes that there is a disanalogy between arguments about orientation selection and arguments about the use of genetic technology to prevent the birth of babies with serious 'disorders'. Such disorders, he notes, may dramatically decrease life expectancy, cause great suffering and intrinsically undermine a person's quality of life. Homosexuality and bisexuality, he points out, are not like this. In particular, he argues, the primary negative features of being lesbian, gay or bisexual have to do with societal attitudes towards sexual orientation, not with intrinsic features of homosexuality and bisexuality. Thus Stein constructs the 'problem' of sexual orientation as stemming from societal structures, whereas disability is constructed as a problem intrinsic to the individual (p. 22).

Clearly, this argument mirrors the traditional divide between medical and social model explanations of disability (Oliver 1996). So, why should sexual orientation be accommodated by a societal adaptation model and disability not? Further, if we do discover that being gay is indeed related to genetics, how can it not be intrinsic to the person? Stein claims that disabled people would naturally prefer not to be disabled but that gay people do not wish to be straight. Yet, as the international disabled people's movement has shown, many disabled people do not feel that they would necessarily be better off if they were 'normal'.

In the West, the positions of women, gay men and lesbians are now widely viewed within a social model, suggesting that the disadvantage they experience is caused not by an intrinsic characteristic of being female or gay but by the behaviour of male/heterosexual-dominated societies towards them. The disadvantage experienced by disabled people, however, is seen to be a problem caused by an intrinsic characteristic of the embodied individual, viewed within a medical model. This difference in perception allows a distinction to be made in the way that society treats women, gay and disabled people with respect to eugenic decision-making. Disabled people's options are of a medical nature – termination or cure – whereas the responses to women, gay men and lesbians are increasingly an adaptation by society. This is the underlying problem, at the root of explaining the acceptance of eugenic measures targeted towards the characteristic of 'disability'. The suffering of women prompts a societal solution; the suffering of disabled people prompts a medical solution.

Influencing the debate

As these examples show, eugenic practices in technological societies are increasingly targeted at characteristics disability and disease, despite the fact that most of the arguments used to justify special protection for non-disability characteristics are untenable. The use of such arguments to manifest a societal, cultural, eugenics of disability and disease has gone largely unchallenged, primarily because disabled people have been excluded from the debate on bioethical issues.

On the governmental decision-making level disabled people are excluded because they do not normally sit on the committees and decision-making bodies that influence genetic or eugenic policies. For example, the Canadian Biotech Advisory Committee has no disabled members at all. Exclusion at this level goes against international recommendations such as the UNESCO World Conference on Sciences, which clearly stated that disabled people should sit on decision-making bodies (*see also* Rock 1997). On the academic level, disabled people have been mostly excluded (a) because they have not gained access in sufficient numbers to the level of education required, and (b) because it has been difficult to convince universities (particularly in North America) that an academic perspective on the social aspects of disability is required. As one consequence, although feminist theories on bioethics and genetics have become a credible branch of the debate, disability critiques of bioethics remain largely ignored (for examples of this counter trend *see* Pfeiffer 1994; Rock 1996; Shakespeare 1998). Another consequence is that the media have less access to credible bioethicists or other academics working within a disability rights or social model perspective, than those working within a medical model.

Disabled people are often discouraged from contributing to public debate on genetic technologies because they are 'emotionally involved'. Yet, the same argument is never applied to non-disabled people who may be prospective parents or women. Around the world the disability rights movement has been largely ignored in the debate on bioethical issues, such as euthanasia and gene technology. The euthanasia debate has been shaped largely by the 'right to die and 'pro-life' lobbies and the bioethicists, while the gene technology debate has been shaped mostly by the medical profession, anti biotechnology groups, the biotechnology industry and bioethicists. Although disabled people themselves are largely excluded, the various parties involved frequently invoke the characteristic of 'disability' to justify and promote their own agendas.

The disability movement is also excluded because it does not have the resources to educate and empower its membership in the way that other lobby groups can. Most individual disabled people, even in rich Western countries, cannot afford the travel, accommodation and fees involved in attending workshops and conferences. The only way to build this peer education is to have people in every locality who are knowledgeable and willing to share their knowledge. In Canada, that is still largely a dream, although the Internet is beginning to open up new networks (at least for those with access to a computer). The less that disabled people's voices are heard in these debates, the more their lives are in danger. In essence, those who are heard will be able to make claims within a social model perspective. Those who are unheard will be stuck with medical model solutions.

Two recent examples illustrate how the disability movement is beginning to become a player in the debate over bioethical issues. One is the setting up of the International Network on Bioethics and Disability (to join, send an e-mail to *bioethics-subscribe@onelist.com*). The other is the so-called Solihull declaration (DPI Europe 2000), resulting from a recent conference to debate bioethical issues, attended by disabled people from twenty-three countries and organised by Disabled People International in Europe. The declaration affirms and asserts that:

We are full human beings. We believe that a society without disabled people would be a lesser society. Our unique individual and collective experiences are an important contribution to a rich, human society. We demand an end to the bio-medical elimination of diversity, to gene selection based on market forces and to the setting of norms and standards by non-disabled people . . . Biotechnology presents particular risks for disabled people. The fundamental rights of disabled people, particularly the right to life, must be protected.

The consequences of eugenics practices

Through eugenic practices women lose their right to autonomy and reproductive freedom, becoming instead the quality control gatekeepers of human perfection. Thus Hershey (1995) asserts that, although prenatal testing appears to empower women, because it allows for reproductive choices, it is actually asking women to ratify social prejudices. The technology of predictive testing carries with it the possibility of personal eugenics and, in reality, introduces a shift to societal eugenics. Thus we face a society that increasingly functions on eugenic principles; a society where community and government decide which people, with what characteristics, will be allowed to live and which will not. In such a society, we curtail free choice for women in regard to their pregnancy and substitute socially sanctioned, socially defined and socially limited choices.

Second, eugenic practices destroy the human rights movement. It has always been difficult to accommodate the views of different groups in a movement. An equality rights movement that would integrate and accommodate the views of women, indigenous peoples, gay/lesbian/ bisexual people, visible and ethnic minorities, and disabled people – to mention just a few – is a movement fraught with conflicts of interests. However, with the recent arrival of the genetic 'revolution', the possibility for conflict is now heightened. The new gene technologies offer the possibility of attainable 'solutions', based on judgements that we may have already made about each other: the elimination of negatively judged characteristics and the enhancement of positively judged characteristics. Various groups demanding equality and human rights seem now to be in conflict, each questioning the value of the defining characteristic represented by the other. Judgements of 'value' threaten self-esteem and pride, not to mention the lives of offspring with negatively valued characteristics. Groups defined by various characteristics begin to jockey for positions, from which to argue that their specific characteristic should not be considered ripe for elimination or 'fixing' in the genetic revolution, while often accepting that other groups' characteristics are.

What then is the impact of eugenic practices on human rights for disabled people? The spectre of eugenics pits those with differing characteristics against one another. A war of characteristics begins. Women may denounce eugenic solutions for the 'female problem' in India but not for the 'disability problem' in the world. Gay men and lesbians may denounce eugenic 'solutions' for sexuality but not for disability. Deaf people, blind people and dwarves may denounce eugenic practices for their own impairment characteristic but not for others. In resisting the tide of eugenic practices, it is tempting for different groups to see their only salvation in distancing themselves from others – 'Not for me but them'. To quote Andrew Brown of Amnesty International, discussing testing for Down's Syndrome, 'If society regards the presence of such disease as an acceptable reason for aborting a foetus, this makes it harder to preserve equality of respect for those already born. One might argue that their human worth, if not their human rights, have been diminished' (*The Independent*, February 18 1998, p.19). This *Animal Farm* philosophy weakens the potential for involvement of targeted groups in the human rights movement.

Once pre-birth eugenic solutions are established for a certain characteristic (e.g. disability) other consequences will follow for those living with that characteristic. To deal with the 'problem', we will have to establish – and we are already doing so – anti-natal eugenic procedures like infanticide, DNR ('Do Not Resuscitate') and euthanasia. The justification will come from pre-birth eugenic practices. To quote Peter Singer, a well known ethical philosopher from Princeton USA, 'In the modern era of liberal abortion laws, most of those opposed to abortion have drawn a sharp line at birth. If, as I have argued, that line does not mark a sudden change in the status of the fetus, then there appear to be only two possibilities: oppose abortion, or allow infanticide' (Singer 1994: 210). If we consider it justifiable for a woman to kill her foetus in the womb, because that foetus has been shown to have Down's Syndrome, then this judgement must have some bearing on our views about human life immediately after birth (p. 85).

Conclusions

A social model approach to disability acknowledges that the lives of people with particular impairment labels or characteristics have the same value as the lives of people without that label. Although impairment may cause some disabled people pain and discomfort, what really disables is a socio-cultural system that does not recognise their right to genuinely equal treatment throughout the life course. Some governments have begun to acknowledge the social model of disability, and to make some efforts towards facilitating the integration of disabled people into their societies (although these gains are in danger with the increased availability of predictive eugenic tests which are based on the medical model). For most of the world, however, disability is still viewed as a medical problem – and the danger of the medical model is that it seeks medical rather than societal solutions. Eugenics is a 'good' medical solution.

With the increased rationing of declining medical and social resources, bio-medical solutions, such as deselection based on predictive screening and euthanasia, become increasingly welcome to policy makers. Thus, the need to improve the social, economic and cultural environment in which 'disabled' people live their lives is decreasingly addressed. With no convincing arguments to point the way towards an acceptable line in the use of predictive tests and eugenic solutions, a much more thorough debate is needed, with all the parties involved. As disabled people, as a society, we have not thought through these issues very deeply yet. We need to hold this debate urgently, if only to avoid terrible errors. The only protection we have available to us at the moment, the only way to avoid tragedy, is to work for a society that does not view particular human characteristics as disaster, whether it be not having legs, being gay or being female. We need to ensure a place for everyone and to support each other. We need to put an end to the *Animal Farm* philosophy that can only lead to a bloodbath within the equality/human rights movement. We cannot work with each other when some view themselves as superior to others. The society we create is then our only protection against the new 'gene-ism' that, we are told, will make targets of at least 60 per cent of our society in the end (Dixon, Winship and Webster 1995).

REFERENCES

Bumiller, Elisabeth (1990) *May You Be the Mother of a Hundred Sons: A Journey Among the Women of India*, Fawcett Columbine, New York, USA.

Disabled Peoples International Europe (2000) *The Right to Live and Be Different*, DPI Europe, London (http://www.johnnypops.demon.co.uk/bioethicsde-claration).

Dixon, J., Winship, W. and Webster, D. (1995) *Priorities for Genetic Services in New Zealand: A Report to the National Advisory Committee on Core Health and Disability Support Services*, The Core Service Committee, PO Box 5013, Wellington, New Zealand.

Geller, G., Tambor, E. and Papiernik, E. (1993) 'Attitudes toward abortion for fetal anomaly in the second vs. the third trimester: a survey of Parisian obstetricians', *Prenatal Diagnosis*, 13(8): 707–22.

Hershey, L. (1995) 'Choosing disability', *MS Magazine*, 5: 26–32.

Hubbard, R. (1997) 'Abortion and disability: who should and who should not inhabit the world', in, L. Davis (ed.) *The Disability Studies Reader*, Routledge, New York, USA.

Kelves, D. and Hood, L. (eds.) (1992) *The Code of Codes: Scientific and Social Issues in the Human Genome Project*, Harvard University Press, Cambridge, MA, USA.

Kusum, K. Dr (1993)The use of pre-natal diagnostic techniques for sex selection: the Indian scene', *Bioethics*, 7 (2/3): 149–65.

McGee, G. (1997) *The Perfect Baby: A Pragmatic Approach to Genetics*, Rowman & Littlefield, London.

Miller, Barbara (1981) *The Endangered Sex: Neglect of Children in Rural North India*, Cornell University Press, Ithaca, USA.

Oliver, M. (1996) *Understanding Disability: From Theory to Practice*, Macmillan, London.

Pfeiffer, D. (1994) 'Eugenics and disability discrimination', *Disability & Society*, 9(4): 482–7.

Renaud, M., Bouchard, L., Kremp, O., Dallaire, L., Labadie, J., Bisson, J. and Trugeon, A. (1993) 'Is selective abortion for a genetic disease an issue for the medical profession? A comparative study of Quebec and France', *Prenatal Diagnosis*, 13(8): 691–706.

Rock, M. (1997) 'Genetic norms, eugenic logic and UNESCO's international bioethics committee', *Eubios Journal of Asian and International Bioethics*, 7: 108–10.

Rock, P. (1996) 'Eugenics and euthanasia: a cause for concern for disabled people, particularly disabled women', *Disability & Society*, 11(1): 121–8.

Shakespeare, T. (1998) 'Choices and rights: eugenics, genetics and disability equality', *Disability & Society*, 13(5): 665–81.

Singer, P. (1994) *Rethinking Life and Death*, Oxford University Press.

Stein, Ed (1998) 'Choosing the sexual orientation of children', *Bioethics*, 12(1): 1–24.

Wertz, D. and Fletcher, J. (1989) *Ethics and Human Genetics: A Cross-Cultural Perspective*, Springer Verlag, New York, USA.

Williamson, B. (1998) Presentation at the conference 'The pregnant woman with an anomalous fetus: is current management ethically based?', February 13 1998, Melbourne, Australia.

5   A complicated struggle: disability, survival and social change in the majority world

Emma Stone

In thinking through my ideas for this chapter, I went back to an old issue of *New Internationalist* magazine on disability in a global perspective. Re-reading some of the articles, I was struck by something that I had not noticed before, an apparent contradiction. Compare these two quotes.

Independent living . . . is fine in rich countries. But it does not mean very much to the poor disabled person in Bombay or Bogota or Bulawayo whose main problem is getting enough to eat. Zimbabwean activist Joshua Malinga is blunt about it: '*While people in the rich world are talking about Independent Living and improved services we are talking about survival*'. (Baird 1992: 7; *italics added*)

A few pages on, in another article, Joshua Malinga writes:

Disabled people in Zimbabwe only want equal opportunities and full participation. We want to enjoy the same rights as those enjoyed by other citizens. We must keep working and using our organisations as vehicles of self-help, self-expression and self-representation. *We need to fight for freedom, full participation, and independent living*. We are not alone in this struggle. (Malinga 1992: 13; *italics added*)

Joshua Malinga's words go straight to the heart of what disability is all about in the majority world. What first appears to be a contradiction is in fact the perfect way of conveying why the struggle of disabled people is 'a complicated struggle'. It is a struggle not only for survival but also for social change. Understanding survival means thinking about disability in relation to poverty and development. Understanding social change involves identifying how a society views and responds to impairment in ways that disable people, and often their families too.

In this paper, I have tried to bring together approaches and examples from others who have worked on disability in the majority world and from my own research in China. The approaches have been around for some time but have not necessarily found their way to wider audiences in disability studies, international development studies or life course studies. While the examples are intentionally about disability in the majority world, I hope that those who focus on minority world issues might also find something here that is relevant to them.

Finally, the approaches set out in this paper need to be held together within the framework of the social model of disability. For me (though not for everyone whose work has informed this paper), the social model distinction between 'disability' and 'impairment' has to be the starting point and the fundamental principle for action on disability in the majority world. The social model of disability is a radically different way of thinking about disabled people and society. Its essence is a total redefinition of the word 'disability', and the critical separation of 'disability' from 'impairment' (*see* Oliver 1996; Thomas 1999). Within a social model framework, disability is redefined as social oppression experienced by people whose bodies and minds are labelled as different or impaired. Society disables people with impairments, through negative attitudes, environmental barriers and institutional discrimination. The result is that people with perceived impairments become disabled people, denied the opportunities and support to take up the rights and responsibilities of full citizenship, to follow ordinary life course pathways, to enjoy ordinary life chances.

Using the social model of disability as an analytical framework is not the same as using it as a blueprint. A framework allows the possibility that disability (as social oppression) may or may not exist in any particular context, or that it may exist differently across cultures and over time. Using a social model framework need not be Eurocentric, or dismissive of cultural and conceptual diversity. To my mind, separating 'disability' and 'impairment' makes sense in the majority world as well as in the minority world. In separating the individual body/mind from social responses to the body/mind, it becomes possible to unlock the different dimensions of disability that exist in different cultures and communities. The distinction may be blurred in real life, but we need to hold on to it if we are serious about understanding how societies disable people (the struggle for social change) and why disabled people are often among the poorest of the poor (the struggle for survival).

Survival, disability and impairment

Disability creates and exacerbates poverty by increasing isolation and economic strain, not just for the individual but for the family: there is little doubt that disabled people are among the poorest in poor countries. (Coleridge 1993: 64)

Given limited space and the knowledge that Anita Ghai's chapter in this book explores issues of survival in the majority world, I have restricted this section to a few points (*see* also Beresford 1996; Chambers 1983; Coleridge 1993; Stone 1999).

First, holding onto the distinction between impairment and disability is vital when thinking about poverty and development. There are the obvious ways in which impairments are created and compounded through poverty (lack of access to resources, to basic healthcare, to adequate nutrition, to appropriate support) and through conflict. Then there are the less obvious ways in which impoverishment is experienced by people who are disabled by social, state and cultural responses to their impairment: through denial of access to education, employment, training, involvement in decision-making, and so on. Very different strategies are required to tackle these very different issues.

Second, understanding the links between poverty and disability should encompass what happens to, and within, households – as well as a more structural understanding of the poverty experienced by entire communities and countries. As Joseph Kisanji asks:

The question still remains: how can disabled people have equal opportunities in developing countries in the face of rapid cultural change, worldwide recession, armed conflicts, continued imbalance of trade, structural adjustment and the ongoing rapid technological advances of the modern world? (Kisanji 1995: 199)

Third, it is widely recognised that there is a vicious cycle whereby poverty produces impairment, and impairment, in a disabling society, results in poverty. Again, there is a need to emphasise that having an impairment does not always, and need never, result in greater poverty than that experienced by people who do not have impairments (*see* Beresford 1996). What is less understood is the complicated nature of poverty in the majority world. In order to illustrate this complexity, a revised version (taking better account of impairment and disability) of a framework on rural deprivation in the majority world, developed by Robert Chambers, is useful (*see* Figure 5.1).

The concepts suggested within this framework may be understood as follows:

- Powerlessness is lack of political influence or leverage, exclusion from community and national decision-making, and denial of opportunities for self-representation.
- Poverty, in the basic material sense of the word, is lack of individual and household resources, assets and income (it is often but not always related to poverty experienced by communities and whole regions).
- Disability is institutional, attitudinal and environmental discrimination by a society (community, culture, state) towards people with perceived impairments.
- Impairment is culturally perceived difference in the body/mind; this might also be extended to ill health and weakness that result from malnutrition and overwork in the majority world.

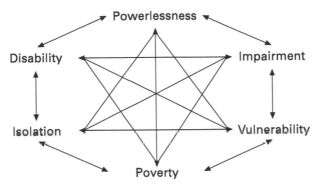

Figure 5.1 Revised version of the 'deprivation trap'

- Vulnerability is living in a situation whereby any unexpected expense (e.g. on medical treatment, a dowry, a burial) or disaster (poor harvest, loss of livestock to disease, conflict) can tip the balance from survival into extreme deprivation.
- Isolation is about lack of access to support, information, education, healthcare, markets, infrastructure, and so forth.

The more we recognise the complexity of poverty in the majority world – its causes, consequences and the ways in which people become locked into deprivation – the more evident it is that rights-based strategies for development and social change are what is needed, and not charity (Malinga 1992; Williams 1995; Coleridge 1993; Hurst 1999).

Society, disability and impairment

Socially accepted definitions of who is a valued member of the community, who is undervalued, and who is not valued at all vary across cultures and over time. As academics, we know this to be true from accounts that document cross-cultural variation in the treatment of people with perceived impairments. As activists, we need this to be true because it allows room for the possibility of social change. As human beings, we feel instinctively that it must be true because cultures are different. So, how is it that a Westerner can travel to another country and see little in the treatment of disabled people that appears to differ from their hometown, even where the cultural, historical and socio-economic context could not be more different? In such cases, how can researchers begin to identify the role of culture and communities in producing disability differently?

Contributors to Ingstad and Whyte's (1995) collection *Disability and Culture* looked to local socio-cultural definitions of the body/mind, of difference and of personhood in their attempts to grapple with these issues. In the sections that follow, I have set out these approaches with some additions. In particular, I want to emphasise the value of considering the state/social dimension (macro-level) as well as grassroots conceptualisations; and the different ways in which the body/mind is defined as 'capital'.

Body/mind and difference

. . . we need to . . . analyze the cultural perception of the biological constitution of the human being itself, in order fully to grasp the meaning of disability in a given culture and its social significance (Nicolaisen 1995: 39–40)

Western bio-medical definitions of impairment are not universal. Nor are Western notions of a 'normal' body, mind or behaviour. Perceptions of the body/mind vary across cultures and change over time (for example, changing and different definitions of beauty). In fact, in many historical and contemporary cultures, the body/mind holds a significance that goes beyond current Western notions of the functional body-as-machine and the dualism of body and mind. In this context, the following questions may help frame inquiry: What are the dominant constructions of the body/mind in a given society or culture? How far do notions of a 'normal' body/mind exist, and to what end? How does the body/mind fit into wider belief systems or worldviews, into political economies and social organisation? What differences in the body/mind are viewed as significant? Why and with what implications for the lives of individuals and their families?

Understanding how a culture (society, state) perceives the body/mind and its variations has proved a useful starting point in disability research in both minority and majority world settings. As Garland Thomson (1997: 282) has written in relation to Western culture, the body is 'a cultural text which is interpreted, inscribed with meaning, indeed made, within social relations of power'. Different social and cultural constructions of the body/mind may be more or less oppressive. They are increasingly likely to feature an array of old and new, indigenous and outsider, personal and public constructs. So, while it is important to recognise that Western definitions are not universal, it is also important to look for the impact of Western constructions on local constructions, particularly where Western-led or Western-style interventions are creating new categories of 'disabled people' (Kisanji 1995; Ingstad 1995).

Example: A continuum of definitions – cerebral palsy in Nepal (*see* Saul and Phillips 1999)

Nepal is a heterogeneous society in terms of religion, caste, ethnicity, geography, socio-economic development, and exposure to outside ideas and technologies. In such a society, it is impossible to identify one dominant conceptualisation of a specific impairment: cerebral palsy. Instead, the researchers learned about a range of different conceptualisations that might be located along a continuum of 'cosmologies' (belief systems): from rural, through urban, to cosmopolitan.

A rural cosmology is based in 'traditional values' and influenced by 'beliefs in ghosts, spirits and witchcraft'. An urban cosmology is influenced by 'systematic belief systems based on the written word, often associated with Hindu, Muslim or Buddhist teachings and with ayurvedic medicine'. A cosmopolitan cosmology is influenced by exposure to 'modernity' and 'western biomedical teachings', and is also shaped by Hindu religious beliefs and practices. Each of these cosmologies implies different views about causation, the nature of impairment, and appropriate actions. Moreover, no cosmology is exclusive: 'individuals often simultaneously hold several different (and sometimes contradictory) beliefs from all three points on the rural-cosmopolitan continuum'.

Identifying how differences in the body/mind are understood is the first step. The second step is to learn how such variations are 'socially and culturally constructed as a "difference" *implying notions of hierarchy and requiring extraordinary actions and practices*' (Talle 1995: 59, italics added).

Responses to difference also vary between cultures and over time. In any particular context, perceptions of specific impairments may invite specific interventions (e.g. acceptance, abandonment, celebration, extermination, ridicule, rehabilitation, or healing). The precise form of response and the extent to which it is disabling will be shaped by a wide range of factors including shared and idiosyncratic beliefs (e.g. about the perceived causes of an impairment), household or community assets, available support options and technologies, information networks, and so on. These responses can impact directly on an individual's life course and life chances through establishing entitlements to the resources, roles and relationships that constitute 'personhood'.

Personhood and life course

The concept of personhood is one way of grasping local socio-cultural expectations of what it is to be a child, an adult, an elder, a woman, a man. It is useful to ask how cultural responses to perceived differences in the body/mind impact on access to valued personhood and on life course pathways. As Ingstad and Whyte (1995: 11) point out:

If personhood is seen as being not simply human but human in a way that is valued and meaningful, then individuals can be persons to a greater or lesser extent. There may be kinds and degrees of personhood, and the qualities of a person are evolved and confirmed throughout life . . . So what are the significant characteristics of a person? Individual ability? Community membership? Family? There is no single answer for any culture, nor is there a universal set of priorities.

Research into socio-cultural constructions of personhood involves digging deep to uncover 'basic assumptions about what it is to be a person, and what kinds of identities and values exist' in a society (Ingstad and Whyte 1995: 7). It involves identifying the criteria used to confer personhood, and how this process is affected by perceived impairments and disabling barriers. For example, criteria for conferring personhood might include: specific attributes or personal qualities; marriage; having children; having male children; fulfilment of certain rituals; fulfilment of family or social obligations; socially valued labour; socially valued achievements (military, academic, sporting, financial); social belonging (to a caste, ethnic group, guild, family, clique); possessing specific material goods or assets; being of a certain age, gender, sexuality, and so on.

Where someone is denied the opportunities to attain personhood – through laws, policies, practices and prejudices – because of a perceived impairment, then we are confronted with a disabling society (and often a disabling construction of personhood). Thus, for example, state legislation and socio-cultural practices that exclude disabled people from opportunities to marry and to have children, particularly in societies where marriage and children are core criteria for personhood, are disabling. The sort of institutional discrimination that denies opportunities to work or to attend school in societies that prize income and education is likewise disabling.

In this context, it is important to remember that there is an important difference (albeit often blurred in everyday life) between the ways in which one's life chances and life course are diminished as a direct result of impairment, and the ways in which one's life chances and life course are diminished as a direct result of *disabling responses* to that impairment (*see* Thomas 1999 on 'impairment effects' and 'disability effects).

Second, in many cultures personhood is inherently relational (for example, the Chinese character for 'person' depicts two people side-by-side). This is about more than simply being in relationships; it is about

having the resources and undertaking the roles that arise from relationships. There is thus a need to set analysis of individual capacity,
appearance or attainment alongside analysis of a more relational notion
of personhood. In some cultures, full personhood is impossible without
one's family. In addition, perceived impairment in one member of the
family may reduce the status and prospects of the entire family; disability can be a family affair.

Third, as noted earlier, personhood is more complicated than the
simple distinction between persons and non persons. There are degrees
of personhood (Ingstad and Whyte 1995). It can therefore be helpful to
consider how the point in the life course at which impairment occurs,
and the type or degree of impairment, affects life course pathways or life
chances (for example, there may be differences between the status of a
man who has acquired impairment through military service and a girl
who has had an impairment since birth). We also need to examine how
links between impairment and other factors (such as gender, age, class
or caste, or the economic and political standing of one's family) may
affect access to the roles, resources and relationships that constitute
personhood in a given society.

Finally, there is clearly an overlap between notions of personhood and
the life course. Most obviously, personhood varies according to generational location within the life course (child, adult, elder). In addition,
the fulfilment of personhood may be contingent upon following a
prescribed life course pathway or 'socially significant career', as explored
in the following examples (Nicolaisen 1995).

Example: Impairment and personhood in Central Borneo (see
Nicolaisen 1995)

*For the Punan Bah of Central Borneo, the social system includes both
the living and the dead. Full personhood involves: a) being human
(witches are nonhuman); b) being legitimate (illegitimate children are
labelled as 'children of dogs' and occupy a much weaker social position
due to their lack of belonging to a paternal kin group); and c) a 'socially
significant career'.*

*In Punan Bah society, a 'socially significant career' involves marriage
and having legitimate children. Children are the personification of
ancestors and the key to the continuation of the family and the ethnic
group. The different names and labels ascribed to members of the Punan
Bah reflect these beliefs. The labels denote a combination of age, gender
and marital status. In this way, they denote the degree of someone's
personhood. The implication of not marrying and being childless is*

diminished personhood. This is signified in additional restrictions: restrictions on performing rituals, on engaging in certain social roles, and on securing economic independence. Physical, mental and sensory impairments make it harder to find a marriage partner and have children. So also can other physical attributes (e.g. ugliness) and personality traits (e.g. laziness).

Example: Impairment, gender and personhood in Uganda (*see* Sentumbwe 1995)

In Uganda, blind women are generally perceived unsuitable to be wives/housewives due to dominant perceptions of visual impairment and socio-cultural definitions of the roles of women and required attributes. The difficulties they face in accessing marriage stand in contrast to the view that they can be suitable sexual partners (though such relations are regarded as low status). If a blind woman becomes pregnant, her social position and networks improve through the positive values attached to motherhood in Ugandan society and culture.

Sentumbwe's research with Ugandan blind women who were married (mainly to blind men) and successfully performed the expected domestic and parenting roles illustrates that cultural restrictions on access to these roles did not result from the functional limitations of visual impairment. Negative perceptions of blindness, combined with gendered expectations of the roles and prerequisites for fulfilling these roles, result in the situation whereby women's opportunities to attain personhood are reduced. The effects of this are far-reaching since marriage is a key to unlocking further aspects of personhood – having a home, motherhood, and specific roles that confer social and domestic status.

Body/mind as 'capital'

In contrast to the relationship between body/mind and personhood, less use has been made of the concept of the body/mind as 'capital' in majority world disability research. This is surprising since 'human capital' and 'social capital' have proved powerful concepts in planning and researching socio-economic development more generally. It is also worrying, since I suspect that some uses of 'human capital' would reveal Western and disabling assumptions.

State–social constructions of capital may be constructed in relation to capacity for productive and/or socially valued labour, military service, child-bearing, socially valued knowledge and skills, and so on. In relation to disability, there is a need to investigate state–social policies, legislation, institutions and practices. How do state–social definitions of the body/mind as capital manifest themselves in state or social policies, practices and institutions? To what extent are these definitions disabling? Do they reduce or restrict the life courses and life chances of people with impairments? What are the dominant forms of state–social investment in human capital and who is deemed worthy of investment? In broader historical and political perspective, what relationships exist between definitions of the body/mind as capital and wider state–social projects (e.g. projects of empire, expansion, national development planning, population control, genocide)?

Some may feel that state–social constructions of the body/mind as capital are less relevant to majority world settings. I would caution against jumping too quickly to such conclusions. Most majority world countries have institutional infrastructures and ideological legacies that stretch back for centuries. Some of these will include explicit or implicit state definitions of 'normal' body/minds and personhood. Where such definitions exist, further inquiry will be needed to determine how far these definitions impact upon people's lives. We should not limit our inquiry to grassroots concepts, and keep our eyes averted from political institutions, social policy, modes of production, and the interests of power-holders (be they military, medical, legal, religious, or educated bureaucrats).

The concept of the body/mind as capital is also useful in understanding grassroots responses. The final example, taken from my own research in China, illustrates three different but related ways in which the body/mind is constructed as capital. The first two are kinship (lineage) capital and household (economic) capital. Both operate primarily at the micro-level of family and community; both can be situated in discussions of household survival and social change (Stone 1999a). The third – national capital – is most evident in state ideologies, macro-level policies and provision. Again, there are connections to be made between discourses of nationhood and the body as national capital, and disabled people's struggles for survival and social change (just as such connections have been made in research on the minority world).

Example: The body/mind as capital in China (see, Stone 1999, Stone 1998)

(a) *Lineage capital: The body/mind is the basic asset for fulfilling family obligations: marriage, male children, providing for and burying family elders. Negative perceptions of variations in the body/mind and disabling responses may prevent fulfilment of these critical roles.*

(b) *Household economic capital: Impairment and disabling responses can threaten household survival and limit opportunities for financial security for the whole family. The additional costs of impairment and expenses incurred through seeking treatment can lead to debt and long-term deprivation. Where alternative support is limited, providing support for one or more disabled family members takes time away from household survival strategies. Lack of access to education, training, credit and income generating opportunities compound impoverishment. For some, though, the body is a means of generating income in so far as impairment legitimates certain activities (e.g. seeking alms).*

(c) *National capital: Research into state constructions has revealed the involvement of the Chinese state in defining a 'normal' body/mind. State definitions have built on age-old ideologies as well as recent developments (e.g. the rise of nationalism since the nineteenth century and the current push for capitalist economic development). Population policies aimed at maximising human capital have been a feature of Chinese social policy since the 1950s. In the 1980s and 1990s, a policy discourse of turning disabled people from national 'liabilities' into 'assets' has been influential in supporting rehabilitation, education and work opportunities, whilst simultaneously promoting the prevention of impairment, including via eugenic policies and legal restrictions on some disabled adults to marry and have children.*

Making space for diversity and resistance

Cultural constructions and definitions can be at once dominant and contested. Identities can be both accepted and rejected. Life course pathways can be both imposed and negotiated. Individual agency and identity, family background, location, access, assets, support networks, age, gender, ethnicity, impairment, social movements and social trends, state ideologies and provision, information, economics all play their part in shaping and subverting perceptions and responses, often in ways that are neither straightforward nor predictable. Macro and micro-level changes (social, economic, political, cultural, geographical) also impact on perceptions of and responses to impairment, on the nature and extent of disabling barriers, and on individual and family lives. Further, Western-led or Western-style interventions impact on local constructions of disability and personhood in ways that are complex and even contradictory. All these variables and the potential of individual agency and collective action need to be borne in mind when using the approaches set out above.

Conclusion

Our problems were not solved by the war of liberation because ours is a different war altogether. It is a complicated struggle, but we understand the process. We want to be involved in the development process and not treated as charity cases. (Joshua Malinga 1992 on disabled people's struggle in Zimbabwe)

If we are talking about disability in the majority world, then we need to talk both of survival and of social change. It does not ring true to call for better policies, provision and attitudes without also pointing to the global structures that keep millions of people locked in poverty and powerlessness. Likewise, the experience of disabled people in the minority (Western) world shows the abject failure of economic development as a stand-alone strategy for alleviating poverty or dismantling disabling barriers.

Talking about survival means teasing out the difficult links between poverty, development, impairment and disability. It requires us to think about poverty at the level of people, their families and their communities; and then to situate this within regional, national and global structures of wealth and power. There is nothing straightforward about poverty, nor about the links between having an impairment and being poor.

Talking about social change means unlocking the ways in which societies (families, communities, cultures, states) disable people whose bodies or minds have been labelled as different or impaired. This is even less straightforward. Identifying the ways in which a society views differences in the body/mind is a starting point. This leads onto learning about what it takes to be a 'person' in a given society, and whether social constructions of personhood or impairment create disabling barriers that restrict life course choices and reduce life chances.

It can also be useful to think about the body/mind as capital in the context of the family or community, and in relation to state–social definitions of whose lives are worth investing in. To date, there have been few inquiries into these forms of discourse (governmental and non-governmental, national and supranational) in the majority world. In this era of capitalist development, globalisation and rapid expansion of the disability and rehabilitation industry, this surely warrants further investigation.

Finally, in putting forward these approaches and suggesting that they have cross-cultural validity, I want to underline that none of this is to support the unthinking export of Western approaches to majority world contexts. Criticisms of Eurocentrism and cultural imperialism must be taken seriously and used to scrutinise our actions and assumptions. Nor is it to suggest that disability exists in the same way in all contexts. It is, though, to stand up for disability as a framework that has value and power in the majority world, and that captures something of the complicated struggles of disabled people for survival and social change throughout the life course.

REFERENCES

Baird, V. (1992) 'Difference and defiance', *New Internationalist*, 233: 4–7.
Beresford, P. (1996) 'Poverty and disabled people: challenging dominant debates and policies', *Disability & Society*, 11 (4): 553–67.
Chambers, R. (1983) *Rural Development: Putting the Last First*, Longman Scientific and Technical, Harlow.
Coleridge, P. (1993) *Disability, Liberation and Development*, Oxfam Publishing, Oxford.
Devlieger, P. (1995) 'Why disabled? The cultural understanding of physical disability in an African society'; in B. Ingstad and S. Reynolds Whyte (eds.), *op cit*.
Garland Thomson, R. (1997), 'Feminist theory, the body, and the disabled figure', in L. Davis (ed.), *The Disability Studies Reader*, Routledge, New York, USA.
Helander, B. (1995) 'Disability as incurable illness: health, process, and person-hood in Southern Somalia', in B. Ingstad and S. Reynolds Whyte (eds.), *op cit*.
Hurst, R. (1999) 'Disabled people's organisations and development: strategies for change', in E. Stone (ed.) (1999) *op cit*.
Ingstad, B. and Reynolds Whyte, S. (1995) (eds.), *Disability and Culture*, University of California Press, Berkeley CA, USA.
Kisanji, J. (1995) 'Growing up disabled', in P. Zinkin and H. McConachie (eds.), *Disabled Children and Developing Countries*, MacKeith Press, London.
Malinga, J. (1992) 'A different war', *New Internationalist*, 233: 12–13.
Nicolaisen, I. (1995) 'Persons and nonpersons: disability and personhood among the Punan Bah of Central Borneo', in B. Ingstad and S. Reynolds Whyte (eds.), *op cit*.
Oliver, M. (1996) 'Defining impairment and disability: issues at stake', in C. Barnes and G. Mercer (eds.), *Exploring the Divide: Illness and Disability*, The Disability Press, Leeds.
Reynolds Whyte, S. and Ingstad, B. (1995) 'Disability and culture: an overview', in B. Ingstad and S. Reynolds Whyte (eds.), *op cit*.
Saul, R. and Phillips, D. (1999) 'Ghosts and germs: cerebral palsy in Nepal: a preliminary exploration of cosmology and disability', in E. Stone (ed.), *op cit*.
Sentumbwe, N. (1995) 'Sighted lovers and blind husbands: experiences of blind women in Uganda', in B. Ingstad and S. Reynolds Whyte (eds.), *op cit*.
Stone, E. (1998), *Reforming disability in China: A Study in Disability and Development*, PhD thesis, University of Leeds.

Stone, E. (1999) 'Making connections: using stories from China as an example', in E. Stone (ed.), *op cit.*

Stone, E. (ed.) (1999), *Disability and Development: Learning From Action and Research on Disability in the Majority World*, The Disability Press: Leeds.

Talle, A. (1995) 'A child is a child: disability and equality among the Kenya Masai', in B. Ingstad and S. Reynolds Whyte (eds.), *op cit.*

Thomas, C. (1999), *Female Forms: Experiencing and Understanding Disability*, Open University Press, Milton Keynes.

Whyte, S. and Ingstad, B. (1995) 'Disability and culture: an overview', in B. Ingstad and S. Whyte (eds.) *op cit.*

Williams, L. (1995) 'Rights not charity', in P. Zinkin and H. McConachie (eds.) *Disabled Children and Developing Countries*, MacKeith Press, London.

II

Methods and stories

6 Life event histories and the US independent living movement

Devva Kasnitz

The goal of this chapter is to introduce a life course event history approach to leadership development within the US independent living disability rights movement. This approach is one that I developed while working with colleagues, at the World Institute on Disability, on a qualitative study to trace the various ways in which knowledge of, contact with and identification with other disabled people impacts on leadership development within the disability movement.[1] What is unique to this research is its approach, which seeks to analyse the occurrence and sequencing of significant events and changes in peoples' lives through the construction of leadership development 'event histories', a concept borrowed from the quantitative technique of Event History Analysis (Mayer and Tuma 1989).

Over the last five years the World Institute on Disability (WID) in Oakland, California has conducted research on the relationship between peer support and leadership development, in a nationwide exploratory study of the independent living movement (utilising focus groups, life history interviews, expert review of reports and pilot sample case studies). The leadership study is important. It is vital that we understand the processes that create leadership, so that they may be encouraged in shaping the institutions, policies and opportunities that constrain our lives. We know that effective individual strategies and effective group leadership are not separate processes; rather they lie on a continuum from self-advocacy to systems advocacy. Social and cultural contexts, beliefs, attitudes and experiences mediate any individuals' position on, or transition along, this continuum.

The initial leadership study could not represent the diversity of people involved in the independent living movement, but strives to be illustrative of a wide range of variation. It identifies issues for further research, including a possible quantitative event history analysis approach with a larger sample, and suggests some strategies for leadership development that apply to policy making, and to leadership training. We need to know more about the context in which to interpret individual impairment and disability careers or event histories, including the larger social history of disability. To start this process I consider the lives of a group of thirty leaders, chosen by a formal peer nomination process, who exemplify the history of activism of disabled people in the United States starting in the 1950s and continuing up to the present.

The study relates personal and contextual factors (the historical context, the individuals' personality and familial predisposition to leadership, the nature, onset and course of their impairment, their experience of societal stigma, their life opportunities and access to disability peers) with the assumption of an identity as a disabled person among others. Broadly sketched, these interrelationships suggest practical action that can be taken in policy development and implementation affecting the lives of disabled people.

A life course approach

While I approach this project using a version of the social model of disability (Kasnitz and Shuttleworth 1999), it is a model drawn from life course and event history analysis research methodology that I wish to describe here. Mayer and Tuma define life course research as ' . . . the study of social processes extending over the individual life span, or significant portions of it, especially the family cycle . . . educational and training histories, and employment and occupational careers' (1989: 3). I want to suggest here that we look at individuals' personal impairment and disability history (age at onset, duration, or exacerbation of impairment, experience of exclusion, assumption of disability identity, etc.) as another interweaving life course trajectory to be analysed in addition to those factors listed by Mayer and Tuma.

Borrowing from marketing theory, Mayer and Tuma (1989) propose the use of a statistical technique, *Event History Analysis in Life Course Research*. This approach identifies and chronologically maps essential 'events' in individuals' lives creating an 'event history'. It then examines how these events relate to 'transformations of status' and to 'roles' in someone's life. The model suggests that changes in life are step-like. In this sense, we hold a certain status and role for a period of time and then experience either a fast or a gradual transition to a new status and role, with all of the attendant rights and responsibilities that flow from that new role status. Using life course event history analysis, a researcher may select to study specific key transitional events, their sequencing and the role incumbencies inherent in those status transitions. Figure 6.1 provides a simplistic, overly linear, rendering of this idea.

I believe that a qualitative visual reworking of event history analysis

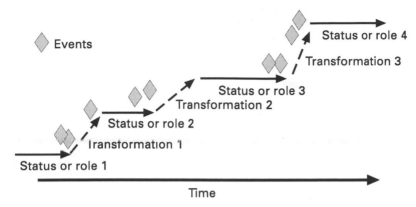

Figure 6.1 Life course event history model

helps to elucidate factors contributing to the disability movement leadership experience. We can look at patterns in the sequencing of life history events, at transitions in identity and experience related to impairment and disability, and at the temporal placement of impairment and disability events in the context of other dynamic life course processes. Along with an analysis of basic demographic characteristics, we should be better able to tease out the configurations of life events that demonstrate the development of identification with Independent Living philosophy, the achievement of personal goals and leadership skills. Although this type of study is qualitative, it may also suggest a future research design that includes more formal statistical Event History Analysis.

The leadership study

In order to capture a wide range of variation, the sample selection design included four sets of filtering criteria: membership of a historical cohort, attributes of leadership, a nomination process and a focused recruitment for diversity (Kasnitz, Bruckner and Doe 1996). We defined three cohorts of leaders based on their participation in the legislative process that culminated (in 1973 1990 and 1992) in national legislation recognising the civil rights of disabled people in the US. Attributes of leadership refer to three sets of leadership styles and skills, the 'motivator', the 'spokesperson' and the 'organiser'. In the formal nomination process, leaders in the movement were asked to nominate thirty peers from a pool of over 100, using an iterative process. Focused recruitment for diversity assured that racial and cultural minority groups were oversampled. Groups identified for this focused recruitment included His-

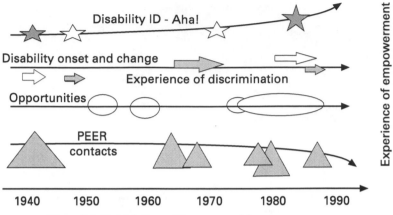

Figure 6.2 Multiple linear life course model

panics, African Americans, Asian Americans, people with developmental disabilities, people with HIV/AIDS and Deaf people.

The uni-linear model presented earlier in Figure 6.1 clearly oversimplifies the complexity of life course histories. Figure 6.2 provides more detail, showing one line for each of the main life domains of interest in the leadership study – disability identity, impairment and disability onset and changes, opportunities and peer contacts.

This model allows for the analysis of patterns both horizontally (within a single life domain) and vertically (to study patterns of domain interaction). It was this conceptual model that drove the initial leadership study questionnaire design. The essential domains, under which more specific codes were grouped, were then re-identified in the analysis as follows:

> PREDISPOSITION to leadership and HISTORICAL CONTEXT: people begin in a historical time and with ability or potential towards leadership, regardless of their impairment. Communication skills, self-esteem, family support, personality, pre-disability experience and expectations, and the drive to achieve were among the factors identified as contributing to predisposition for leadership.
>
> Other SIGNICANT LIFE EVENTS: this included education, marriage, employment, and so on. Exposure to injustice about race, class and gender discrimination was also identified as significant, leading to awareness that impairments or functional limitations are grounds for creating 'disability' oppression.

DISABILITY EVENTS: the ONSET type, change, extent, stability and other key variables of impairment and/or disability (Kasnitz 1994) affect a person's awareness of and identification with other disabled people. The nature of impairment also affects the social stigma cast upon it.

DISABILITY STIGMA and DISCRIMINATION experience: stigma and the experience of discrimination, in school, family, work, or generally in society is a critical factor in the development of leaders.

An 'AHA!' experience: a speedy or sudden appreciation of a fundamental identification with the independent living movement. The 'Aha!' experience is that of connecting one's disability experience to a collective status, with shared issues, within a civil rights movement.

DISABILITY IDENTITY assumption or change: identification as a disabled person and identification with a group of disabled people is part of the ongoing process of constituent identity.

PEER contact: mentor, mentee and role model experiences.

OPPORTUNITY for peer contact or support and skills related to leadership: opportunities and peer experiences interact, occur repeatedly and in combinations to provide support and skills, which in turn lead to 'roles' in the formal or informal disability network, or to other mainstream leadership positions.

Using these analytical domains, I created what I call Life Course Event History Charts, which graphically represent significant life events. Figure 6.3 provides a key to reading these charts. Each type of event is assigned a geometric symbol as shown.

Figures 6.4 to 6.6 represent the occurrence of such life events in a sample of three peoples' actual lives. The three people were chosen to illustrate variety. John became disabled as an adult, Annette and Barbara as children. Barbara is a woman of colour; John and Annette are white. In fact, the resulting Life Course Event History Charts show great similarity between Annette and Barbara. Their age at onset of impairment is the same, with experiences of discrimination coming significantly later in life.

Barbara's story is one that shows the intersecting multiple layers of a person's life. Her family background and her own personal experience with disability interact in a way that promotes her ability to become an active leader in the disability rights movement. Her family is large and has a history of arthritis. Barbara and Annette both attended a rehabili-

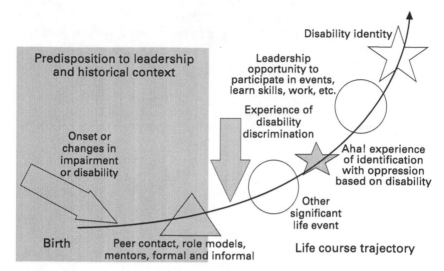

Figure 6.3 Model key

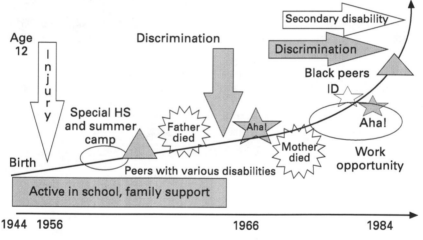

Figure 6.4 Barbara's life event history

tation unit or special summer camp for disabled children. Through these contacts with other disabled young people, they began to develop a sense of identification with disabled others.

John's experience was more compressed in time. The Veterans Administration hospital, immediately after his injury, contributed in many ways to his leadership development. He had contact with other

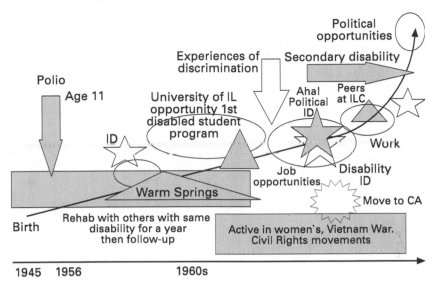

Figure 6.5 Annette's life event history

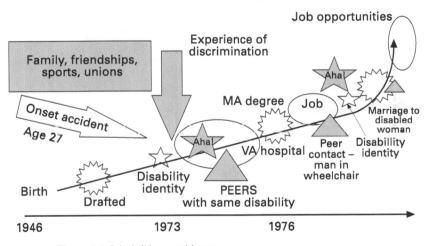

Figure 6.6 John's life event history

disabled people and, immediately after leaving hospital, returned to
university to pursue a master's degree – something he said that he
probably would not have done if he had not been injured. Directly after
graduating John became a service delivery staff person for disabled
students. For John, there is one particular man, who uses a wheelchair,
who acted as a role model and involved him as a volunteer in a coalition

for barrier-free living. Through that experience, John became familiar with disability rights and organisational issues. Another significant life event, which also created opportunity and peer support for John, was his marriage to a disabled woman.

When looking at leadership and life histories we try to identify significant events or factors and their pattern. John was in the military but tended to avoid structured organisations, whereas Annette and Barbara were active in high school. However, John's family is connected with twenty couples in a tight friendship group, and his grandparents were particularly active in the trade union movement. The friendship group not only socialised and supported his parents but also provided him with assistance, acting much like an extended family or support network. The family involvement with unions and civil rights quickly led to his disability movement involvement.

JOHN: I've always been able to write and things like that. The speaking stuff's really been mostly post the – my injury, and I don't know if that's just my ageing or it's the disability . . . I was always very very quiet and shy. Now they can't shut me up, so I don't know . . . I was about twenty seven when I broke my neck, so it was just sort of a, moving out of – um, being shy and . . . not wanting to do much speaking or whatever, or, it was just the disability and . . . becoming more righteous about, you know, the rights issue.

Identity as a disabled person, or as a member of a racial minority, is not usually rewarded by society. It is stigmatised. However, for many disabled people it is a relief to finally find a movement where acceptance not only allows for disability, but also supports and nurtures disability as part of human nature.

BARBARA: So from college on it's very interesting that my friends again (you know, I went from like all black in elementary school in Texas, to kind of a mix in junior high and high school to basically all white . . .) . . . [there] was a point a few years back when I realized almost all my friends were white, and in . . . the last ten years have I become very very conscious again of meeting and being with black people, and that has a lot to do, I think with the movement, with having gotten in the disability movement.

Preliminary findings

The use of the concept of disability event histories produces interesting results. For example, our data suggests that the leaders interviewed fit into two broad categories. One group consists of those predisposed to leadership roles by early life experiences. These are people who would probably have become leaders in any case, and for whom disability status provided a focus for leadership activities. The other group comprises those for whom the disability experience propelled them into a leadership position. This useful distinction holds true even among people with a young age at onset of impairment/disability. Some demonstrate a propensity for leadership roles in arenas unrelated to disability, and despite any stigma or discrimination attached to their impairments. Only later do they come to a leadership role in the disability movement. Others, by contrast, describe how their impairment itself kept them from being wallflowers – there was no wall into which they could blend, no fence on which they could sit. Disability itself can make a leadership role very compelling.

One unexpected finding is the direct way in which impairments can provide individuals with an opportunity to be in a visible community role, leading to leadership. When asked, 'Has your disability affected your leadership role? Is your disability an advantage or disadvantage?' answers were striking. Annette's inability to fulfil expected social roles freed her to look elsewhere for direction.

ANNETTE: . . . if I have leadership abilities it's because I have a disability . . . if I hadn't become disabled, I can't imagine what would have happened to me. I cannot imagine where I, what direction I would have gone in. I lived in a southern, racist town, you know, and I was expected to come out, get married, and grace somebody's home.

Darla describes how she was offered opportunities to take on visible roles in the disability rights movement precisely because of her deafness. Ronald talks of invitations to sit on committees that he receives because he is both a disabled person and a Japanese-American. As disability rights movements grow, and become increasingly diverse, individuals with under-represented impairments and from ethnic minorities may have unusual opportunities to represent their constituencies.

KATIA: I wouldn't be a leader of anything much if I didn't have this disability because my particular skills or visions wouldn't have been as essential to any other group. Since people with environmental and chemical disabilities are so horribly desperate, even what I have to offer came in handy, it was usable. And it actually provided me with an opportunity to get my bearings and see where we fit in and get to know people who had better skills and so forth, who had other disabilities. I don't think I would have been forced into the role into which I have been active if I had a different primary disability or none at all.

Policy recommendations

I believe that it is incumbent on researchers to state how they want to see the results of their work utilised, and other papers include full policy recommendations from this research (Kasnitz, Bruckner and

Doe 1996). Briefly, our findings emphasise the importance of disability identity and of the visibility of disabled people in public life. Many disabled people continually explore different layers of their identity. As a result of exclusion from the mainstream, and inclusion in impairment and/or disability-specific experiences, including disability culture and disability industry employment, disabled people may come to recognise, defend and efficiently extend their rights as disabled people in society.

Research has shown that even a casual knowledge of peers and role models can have a profound impact on people's attitudes and life course pathways. This marks the importance of considering the policy implications of individuals' isolation from disability peers versus their integration with non-disabled peers. The opportunity to be in a critical mass of disabled people may be as important as being integrated within the larger non-disabled society. This suggests applications in the structural ordering of education and peer contact: peer contact in medical and engineering rehabilitation; peer contact and independent living programmes; cross-impairment and disability peer contact development; and other general peer contact opportunities. In order to do this, it will be necessary to build the movement and to create a new cohort of trainers and role models, to extend programmatic mainstreaming and thereby increase life opportunities.

Conclusion

In marketing research, with large samples, event histories are expressed mathematically. Here I have emphasised the qualitative use of the graphic models to allow visual comparison. Future analysis to develop a computer modelling technique to store, arrange and abstract the charts of the thirty participants is also underway. In order to demonstrate the preliminary research findings from an analysis of the highlighted domains, and to make the research accessible to leaders and aspiring leaders, we brought a preliminary event history model to the Society for Disability Studies conference in June 1995. To develop the model we spent many hours reviewing the text and the context of the interviews, seeking to understand cause and effect and the sequencing of key events in the data, and validating concepts with other disabled people. The result is a fluid event history model, which identifies factors that have an impact, and the ways in which these factors interact with one another at various times of transition. The benefit of developing this model is in making the development of leadership accessible as a visual/physical model to assist the lay reader in understanding the processes involved. It also provides a basis for intervention, since the model identifies certain kinds of opportunities and events as significant in the development of leadership.

We now know that the peer contact that occurred in separate schools and summer camps, and the long stays in rehabilitation hospitals, had a powerful impact on a generation of disability rights leaders. We also know that the next generation had fewer of these experiences and more opportunity for peer contact at centres for independent living and other community organisations. As universal access expands, as services to disabled people become more mainstream and more distributed, how will the coming cohorts of disabled people have the opportunity for the critical mass of disability peer contact that is so empowering?

Peer support means, it means my life, – everything, it's everything that's meaningful to me, it's everything that's given me anything. Before I was involved in our movement I was in the worst pain and enduring abuse and oppression, and terrible treatment and loneliness – and homelessness and moneylessness and friendlessness; and being involved in the movement, both the mental patients, consumer survivor, disability rights, independent living movements, civil rights movements, since being involved in that I've had everything that's meaningful in life, or almost everything except my Lear jet – a home, a job, friends, you know. And a purpose in life. (Howie the harp 1953–95)

Note

1 The research team for the leadership study included Tanis Doe, Bill Bruckner, and Raffi Aftendelian. The research was supported by the National Institute on Disability and Rehabilitation Research, Research and Training Center Program.

REFERENCES

Kasnitz, D. (1994) 'Personal disability history variables in disability research, theory, and advocacy', in E. Makas and L. Schlesinger (eds.) *Insights and Outlooks: Current Trends in Disability Studies*, Society for Disability Studies/ Muskie Institute, Portland, ME, USA.

Kasnitz, D. and Shuttleworth, R. (in press) 'Anthropology in disability studies', in B. Swadener and L. Rogers (eds.) *The Semiotics of Dis/ability*, SUNY Press, Buffalo, USA.

Kasnitz, D. and Shuttleworth, R. (1999) 'Engaging anthropology in disability studies', *Position Papers in Disability Studies*, 1(1): 1–35.

Kasnitz, D. and Doe, T. (1998) 'Leadership and peer support in the independent living disability rights movement,' in E. Makas, B. Haller and T. Doe (eds.) *Insights and Outlooks: Current Trends in Disability Studies*, Society for Disability Studies/Muskie Institute, Portland, ME, USA.

Kasnitz, D., Bruckner, B. and Doe, T. (1996) *Leadership and Peer Support in the Independent Living Disability Rights Movement: Executive Summary*, Research and Training Center on Public Policy and Independent Living at the World Institute on Disability, Oakland, CA, USA.

Mayer, K. and Tuma, N. (eds.) (1989) *Event History Analysis in Life Course Research*, University of Wisconsin Press, Madison, USA.

7   A journey of discovery

Swapna McNeil

I was born in 1944 in Jamshedpur, in the state of Bihar in the North East of India, the third child and the only daughter in the family. It was one of the major steel towns and my father, a Chemistry Honours graduate, was a metallurgist. That was in the years before independence, in the middle of the war and towards the end of English rule. One of the first things I remember is the Hindu-Muslim war. I remember the tension in the house. We were Hindus but my father had a close friend who was a Bengali Muslim. They worked together at the steel plant and there were problems there, and so he hid his friend. I remember that Baba (father in Bengali) was really worried about him and worried about us too, because we were his family and if anybody found out . . . My parents were very cosmopolitan and did not believe that religion or difference should separate people. That may be an important factor in my own story too.

I was born an albino and I think that this was the first 'problem' in the family. They had never come across it before and did not know anybody else with that condition. I had no one to relate to. I never met anybody who was like me, although later in my teens people told me that there were others in Calcutta. I think my parents were very positive though. My grandfather had been chief medical officer and my uncle was a doctor. So I was in a medical environment and that must have had a positive impact. It would probably have been different for someone of a different caste or in a more rural area. Being born in a middle class family made a big difference. I think I was cushioned from some of it.

Family

Within six months of my birth my mum had her first heart attack. She had a heart condition already and was a rheumatic patient but it had never really surfaced until then. My mother was quite anxious about me and I can remember in my teens that I became quite an anxious person too. However, she was determined that I should be independent and did

79

not want me to feel that I should be a burden, just because I was different. She had gone to a missionary school and was very Western in her thoughts. She was a strong woman but after her first heart attack she knew that she would not be around for long. She wanted to prepare me. She did not want people to feel that they should pity me. As a mother, I think she just wanted the best for me.

So, I had a really difficult start. Not only was I different to look at but also, because my mum had a heart attack, I was passed around. There was nobody to look after me. So, I went round the houses to anybody who would look after me. There was one auntie who looked after me when I was very young and I used to call her my new mother for a long time. She had a daughter about my age and we became close friends. I think most of my friends were cousins when I was young. I come from quite a large family and that was sufficient. You grew up with them. The eldest boy was kind to me and I looked upon him as if he was my own brother. I was very close to them up to the age of six or seven, but when we moved away from Calcutta, I started to make friends at school.

Some of my relatives did not really want people to know that there was someone in the family 'like that'. I was very much a hidden factor, pushed away. Recently, my cousins told me that when we went out in the car, and someone was coming, they would push me down, out of sight. When I was growing up in my auntie's house in Calcutta, some of the servant children would scream if they saw me. I must have felt very hurt because by the age of twelve I felt really bad. I was very suicidal, despite the fact that my parents were so positive. That was there all through my childhood. I remember all sorts of questions about my identity – Who am I? Why am I like this? Why am I so different? That played a big part all through my childhood. I remember when I was twelve I wanted to learn swimming but my mother was worried. There was nobody to accompany me. To be seen with me would mean exposure to more awkward staring. Those kinds of things leave scars. You don't trust people any more. In some ways that made me quite independently minded.

My brothers were very sporty, as young boys are at that age. They were never in and my parents had to make special arrangements for me to go with somebody but there is only so much you can do for one child. So in some ways I missed out a bit on childhood. I had more adult company though. The younger couples that worked for Baba would come over. They would have been in their twenties when I was 13 or 14, and I saw more of them than anybody near my age. I was quite an isolated individual, quite fond of my own space, and once I got into reading I became a voracious reader. I used to sit up in a tree and read books. I didn't really miss the company.

The other problem was obviously my sight. Nobody understood how little I could see and I never told anybody, because I thought everybody could see the same. I didn't understand that other people could see. So, all through those first years, I used to muddle through stuff. Life was not very easy as far as my sight was concerned, because I could not go out on my own. I had to be very dependent. That was one of the worst things for me because I wanted to be independent.

In other ways, sight was the least of my problems. Disability for me was as much about my colour. It was like racism. Everybody used to stare at me, although I could never see their expressions. The older children would say, 'Oh, look at your hand' and they would put their hands next to me to show how light skinned I was. They thought they were helping me, trying to praise me, but it hurt my feelings when it was constantly pointed out. Under other circumstances there might have been a status attached to lighter skin. If you were fairer you were usually good looking, but being albino is too much. You are so separate from everybody else, and so you have to build your own kind of life. It was ironic to come to England much later and find other people suffering from colour prejudice, when I had experienced it with my light skin in India.

Education

I first went to school at the age of six. It was quite a small cosy school that my mum chose, rather than the bigger missionary school. There were no nuns in my first school. I went to Loreto Convent afterwards, the best chain of girls' schools in India. I think that because my mum went to a missionary school, she preferred the same for me. She was anxious that I should get the best and she felt that they would cope better with my sight. In reality, the only concession I had was to sit on the front row of the class – I used to walk up to the board to read. Later, when I was 12, I found it harder and was given a small orange magnifying glass. The other children were tolerant and never picked on me there.

On the first day I moved up three classes within one hour. My mother had taught me at home, although I don't remember it, and so when they placed all these sums in front of me I could do them. I could do all the additions and subtractions. So they moved me right from the kindergarten to Preparatory B within the hour. I felt very confident. I remember sitting in the back of Baba's car and him saying, 'She can't see but she's got a good head'. He constantly reinforced that and praised my intelligence. I may have become a bigheaded child but it was because I liked listening to stories and loved to read books.

When I was 12 my dad went to work in Europe. Up to that time I had always thought that my mum was fonder of my brothers and that my dad was fonder of me. As a parent, that is something I can understand more now but at that time it was very difficult when my father went away. Lots of things happened around that time. I remember that my eye surgeon died and that was a big blow. We moved back to Calcutta and I changed schools. I had terrible headaches, and my eyes used to water. I couldn't concentrate and the end result was that I had to leave the school and my friends. I never went back and that was the end of my school career – at 12 or 13. It was really bad at that age, compounded by the problems of my colour and my sight. I think I would have destroyed myself if I had not had support from my cousins. I would have finished my life then. I don't know what made me go on but I think it was education, a determination not to remain uneducated. I think that was the thing that made me go forward.

When my father came back from Europe, we moved to a new steel plant down in Orissa state, where there were no English schools. I had a tutor at home but I hated him. He was Bengali and knew nothing that I wanted to learn. However, I was determined to take my school final exam privately in the same year that I would have done it at school. I didn't want to lose a year. I couldn't take the public exam that was offered in the missionary schools, where the papers were sent to London, so I had to take the school final conducted by the board of secondary education in West Bengal. For that, I had to learn, or rather to teach myself, Bengali. I was very weak in Bengali. It was my mother tongue but I had never studied it because I went to an English school and English really was my first language. I read film magazines to get the spellings. In the end I scraped through Bengali and came out with flying colours in English, maths and the other subjects – and all with that tiny little magnifying glass!

Although my formal Western education was going quite well, I missed out on some of my culture and my religious education. My parents were very liberal Hindus. We went to festivals but we never had the daily ritual of worship and ceremony. I saw my aunties spending hours over religious work and couldn't understand why they never paid us any attention. As a child, I didn't want to know and denied myself some of the things that I should have known. There were strict codes for religious festivals and I was never allowed near the ceremonies because I was different. The religious practice was very male dominated and the priests dictated how everything should be done. Although I was a woman, I did not fit into their idea of a normal woman, and I had never learned about social interaction properly because I was so socially isolated. Little things used to affect me very deeply. I used to feel very hurt if somebody said 'Oh you've done that wrong'. When my mum died we had to do the ceremony at home and the priest was unhappy with the way I had made the wicks for the oil burners (I think they were too long). I had never done it before and I remember thinking that was typical of religious people. So I kept away from big religious gatherings.

Leaving home

I was determined that I would go on to further education but my uncle, the doctor, was very concerned that my sight might deteriorate if I studied. He had wanted me to learn braille. I was terribly angry. I remember saying, 'What do you know about me? I want to use my sight. I don't want to learn to braille'. I remember thinking that braille was for people who couldn't see at all. I could see! And I was struggling to use my sight as much as I could (it never did deteriorate).

By the time I was about 16 I was determined not to have anything to do with relatives, and I certainly did not want to stay with them. So, to go to college, I would have to stay in a hostel. My mum tried to send me to this place but they said that I would not fit in to the hostel because I couldn't see. They also thought that my skin condition might be infectious. They came up with some strange excuses, saying that I might take too long to have a bath, but the message was clear. They did not want me there. It was devastating. I told my mum to give up. I did not want to go somewhere where I would not be made welcome.

I could not get a place anywhere. None of the hostels would take me. They all said that they were full up. I had had enough. Then a friend wrote to say that there was a hostel that could take me in a campus university in Banaras (Varanasi). It was one of the best in India and fortunately one of the men who worked for my father had an influential family there. I went and that was that. I had found my new life. I completed my pre-university course and then my three-year degree – and all with the same little magnifying glass.

In the hostel we were three in a room and I made friends quickly. I started to learn about the social side of life. That was my first exposure really. The hostel was very cosmopolitan and there were many different communities from all over India. I knew very little Hindi when I arrived and they used to tease me about my broken speech but I soon picked it up. However, I was very good in English and this was an advantage. We had group reading sessions and I would help them with their essays. It was a good life and I made good friends. I never met anyone else who was disabled.

Sanskrit was compulsory at university, even to sit for the BA exam, and, because I did not know the Indian languages well, I found it difficult. Everyone knew that if I didn't pass then that was it. Then, just before my Sanskrit exam, my little orange magnifying glass was stolen. I never found it again. I thought that I would not be able to read the couplets without it but somehow I managed. I don't know how. I must have put some other kind of energy into it. So, I finally completed my BA in English and philosophy. Unfortunately, my mum died just after the exam and never heard my results.

My marks for the two subjects were the same and my philosophy tutors wanted me to continue with an MA. I really enjoyed Western philosophy. My whole focus was on the West. I don't know whether it was due to my school education, although I was never particularly interested in going there. That came much later. In the end I chose to take my master's degree in English Literature.

However, with my mum's death, I was needed at home. My dad was now head of his department and the general manager knew that he needed someone to look after him. It was the norm. He was unhappy that he had been left on his own after my mother's death, so I stayed with him. After my mum died I was very much the daughter who looked after the father. I would accompany him on trips because he did not like to be on his own. I went back late to join the MA course and my first marks were not very good. I had to depend on my friends' notes, but I caught up. By then I had made really good friends, some of whom I still correspond with.

When I finished the MA I had my first offer of work, teaching, but I did not feel confident enough to face a classroom full of children. To be honest, I was frightened of children, even the older ones. I had never had younger brothers and sisters and I remembered the way that young children would scream when they saw me and run away. My head wanted me to stay and to do a PhD but I was torn between the university and my dad, who was far away. My father had created a job for me, teaching English to the apprentices. So I gave in and went back. I was terribly bored.

Two years later I went back to Banaras and was persuaded to take a temporary teaching job there, and to enrol for a PhD (on the writings of William Faulkner). It was very new to me, and when the three-month post was up, I had to go back to my father. But I kept thinking about my studies. It was 1968 and India was changing. I applied to Yale and they accepted me. Unfortunately, someone forgot to send the papers and I was unable to go that year. Things change quickly. My uncle died and Baba was devastated. Both my brothers were in the army and had an accident. My dad's ulcer burst and he retired. All sorts of things happened. It was horrendous and I was left holding the fort. I went back to the daughter's role and forgot about America.

In 1969 my eldest brother left the army and went to work in England as a doctor. He got a little flat and wrote to me, asking if I wanted to come for a holiday. I was totally against spending my father's money. I didn't have enough myself, although I was doing private tuition and earning more than I had ever earned in my life. My father persuaded me in the end and we both came together. I came for a holiday but also asked my brother to go to Leeds University and ask whether they might accept me for a PhD in American literature. I didn't impress them with my Indian education but there was a Bengali man there who suggested I should enrol as an MA student instead. I agreed and renegotiated my visa (which was much easier in those days). I found it very difficult in England. I was unable to bring money over and we had always been quite well off in India. I had also lost my independence and was now dependent on my brother. I hated that. Staying at home was something that I did not appreciate and the sister's role did not fit me at all. I really wanted to break out.

Becoming disabled

To cut a long story short, I stayed on in England, married and had two children. I did not know anything about the kind of help available to people with limited vision. During the first fifteen years in England I never met anyone else with a visual impairment, until I started to work. I never thought of myself as blind or disabled. I knew my limitations but I did not relate to any kind of disabled identity. Even when I married in England, my in-laws always saw me as an individual. They never thought of me as disabled. They never expected me to put my impairment forward and say 'look at me I can't do this, will you help me?'.

I still felt very different though. I still asked 'Why me?' Why did I have to be different? I think the big difference was that I was accepted in England. Because of my skin colour, nobody made me out to be different. That difference wasn't there any more, except when I was with my brother's friends. My visual impairment was still 'my' problem because I had never shared it with anybody. I had never spoken about it. I never wanted anybody to draw attention to it. It was my problem and I had learned to cope with it.

Meeting other disabled people in England really changed things. It opened up a whole new society that I never knew was there. I was in my mid-40s before I met another blind person. My children were growing up and I was desperate for a job. I did various things and eventually became a patients' advocate. The assistant director said to me 'If you're going to be an advocate, are you registered yourself?' It was the first time I heard the word and I had to ask what it meant. She said that if I went through the process of registering as a blind person I might be more able to tell other people what it meant.

So, I went to my doctor and then to the consultant at the hospital. When I got there, I forgot that I had come to be registered. I read everything with the magnifying glass but they put me on the partial sight register anyway. They should really have put me on the blind register then but they must have thought that I could cope. Perceptions are very important. I never thought of myself as a blind person. So it was hard for me to go through the process of accepting that I was disabled. However, once I got through that I wondered why I had never known about it before. I started a learning process then, but I would still not work with other disabled people. I resisted that for a long time. Later, I began to think that I ought to do something because, if I had this problem finding out about services, what chance did others have?

I had lived in England for seventeen years and had never heard anything about services for blind people. Thinking back, I could really have done with some help, especially when the children were growing up. The social worker that visited me after registration suggested all kinds of things but the only one that interested me was a local drama group. That was where I really met other blind people – for the first time in my life. I didn't really want to know until then because I didn't consider myself disabled.

They made me very welcome and for the first time I felt that I was part of something in England. I was not on my own, struggling. Then one of the women told me about the Monoscope. She knew that I went to the theatre and she told me about low vision aids. So, they were the people that tutored me, from their experience, not the social workers. Since then, I have gone through a whole metamorphosis. I wonder how I could have been so insular.

I was very nervous in England. Even at work, I would rarely speak because I was afraid. My disability had become internalised, emotional. All through my university life I made sure not to put myself in situations where I might be hurt. I avoided that and tried not to talk about my difficulties. When I went for job interviews I would never tell them that I could not see their faces, that I had to sit away from the light. Now, for the first time, people were saying to me 'Take your magnifying glass out, make them aware how little you can see'. They started to influence me and I started to learn. I started to talk about disability.

It was about then that we first had the idea to start a local group for blind Asian people. A blind English man, who had a job with the council, asked me if I had heard of the Association of Blind Asians in London. My family's attitude was to keep away from disability organisations but I began to think about my own experience. If it had taken me so long to find out about information and services in England, with all my education, what chance did other blind Asian people have. One of the social workers introduced me to a blind Asian man and together we arranged the first meeting. My husband helped out with the transport and we began to meet regularly, every month. Later, when I started to meet the women, that became my main focus. As a health advocate, I began to see how Asian people were not given the information that they needed in England.

The National Federation of the Blind backed us and we had a lot of support from the community development worker. I can see now that that must have helped his work as well, to have an Asian minority group forming in the area. Things were progressing and my boss at work encouraged me to work more and more with other blind Asian people. We secured some funding to produce a report, along with a researcher from the university (Priestley 1994), and this helped us to get funding for a co-ordinator's post.

I did not feel that there was any real need for a big organisation at that time, but when I compared my life experiences with those of the people I was meeting, I realised that there was a lot to be done. I met so many people who had not been given that positive attitude towards education. They felt as though they were not valued. Back home, if you had ability they would try to develop that. Education has to be a priority. The opportunities are simply not there for disabled children in England and the schools are not interested in developing them. I am not sure whether it is society that makes people like that, but it becomes an ever-decreasing circle where everyone suffers. I still feel that my education in India, and my help from the doctors, contributed to me becoming an advocate.

It is difficult to know how we become what we are, but I feel now that it has been worthwhile. The weekly meetings at ABA are mostly elders but the group has also brought different age groups together. We have managed to get the community involved in festivals, because the Indian community have failed with that in the past. We are doing various things and I feel happy that I am a part of it. Sometimes I have taken on too much and I don't know how much I can continue to deliver, especially when I get tired and my health is not so good.

I wonder what would have happened to me if I had agreed to follow our Indian tradition of marriage. My father's sisters had felt that they should marry me off and began sending out wedding proposals, without consulting me. My father had seen this and used to send the letters on to me, 'You deal with it!', 'You can tell your aunts what you want'. Most Indian parents would have forced you to do things but he was so liberal. He had a totally different attitude.

REFERENCES

Priestley, M. (1994) *Organising for Change: ABA (Leeds) research paper*, Association of Blind Asians/Leeds City Council Health Unit.

Using life story narratives to understand
disability and identity in South Africa

Ruth Morgan

There is a rapidly growing body of research focusing on how people use
language to construct personal meaning and identity (de Certeau 1984,
Miller *et al.* 1990, Rosaldo 1993). Accordingly, scholars have renewed
their interest in life story narratives as a way to access the construction of
self (Gee 1991, Linde 1993, Sun 1998). Life stories are a type of
narrative, providing a window through which we can examine the ways
that individuals actively interpret and negotiate their reality. In the
process of telling their life stories, people construct meaning by selecting,
evaluating and emphasising significant experiences (Linde 1993). Thus
life stories are important sites of social-cultural identity construction, in
which people make sense of their relation to themselves and to others.

Life stories as a research tool in disability studies

The analysis of life story narratives is an exciting qualitative research
methodology, yielding rich and textured data on the lives of disabled
individuals, in the context of the broader society. Although life stories
have been used increasingly by social scientists to document the lives of
marginalised groups (Lincoln 1993), they have not been used a great
deal in research focusing on disabled people. Disability research frequently privileges the voices of able-bodied outsiders and excludes those
of disabled people. Considering that research is often conducted by
outsiders, life story narratives provide an opportunity for collaboration
that privileges the voices of insiders.

As an outsider involved in a large disability study for the Department
of Health in South Africa,[1] I was interested in using life stories to access
the worldview and construction of identity of people who have been
disadvantaged and silenced by the dominant South African society
during the era of apartheid. Their life story narratives also provide us
with a window into their experiences of the transition to a democracy
since 1995.

Le Compte (1993) points out that life story narratives can be used for the purposes of research as well as for that of social advocacy and activism. Life stories are a means of giving voice to groups that have been oppressed and thereby silenced by the dominant society. Accordingly there were two reasons for including life stories in this study. The first was to complement quantitative data with qualitative data that would provide policy makers with direct access to the stories of previously silenced people. These stories are powerful testimonies in their own right that need to be heard by the people currently in power. They provide colour and context to the quantitative data, which often provide only an *averaged* or *aggregated* view of the disability experience. The second reason for their inclusion was to empower the narrators through the process of telling their stories. The narrators spontaneously commented on the importance they attached to the experience of telling their stories after they had been interviewed. Furthermore, the analysis of these stories allows an examination of the repressive impact of apartheid on the lives of disabled people and the current disjuncture between the experiences of individuals on the ground and the new policies that enshrine the rights of disabled people in line with the equality clause in the new constitution.

For the purposes of this chapter I will discuss three life stories, collected in Johannesburg during 1997 and 1998. A Deaf person using South African Sign Language interviewed the Deaf participant. The other two were interviewed in English. The interviews were semi-structured, tape-recorded and lasted about one hour. They were then transcribed and translated where necessary.

Thuli

Thuli is an African woman who is now in her early 50s. She was an exiled member of the African National Congress representing the church, the women's league and the youth league. Thuli was a journalist before she had a stroke in 1989. She comes from a family of political activists. Her brother was killed in police detention in the early 1980s, while she was injured in an assassination attempt. In 1989 she had a stroke that left her aphasic. Consequently she finds it hard to talk in more than fragmented words and phrases and is struggling to learn how to read and write. In 1995, her mother was killed in a car accident in Soweto. It is impossible to separate out how Thuli sees herself and her activism from the way that she sees her disability experience and its relationship to the broader South African society.

Thuli sees herself as 'completely blank' after her stroke and uses this phrase to describe her difficulty in communicating.

long time ago,
nothing,
completely blank,
nothing

She then uses this phrase to describe the state's silencing of herself
and her family during the 1980s, when extreme measures were used
against the opposition such as detention without trial and death during
detention. Her brother was killed after being detained and even the
Truth and Reconciliation Commission hearings did not produce the
answers Thuli's family wanted. She attributes both her brother's and
mother's death to the former government who had to kill them to
prevent them from speaking out, rendering them 'blank'.

Ya same story
And why nobody (did anything) eh?
Eh Mandla died *blank,*
Mamaza eh . . . *blank completely,*
So me no speech *blank,*
My husband two years jail, same thing, *blank.*

Thuli does not see her own stroke and resulting aphasia as an isolated
incident but as part of a pattern of state induced violence, which she
refers to repeatedly using the phrase 'suspect racism somehow'. This
racism aimed to silence her entire family. As a religious person, her way
of making sense of her stroke is by giving agency to God whom she
regards as ultimately responsible for allowing this racism to occur.

Suspect racism somehow
My mother drive and truck crash

Thuli goes on to attribute her brother's death to:

Something missing . . .
Suspect racism somehow.

Thuli has always constructed herself in relation to God. She sees
racism as having historical roots. Something went wrong with the world
when God fell asleep and did not prevent South Africa from being
colonised and subsequently ruled by the apartheid government.
Another refrain is her questioning 'why' God allowed these things to
happen as well as her conclusion 'something missing' referring to the
fact that she is living in a world lacking justice.

Ya ya that's why God
Something wrong here
Long time ago anyway
Long time ago
Something got wrong
Racism
God himself

> Ya *why* stupid
> *Something missing*

Thuli continues this refrain 'something missing' with a more recent episode in the liberation struggle when another exiled ANC leader Oliver Tambo had a stroke. She asks why God forgot Tambo? She then concludes 'something missing'.

> Oliver Tambo beautiful but somewhat forgotten
> My mother gone completely, so eh forgot
> I travelled with Tambo who also had stroke
> But he could still read and write
> And what happened?
> And why this thing?
> *Something missing.*

She emphasises that Tambo could still read and write after his stroke and was therefore better off than her. Thuli finds her inability to read and write more debilitating than not being able to speak properly. She expresses her anger at not being able to do so.

> Wheelchair
> But now angry, angry
> And then walk
> But (can't) read and write
> Angry. . . .

Thuli perceives herself to have twenty per cent of the capacity that she had before her stroke. She cannot work since she had her stroke.

> But long time ago hundred
> But now aphasia, disability
> Eh twenty per cent . . .
> No speech
> No work
> Nothing
> Gone
> Ya disability
> At least (if I could) read and write
> Speech, I don't care
> At least work and talk, read
> But long time ago
>
> Why, I mean?
> Ya but (can't) read and write why?
> Ya, read and write no
> But now no speech
> Aphasia read and write gone

Thuli also links her inability to read and write to her inability to work as a writer. She wants to complete her book but cannot do so. Thuli does not realise that it is in fact the larger society that is exacerbating her impairment. As an unemployed person without a disability grant, she is struggling to survive and does not have the resources to buy a computer with the appropriate assistive technology. She could in fact use a computer with a voice synthesizer.

She goes on to discuss the fact that despite the advent of a constitution that prohibits discrimination on the basis of disability status, she is not aware of any changes on the ground that will improve the quality of her life. She has spent three years unsuccessfully trying to get a disability grant through the Department of Welfare. Nkeli (1998) discusses the disjuncture between the legal and constitutional protection that the new South Africa provides for disabled South Africans and the discrimination that still exists to prevent these rights being realised.

From this life story, we can see how macro level political changes have shaped Thuli's interpretation of the significant events that have impacted on her life. She roots herself firmly in the past as an African woman whose heritage has been stolen by white outsiders while God was sleeping. Subsequent generations of white people have waged war against her people and her family, resulting in the death of two close family members. She closely escaped death but was silenced in the end by a stroke while she was in exile, evading the former government who tried to assassinate her. She cannot read and write, and therefore cannot communicate her story to the world. She also cannot tell it verbally due to her speech problems. Moreover, she is disabled by a society where she has difficulty getting her disability grant, access to assistive technology, occupational support or employment opportunities. She has become disillusioned with her comrades in the struggle who now occupy positions of power in the current government and who seem to have forgotten her.

> Shuttle all over the world
> But long time ago
> Shuttle all over the world
> And now nobody

Thobile

Thobile is a Deaf African man who uses sign language. He is in his early 40s and became Deaf at the age of seven as a result of a childhood illness. He is a Deaf activist and the leader of a grass roots Deaf organisation.

He starts his story by describing the segregated Deaf school for black children that he attended as a child. Because of the Group Areas Act, he was not allowed to attend the white school in Johannesburg. Instead, like other Deaf children from Soweto, he had to go to a school specifically designed for his ethnic group. He was therefore forced to go to a school a two-hour drive away that catered specifically for seSotho speaking black children.

Long ago I went to a Deaf school near Rustenburg called Kutlwanong School for the Deaf . . . When I arrived at the Deaf school, I saw other Deaf children. I lived at the Deaf school and only returned home to Soweto for holidays.

During school holidays in Soweto, he connected with other Deaf children who had returned from schools located all over the country. It is to this time, that Thobile attributes the beginnings of his activism and leadership role.

My mother asked me why do you help Deaf people? My mother remembers that when I was young, eight years old, many Deaf always visited my home. My older brother was also Deaf but never became an activist. Although I was younger, I was the one who became involved with other Deaf.

However, when he was twelve years old, he was expelled from the Deaf school. He is still not sure why that happened and thinks it may have something to do with the Group Areas Act. He remained at home in Soweto for three years due to the lack of educational and employment opportunities, spending his time playing soccer with other Deaf children.

He emphasises the fact that there was no space where Deaf people could gather at that time to seek help or support. Playing soccer gave him an opportunity to consolidate his leadership position among his peers. During this time he only mixed with black Deaf people due to the strict segregation policies of apartheid.

Many Deaf people visited me that year in 1972 as they wanted to play football . . . In 1972, I was expelled from Kutlwanong. Between 1973 and 1975 the Deaf had no office. We only played football. Other Deaf people asked me why we never met white Deaf people. They were mean during apartheid. Everyone was segregated.

Thobile's expulsion from school, at a time when Deaf black people were so marginalised by society that it did not matter if they attended school, served to politicise him about the extent to which Deaf people were oppressed and motivated him to take a leadership role in the Deaf community.

Although Thobile did not go to high school, he informs us that his situation is not different from those Deaf learners who completed high school, as they were taught a vocational trade such as carpentry or welding and left school with minimal literacy skills. His account of

Deaf schools focuses on the inequity between hearing and Deaf education.

Deaf people are not taught in schools . . . School was never good because they only taught us until noon when we had to go and do vocational training – painting, woodwork, welding and gardening. The problem at school was that we had to do vocational training at the expense of academic training.

The schools for the Deaf were not the same as the schools for the hearing where they teach people properly. Hearing students never had to do vocational training. Deaf students were never educated properly. The problem with Deaf education was not only in Rustenberg but all over the country.

Thobile goes on to elaborate some of the problems that still exist today in Deaf African schools.

Deaf Sowetans have many problems. School teachers make Deaf girls pregnant and when the parents ask who the father is, the Deaf girls say that they don't know. The teachers are never taken to court because Deaf women don't know how (to stand up against harassment).

During the 1976 student uprisings in Soweto, Thobile and other Deaf people were further marginalised by their hearing peers, as they did not know what was going on. Some were shot by stray bullets, some were badly assaulted by police while others were arrested and released the next day due to communication breakdowns with the police. Members of the hearing community were afraid to come to their rescue for fear of police reprisals. Thobile describes in some detail how he and others had the idea of having Deaf identification cards made for Deaf people. This was a concrete way to prevent people being arrested due to a breakdown of communication and could also be used to obtain free access to public transport.

He goes on to say that the predominantly white, and hearing, national Deaf organisation the South African National Council of the Deaf (SANCD) did not provide the Sowetan Deaf with any kind of support, although a white Deaf priest did help them address their problems.

SANCD never had any kind of identification card . . . In 1982 when Jabu Tshabalala came to my own home in order to see me, I explained that the Deaf people didn't have an office or a club or any place of their own. Why didn't the SANCD help us? After all they knew that there were Deaf people in Soweto. They never ever helped us . . . SANCD knew that Deaf people in Soweto wanted an office but they never helped us

Around 1983 Thobile and some of his friends established their own community-based organisation, to serve the needs of Deaf black people in Soweto. They obtained an office with assistance from the Azanian People's Organisation (AZAPO), which was actively engaged in the liberation struggle. Their leader at that time Jabu Tshabalala was also a member of AZAPO. He was murdered in taxi violence in 1984. The early 1980s was a time of political violence as the liberation struggle gained momentum.

Thobile then gave up his job to take over the leadership of the organisation. He did not receive a salary and survived on small donations from members. After he left his job he could not afford to feed the Deaf people who constantly came to his home. He stressed that his life as an activist ruined his marriage but his parents accept his salvation to work for the Deaf cause, as they have watched him do this since childhood.

The SANCD became the Deaf Federation of South Africa (DEAFSA) with the new dispensation in 1994 and Thobile is now a member of the Provincial National Executive Committee. However, he still feels that the national office of DEAFSA is not committed to the needs of the black Deaf community and that in reality not much has changed since 1994. He hopes that in the future, things will change. He went on to say that during the last decade Disabled People South Africa (DPSA) tried to assist Deaf people. However, after communication breakdowns, DPSA quickly withdrew. His perception is that DPSA has not fully committed itself to the needs of Deaf people.

Thobile's vision for the future includes committing his organisation to educating the younger generation in life skills and leadership skills. In this way, the Deaf community will be able to attain self-representation.

Thobile's story, like Thuli's, illustrates the interaction between macro level socio-political changes and key life events. Thobile constructs himself as a Deaf activist and identifies strongly with other Deaf users of sign language who are marginalised by the hearing world. This oppression that originated under apartheid still exists in the new South Africa. Another recurrent theme is his experience of racism growing up under apartheid and being discriminated against as a black Deaf person. Thobile's story also brings out the fact that despite the recent change-over to a democratic government, his life has not changed in any substantive way.

Joseph

Joseph is an African man who grew up in a village in the Eastern Cape. He has a law degree but has been unable to find a job since graduating.

Joseph describes how he grew up in a small village. He then identifies himself as disabled.

I'm the only one with a disability, all of them are pretty normal

Joseph recounted how his father did not want to accept that he could have had a son with albinism and contested his paternity. However, after the women elders had confirmed his paternity, he had to accept that his son had albinism.

My father was disputing eh paternity (laughs) so when they went there. In our tradition you send the old mothers to go and eh check the child, inspect the child and make sure that the child (is yours) to look for the signs, the family signs. So when they got there, my father was angry 'No – I can't get an albino' something like that. So when they got there, they checked under the ears and everything, 'This is our child. So we are satisfied'.

Joseph goes on to explain that disabling attitudes exist in traditional African society.

But I believe it was so difficult for him to accept that because I think it was a taboo of that community. Even the people who were there saying 'you know he was born a monkey, you know'. It was painful and I was the first born and the first child. His first child.

Joseph remembers that his first experience of difference, and being aware of his albinism, came from early childhood when other children teased him. His response was to get angry and to fight back physically.

It is clear from the very early childhood because you'll meet people who'll be teasing you. Calling you albino, in our language *nkau*, you know, which is a monkey in English . . . Sometimes I can say I used to force them not to tease me by beating them. I used to be very strong then, that time.

Despite his leadership skills, Joseph continued to feel peer discrimination in high school where disabling attitudes were more subtly expressed.

They'll be showing those signs of discrimination. Not necessarily teasing. Sometimes to undermine me, to show disrespect. . . . I developed those leadership qualities so even at high school, but at first they seemed to have some problems with me because I'm albino and I used to have some problems, for instance it used to take a lot of time to convince the person there's nothing wrong with me, its only pigment.

There was an assumption that Joseph's pigment differences indicated that he was intellectually impaired. So, he felt compelled to prove to his peers and teachers that he was intelligent.

It was some kind of motivation (to achieve) although it was a painful motivation. I can say so. But I used to convince them that I'm pretty normal. I can do whatever is done by any normal child or normal person.

In fact, people started to think that his albinism was the reason for his academic achievements. However, Joseph worked hard in order to avoid a special school education.

I was a brilliant person. Most people thought that because I'm an albino but it was not like that. I was working. I was a hard worker. I read my books during the day, every day. I had that motivation that if I don't need to go to a special school to prove my abilities, I have to prove them here.

Joseph had to fight for acceptance in his own community, where negative attitudes existed towards disability during the political struggle of the 1980s. He took on the task of educating his comrades in the street committee that he could do the job despite his perceived impairment. At the time when street committees were actively opposing the apartheid government, by making the country ungovernable, Joseph was fighting additionally for the rights of people with albinism, to be treated equally.

I was once a member of the street committee. I was elected there as a general secretary. It was for the first time I was in the leadership (not students) but the community at large. So at first they were very much skeptical but I managed to convince them. Even the adults, they don't understand what disability generally means.

Joseph has always seen himself as equal to others. It is his belief that attending a mainstream school has enabled him to participate fully in society, in contrast to those children with albinism who went to special schools where they never had the opportunity to integrate socially.

I'm a person who's always tried to prove disability as nothing, that is you are a normal person. You think normally, you can do things normally, that is in particular in albinism, you can do things normally except for the visual impairment. Its only a visual impairment and in all my life I've been involved in many activities . . . My life was active . . . but other albinos, you'll see them, they are so withdrawn, always afraid to socialise.

However, when Joseph was nine years old, he was taking grade one for the fourth time. Interestingly, he only added this information as an aside later on in his narrative, which suggests that this was not perceived to be a problem by himself or his family. In fact, Joseph emphasises that he did not fail, but refused to go back to school after school holidays, which resulted in him having to repeat grade one.

He then relates how his father decided to enrol him in the special school for blind and Deaf children, where there are a number of children with albinism. Joseph attributes the agency to his father, although later it emerges that his teachers advised that he should attend the special school after he had repeated grade one for the fourth time. Joseph was adamant that he did not want to go there and told his father so when they arrived. This is an important event in his life, as it shows his resolve from an early age to cope in a mainstream setting, irrespective of the wishes of the teachers, and to remain integrated in the broader society.

We went there and when I got there, I just told my father "I'm not going to study here." I didn't want that place. Then I went back to my old primary school where I was comfortable until high school.

He feels that it is imperative for people with albinism to be main-
streamed, as it gives them the opportunity of convincing others that they
can do the same things that non-disabled people can do.

Because I believe it is so hard to convince people that you are very normal, you
know you have to do it yourself. For instance when I was at high school I was
given part of the student leadership because I could prove myself in meetings, in
discussion and debates. I could prove myself that there is nothing I couldn't do
because of this pigment.

Joseph feels that prospective employers covertly discriminate against
him on the basis of his albinism. During job interviews he is frequently
asked how he copes with his eyesight. He interprets this question as
indicating that the prospective employer perceives him in terms of his
impairment and that this is the reason that many people have not
offered him jobs. However they will never admit that they are discriminating against him. Joseph now feels that people with albinism are
entitled to disability grants, as a result of the difficulty in getting employment due to discrimination. It is society that is disabling people with
albinism who are quite capable of working.

In my job search this was indicated. Albinos are discriminated in any job. They
think they are weak. That's the first misconception they are having. They think
they are physically weak. They cannot do anything, you know. So I've discovered
these things and most of them (albinos), they find difficulties getting employment . . . You cannot get a job on your own. You have to via a certain agency
which is sympathising with the disabled people. So that's why I'm saying they do
qualify to get disability grants because its so difficult for them to get employment.

 Joseph feels that disability issues are not a priority to the Government,
as most people do not know that the Government is addressing the issue
of disability in any way.

They (government) are not taking it as a priority, that's why most disabled
people, they don't even know that the government is trying to do something
about the problem of disabled people . . . I think the government should put it
as a priority. But it should be taken to the top as one of the priorities like
affirmative action. It should be part of affirmative action.

Joseph's life story focuses on his determination not to let his impairment get in the way of his life. He refused to be ghettoised and to attend
a special school. He would not allow people in authority to label him
and avoided internalising externally imposed feelings of otherness. He
insisted that he was as good as anybody else. This theme of refusing to
allow society to disable him, is central to his success throughout his
schooling and tertiary education. It continues in the present where
he refuses to accept the discrimination preventing him from finding
employment.

Conclusion

In this chapter I have considered the way that three individuals construct their lives in terms of the broader societal changes from apartheid to democracy. A theme that cuts across all these life stories, irrespective of disability is the intolerance of the broader society, which was entrenched during apartheid and persists despite the constitutional changes assuring equity. What comes through most strongly is the disabling effect of intolerance and prejudice in the lives of the narrators.

Note

1 This chapter is based on data collected for the national baseline survey on disability, for The Department of Health, Directorate: Chronic Diseases, Disabilities and Geriatrics (*see* Schneider *et al.* 1999).

REFERENCES

De Certeau, M. (1984) *The Practice of Everyday Life*. University of California Press, Berkeley CA, USA.

Gee, J. (1991) 'A linguistic approach to narrative', *Journal of Narrative and Life History*, 1 (1): 15–39.

LeCompte, M. (1993) 'A framework for hearing silence: what does telling stories mean when we are supposed to be doing science?', in D. McLauglin and W. Tierney (eds.) *Naming Silenced Lives: Personal Narratives and the Process of Educational Change*, Routledge, New York, USA.

Lincoln, Y. (1993) 'I and thou: method voice and roles in research with the silenced', in *Naming Silenced Lives: Personal Narratives and the Process of Educational Change*, McLauglin D. and W. G. Tierney (eds.), Routledge, New York, USA.

Linde, C. (1993) *Life Stories: The Creation of Coherence*, New York University Press, USA.

Miller, P., Potts, R., Fung, H., Hoogstra, L., and Mintz, J. (1990) 'Narrative practices and the construction of self in childhood', *American Ethnologist*, 17(2): 292–311.

Nkeli, J. (1998) *How to Overcome Double Discrimination of Disabled People in South Africa*, paper presented to the 'Legislation for Human Rights' conference, 24 August 1998, Stockholm, Sweden.

Rosaldo, R. (1993) *Culture and Truth, the Remaking of Social Analysis*, Beacon Press, Boston MA, USA.

Schneider, M., Claassens, M., Kimmie, Z., Morgan, R., Naicker S., Roberts A., and McLaren, P. (1999) *We Also Count! The Extent of Moderate and Severe Reported Disability and the Nature of the Disability Experience in South Africa*, Community Agency for Social Enquiry, Johannesburg, South Africa.

Sun, L. (1998) 'The loss of narrative innocence: the development of narrative consciousness from child to adolescent,' *Narrative Inquiry*, 8(1): 203–12.

9 Social change and self-empowerment: stories of disabled people in Russia

Elena Iarskia-Smirnova

It is necessary to be skilled in falling to be able to stand up and move
further. (Yuri Nikolaevitch Kazakov)

The purpose of this chapter is to explore the subjective dimension of
Russian women's and men's experience of living with disability in Soviet
and post-Soviet times, and to assess the significance of these memories
for current constructions of disability and identity. In my earlier writings
on issues surrounding disability in Russia, I focused on the experiences
of families rearing a disabled child, on the barriers and limits in the
social location of such a family and their children (Iarskia-Smirnova
1997). Addressing the contemporary politics of social exclusion and its
institutionalisation, through an analysis of interviews with Russian
mothers of disabled children, I have looked at how gender stereotypes,
insufficient services and discriminatory social attitudes frustrate efforts
to develop social tolerance, inclusion, and the participation of disabled
children and their families in contemporary Russian society (Iarskia-
Smirnova 1999a, 1999b).

Recently, it has become increasingly evident to me that the needs-
and-resources analysis of disabled children and their families 'in terms
of living with impairment *per se* (that is, in terms of a medicalised
discourse of the difficult "personal" consequences of being ill or impaired)' (Thomas 1999: 47), needs to be balanced with the enabling
aspects of resistance and success in the lives of disabled adults, in terms
of disability as socially constructed phenomena (Oliver 1990). Here I
use a biographical approach and a narrative method (Booth 1996) to
make sense of these aspects in the stories of disabled women and men
recounted to me in Saratov, Russia, during 1999–2000.

This chapter is based on two of twelve oral histories conducted in an
attempt to learn more about the lives of disabled people who lived
during both the Soviet and post-Soviet periods. The respondents nar-
rated their pasts selectively, based upon their values and interests, as
interviewees do – especially in telling about complex and troubling

events (Riessman 1993: 64). Although I had a list of prepared questions, I rarely referred to it, and the interviews flowed according to each person's desire to talk. Sometimes, I discontinued the questioning altogether, as the respondents became involved in their own stories. I decoded and analysed the taped interviews as texts, using an approach that asks how meaning is being constructed and how it might be constructed differently – in other words, analysing the contextual basis of motives (*ibid.*).

Biography is the product of a social world, and the rules that an individual follows over the course of his or her life 'contribute powerfully to the sense that each of us has about "who I am" (or am prevented from being)' (Thomas 1999: 48). Being personally or intersubjectively felt and uncovered in oral history, the effects of social forces and processes actively structure the life course and biography. At the same time memory 'brings forth the "order" and the "rules" thus trans-forming biographical stocks of knowledge into a biographical resource' (Hoerning 1996: 11–12). As Hammersley and Atkinson (1983: 107) suggest, 'accounts are not simply representations of the world; they are part of the world they describe'. The memories that help us to make sense of our life are both socially constructed and personal phenomena, embedded in the subjective experience of each individual.

Anna Vassilievna Semionova and Yuri Nikolaevitch Kazakov, the focus of this chapter, were two of many Russian children who contracted polio in the early 1950s. 'The time of polio' in their interviews sounds as an identification marker: 'now the disabled are different'. Both, although unacquainted with each other, are very engaged in public activity, defending themselves and others in unfair situations, organising cultural or sport events, advocating for the recognition and implementation of the civil rights for disabled people.

Anna

Born in a village of Saratov oblast in 1949, and disabled by the age of 18 months, Anna Vassilievna was a beneficiary of Soviet efforts to advance people of her physical status during the last four decades of Soviet power. Anna Vassilievna remembers her mother as a tormented but dignified woman, who brought up ten children, unlike her father, who 'was drinking hard and behaved like a hooligan'. As a child, Anna spent a long time crawling in the house and the yard until a visitor from the city saw her and convinced her parents of the necessity for treatment and schooling. This is how she got to the orthopaedic treatment centre, to a local school, and later to a special boarding school for children with motor impairments. Special facilities for disabled children were established in Soviet Russia to provide both treatment and education. In addition to clinics, nursing homes and boarding schools for children with different impairments, there were also vocational schools for adolescents, with residential facilities attached to them. Children lived and studied there, gaining skills and certificates for one of a few occupations that disabled people were considered capable of and eligible for.

Although a few of these institutions had much experience, and provided exemplary care, many compromised themselves and have come under scrutiny, by Russian journalists in the 1980s and now by international human rights organisations, for their methods of diagnosis and treatment. However, it would be a mistake to conclude simply that life in these institutions, and the wider society, provided children with only harmful and disabling environments for their socialisation. There were also some significant achievements in the area of special education and vocational rehabilitation. Some staff acted as advocates, making great efforts to help and empower children (for more details on the lives of disabled people in the Soviet Union see Sutton 1980). Anna Vassilievna's interview showed how, when there was nobody else to rely on, disabled children and adolescents also became such advocates.

Early life and education plays a major role in her narrative, and the years spent in boarding and vocational schools remain central to Anna Vassilievna's life history. At the beginning, I encouraged her to recall her whole life for me, starting with early childhood. Having told many stories about those days, she did not seem to welcome the opportunity to discuss details of her working experience and more recent life, although she gave me several short anecdotes.

She is certain that it was at boarding school where she, and other disabled children gained a sense of equity:

We have all been equal. We all had a habit of sharing, communality. When you grow up among the equal, you feel more confidence. We as children were rather free. When the inspectors visited our boarding school, they would come to us, to the children and ask about our lives. For instance, we told them stop buying absolutely same clothes for each us – it was done. But in general, we all kept silent, we were not used to complain.

Her voice sounded confident, even proud, as she strengthened this last thesis with the comparison: 'I never could understand when a physically healthy woman or man complains about aches and lacks'.

Her narrative consists of a series of vivid stories, each of them related to some aspect of her experience of transgressing the boundaries between the disabled and non-disabled. Often, she had to articulate this difference to make herself visible. She recalls how her sister thought she did not need a new dress because she should look as modest as possible. 'But they look at me more often than at you', Anna replied, '[therefore] I need a beautiful dress more than you!'. Frequently she speaks about abuses of power, and about a sense of dignity. In every event in her life the role of resistance seems important in building and re-asserting her own identity:

A teacher at school was harmful, but it made no sense to scream at me because I immediately reacted with wild resistance. I never considered myself lower than a teacher, or even a director. It was so since my childhood, and today, too, I give rebuff, it is probably [because of] my temperament.

When Anna and her comrades graduated from boarding school, some were sent to vocational schools or back to their parents. Those who had no parents, or who were considered to have no ability for further learning, were sent to different nursing homes. Semionova got to the vocational school in Lipetsk oblast:

It was a building with four floors and at first a committee called me up to say that I won't be admitted. Why? Because, they said, "it would be difficult for you here, how, for example, you would climb the stairs?". I must study, I answered, and after you see the results you decide whether or not I am to be here. And I turned my back to this committee because I did not want them to see the tears in my eyes. – "Aren't you a polite girl?", one woman asked: "Why did you turn your back towards us?" And I told them: "It's because I do not want to put myself down by showing you that I am offended!". Well, [the disabled] people resisted, but there were those who got drunk, committed suicide . . .

But there were also cases when orphans found their parents, and Anna Vassilievna tells me a 'happy-end story' of one boy whose mother left him at an institution without telling his father. Later, the truth was discovered and the boy was taken back to Moscow, where he lives now as an adult in his own apartment.

Many of her stories show how different the experience of young disabled people was from that of their non-disabled peers. Anna tells what it was like to arrange for grieving rituals and funerals for friends who had died: the case of a young man in vocational school who had heart problems, and a dramatic story about an unhappy love affair in a nursing home when a young woman committed suicide. Thus, young disabled people gained many experiences of loss and grief, as well as of independent living, while still children. Growing up without parents or supportive services, they had to decide and arrange everything for themselves, often without help from the institution's administration. In such cases, Anna would employ all her energy to prove that her friends deserved respect when they passed away. She would get permission and arrange the ritual: 'These were the first normal funerals for that time'. Such a sad farewell also served as a victory over circumstances, as a triumph of self-assurance and consolation. Anna's stories too offer a kind of memorial to the men and women with whom she spent her earlier life.

Anna emphasises the commonalities of life with disability as well as the universal experience of all people: 'When you have lived among the disabled, you do everything like everybody else, though it is maybe slow . . . The disabled are the same [as other] people, they possess weaknesses and good features, but they have more complexes'. She talks as if disability was not a defining experience ('I do not count myself as disabled'), but it appears central to her sense of identity, a biographical resource. Her stories demonstrate that society has the power to name and define the identities of disabled people, to formulate and maintain definitions of normality:

When we, the disabled, come to a welfare agency, we are to be dressed in rags, we must not make up, we have to look poor and bad, otherwise we'd be told: "Are you disabled? Oh, no, you aren't!" Or [they] would say: "Yeah, we know your business company of the disabled, there is one disabled shop assistant over there, and he used to smoke cigarettes with filters. Is he disabled?!" Hence, they mean, if somebody has impairments, he or she must live their whole life as a pauper, must not work, but live on state charity.

Cigarettes with filters in this context serve as a sign of high income, which according to the powerful, does not correspond with the definition of disabled people as dependent and needy, sick individuals (Hughes 1998). Disabled people are being reminded all the time who they are:

Often somebody would give us change, for instance, when I was in the corridor, waiting in line in the welfare office, a man gave me some change though I didn't ask him for it, he just saw me and my crutches and reacted in such a way. Another time, my husband and me, we were getting gasoline at a gas station. Unexpectedly, a man from a rich car approached and gave us some money. Well, perhaps, it was hard for him to see two disabled at once.

She says, she accepts these charitable moments without irritation because it helps people to find peace in their own souls. She often objectifies the behaviour and attitudes of other people as nature, that one cannot change and to which one must adjust:

[My brothers] would leave me because I would not be able to get along with them in time. It is natural. That's why I tried to go out in advance, much earlier than my brothers, to have more time for the same distance. You see, it is possible to avoid a painful place, that's all . . . For example, I could not get involved in romantic relations so I observed how others did it around me.

Anna repeatedly admits the impossibility of true, romantic love. Rather, she believes in friendship and mutual support. Perhaps, this is due to the effects of stigma, of 'not being interested' in sex, which all our disabled respondents carried and shared with us, 'a heritage traditionally rooted in avoidance, censorship, and suppression of sexual growth and development' (Fitz-Gerald and Fitz-Gerald 1985: 485). Anna's narrative is intricately bound up with 'public narratives and metanarratives concerning gender and disability' (Thomas 1999: 51), where the disabled body is poor, asexual and dislocated, regulated by public discourse and controlled by the state.

In the dispute with agency and choice, the structural often has more influence on disabled lives: 'Yeah, I did graduate from this vocational school but I did not go to college for I was afraid of the stairs I would have to climb there'. In Russia special state legislation concerning building construction adjusted for people with impairments did not exist until the 1990s. Even now, only a few new buildings have been designed for access, while the major part of the built environment, as well as public transportation, remains inaccessible for people like Anna. But social class, and her primary socialisation in boarding school, set up the limits of her choice more than her impairment. Several of my other respondents grew up in their own families, entered and graduated from college. With few exceptions, the boarding school graduates rarely gained any education higher than vocational school.

Anna admits the role of natural networks, interdependence and linked lives at different points of her life course development when she compares the biography of other disabled people with her own. Having little support from her family, but aided by teachers, friends and her self-confidence, she achieved a sense of her own ordinary yet unique qualities (Mairs 1996: 144). Hers is not a 'triumph-over-tragedy story' (though she survived tragedies and had triumphs, too) but, as Nancy Mairs put it, an 'adventure story', exploring uncharted territory and drawing her own map to guide herself and others (Mairs 1996: 145).

Yuri

My first encounter with Yuri Nikolaevitch Kazakov, the director of a Sports Center for disabled children, took place at the Sports Society

'Spartak'. A few days earlier, I telephoned him at his work, introduced myself and set up an appointment. When I entered the two-storey building with the 'Spartak' sign on the door, I saw and heard a sports hall on the right hand side where a team of people without impairments was playing volleyball. I found Kazakov one floor above. After giving his permission to use the tape recorder during the interview, Yuri Nikolaevitch unexpectedly asked me to refrain from turning it on. He wanted to talk, and to pose questions that interested him. Thus, on the first occasion, no one was interviewed but me. Because of that I gained a unique opportunity as a researcher to understand subjective and structural issues through communication. As Lamneck (1988: 200) notes:

The area of interest in social research is the stock of knowledge of the members of a society, and this knowledge is only able to be experienced through communication . . . And it is exactly the inclusion of socio-structural aspects that allows one to grasp social reality by means of communicative methods (cited in Hoerning 1996: 25)

Yuri's questions were about my studies: 'Why were my colleagues and I interested in disability? Was our research effective and in what way? What practical outcomes were caused by our studies?' When we had spent more than an hour talking about these things, sometimes debating concepts and disagreeing on perspectives ('I am an uncomfortable person'), I asked him if I might start recording. I felt as though I had missed several important details, facts and metaphors that flowed ephemerally as our talking continued. Yuri Nikolaevitch rejected this, saying that we had not finished talking yet. I proposed that he did not yet know the reason of my visit. His response was: 'I do. You came for the material, for the lively one'. It occurred to me then that he did not want to be identified just as my informant; rather he wanted me to become his advocate, to increase his status in debates with the authorities. We decided to work together later and he expressed a strong interest in studying to acquire further qualification at our Department of Social Work. He told me that day about the conflict at his work place, which later led him to leave the Director's position at the Sports and Health Centre for Children with Disabilities – a dream that he had turned into a reality in 1993. An Economical Institute graduate, and after five years of leading this programme, he was accused of not holding the diploma of educator and was replaced by the non-disabled pedagogue who heads the Sports Center now.

A few days later we met again and I recorded his life history. The chronological order of the interview shows how important life events shaped his identity through biographical socialisation. That is why, and because of other important contextual details, I have reproduced this part of his narrative as a whole:

I was born 15 June 1951, it was time of polio. I was born as a healthy baby but got infected by nine months. I could not walk at all and until the age of five was lying in bed. After surgery in 1956, I could move only a little. In 1962, in a sanatorium I was the only child from a workers' family. It was sanatorium of the Ministry of Defence and there were only the children of generals and colonels. I got there thanks to the help of the plant's director where my father worked as a turner. The director of the plant paid 3,000 roubles for a course of two months treatment, you know how much it was, if a Moskvitch car was 860 rubles. In that sanatorium I came under personal control of the director – I don't remember her name, she was a Jew – very nice, smart. If I'd go to Crimea sometime, I'd certainly find that sanatorium and ask for her by name, perhaps she is not alive, then I'd go to her grave. Excuse me [with tears in voice] for such a memorial [pause]. So [with raising voice], what she did was a special rehabilitation course for me, including exercises before and after breakfast, baths, again exercises, massage and stretching. After that I was able to stand straightforward. I was told to never stop exercises, so that upon my arrival to Saratov we went with my mother to the regional health and sport center. It occurred that there were no weights, no special facilities. Besides, the employees at that centre were not trained to work with the disabled. They asked me about what kind of exercises I needed and I brought the description for them. I started to go there to do just some simple exercises but there was nobody who would be interested in communicating with me. Once I did my exercises and went to them to say that I am done, and I saw, they were sitting and drinking tea. So, I as a child became disinterested, stopped going there and continued my exercises at home. And approximately in 1987, yes, in November of 1987 – I had already been working by then as an engineer– I came to the regional trade union board and my friend there told me about a plan to organise a sport club for the disabled in Saratov. So by February 1988 we got together for the first meeting, we were 56 people with motor impairments who came to exercise and rehabilitate their health through physical culture and sport. The voluntary sport society with the financial support of the regional trade union board helped us to establish this club. Soon I was elected as chairman of the club. We started dealing with different issues – finance, sport instructors, plan of activities for the year, etc. By December we decided to name our club 'Volga'. The full name was The Sport Club for the Disabled 'Volga', but it was always easier to say I am from 'Volga' for short.

It strikes me that in Yuri's story the rehabilitation practices of child-hood are immediately followed up by his engagement in mobilising events at the age of 36. He then continues on with details of inter-national rules for disability sport competitions. Only later, after much encouragement, did he talk about his adolescence and youth, and I learned about the content of the 'break' in his biography – studies at the economic institute, working experience and marriage.

He tells me a story from his adolescence about riding a bike, when the only hindrance seemed to be starting or finishing his ride without a prop. Every other event in Kazakov's life seems to pale in comparison to the role of physical activities and sport. However, his experience of managing a sports club and organising sports events seems to play an even more important role. Kazakov speaks of his management skills as if they were more significant than other survival skills: 'If I cannot do something, it is no problem for me for I can always find and ask a person who will do that for me, who will help me because I have helped her or him in some other way'. To manage is also to teach and to learn how to overcome difficulties, and Yuri Nikolaevitch understands very well that there are many barriers in the lives of disabled people. He says, 'The disabled must be skilled to fall. We cannot fall the same way as a physically healthy person does, we must concentrate and hide the head, trying to avoid sharp angles. It is necessary to be skilled in falling to be able to stand up and move further'.

By examining his personal accounts, I do not want to give the impression that sport and impairment are the only dimensions of relevance in Yuri's life. For example, he speaks about his beloved wife and daughter: 'I got married very late, by 35. How old, for example, is your child? . . . Fourteen . . . And mine is thirteen. See? You are welcome to visit me and my wife, we'd be happy to receive you at our home'. But it is the mobilisation of the oppressed that is so obviously produced in his stories, as he names his own history, shapes his own identity and defines his reality through resilience and resistance.

Yuri never returned to the history of the sports school for disabled children again in our interview but a few days later he wrote an autobiographical essay for me, where he referred to his experience of working with disabled children, their parents and sports instructors. Today the opportunities for disabled children and adults in Russia to be engaged in physical culture and sporting activities are growing. Yuri was the first in Saratov, although not the first in Russia, to believe and to prove that sport can be a starting point for developing positive identities for disabled children and adults, that it can transform the social, political, cultural and economic contexts within which individuals live.

Yuri Kazakov, who was disabled since childhood and grew up in a totalitarian society, developed himself into the leader of an organisation helping disabled children to raise their self-esteem and their abilities through sporting activities. With his help, sport became a cultural/

political act for children and their parents 'with the aim of building self-identities, while at the same time holding the goal of transforming societal attitudes and beliefs that have acted to stifle the cultural identities of disabled people' (Peters 1999: 105).

From my first encounter with Yuri I learned that he first established the Sports School for disabled kids as a non-governmental organisation. Within a year it became state based, and after a while he was forced to leave his creation. Having experienced pain and loss, however, he did not remain frustrated too long, for there was little doubt what to do next: very soon he established another sports club for children and adults as a non-governmental organisation attached to the All-Russia Sports Society 'Spartak'. Yuri Nikolaevitch says, he likes the name of the society because 'we all must rebel against our own pains and complexes, against the miseries that affect the families of children with disabilities, exactly as "Spartak" who led a rebellion of slaves against oppression'.

Conclusion

As Mark Priestley points out, language is a social phenomenon:

. . . embedded within wider social process and relationships of power. The way we acquire and use language not only reflects our relationship to the wider social world, it also reproduces it. When we speak in terms of gender, race, class, age, sexuality or disability we are also contributing to the production of those same social divisions and categories. Moreover, when we name ourselves, or when others name us within such categories, we too are being produced (Priestley 1999: 92).

The way in which Anna and Yuri produce themselves through the language of their life stories can be epitomised in two quotes, suggesting two different, gendered, strategies of resistance. The first, from Anna, is 'To have more time for the same distance' – a strategy for negotiating disability. The second, from Yuri, 'We must rebel against the pains' – a strategy of non-compliance, a strategy of rebellion. Other respondents adopted their own strategies and produced themselves in other ways. However, none thought of themselves as outcasts, and over the years they have caused the social barriers around them to crumble. Many are eager to promote this process for others and to do what they can towards that end.

Technological advances in the West 'permit disabled people to travel, study and work, and as the media incorporate their pictures and stories into articles, advertising, television programs and films, their presence becomes more familiar and less frightening' (Mairs 1996: 127). In

Russia, much of this is only beginning to happen. We can see this process being played out through and against public narratives of 'normality' (Thomas 1999:51). Both social change and self-empowerment are therefore shaping the biographies and identities of disabled people in Russia, within social contexts of time and space, gender and class, and the availability of services and networks.

REFERENCES

Booth, T. (1996) 'Sounds of still voices: issues in the use of narrative methods with people who have learning difficulties', in L. Barton (ed.) *Disability and Society: Emerging Issues and Insights*. Longman, New York, USA.

Fitz-Gerald, D. and Fitz-Gerald, M. (1985) 'Deaf people are sexual, too!', in M. Bloom (ed.) *Life Span Development: Bases for Preventive and Interventive Helping*, Collier Macmillan Publishers, London.

Hammersley, M. and Atkinson, P. (1983) *Ethnography: Principles in Practice*, Tavistock, London.

Hoerning, Erika M. (1996) *Life Course and Biographical Research: Conceptual Approaches and Methods*, University of Goteborg, Sweden.

Hughes G. (1998) 'A suitable case for treatment? Constructions of disability', in Esther Saraga (ed.) *Embodying the Social: Constructions of Difference*, Sage/Open University Press, London.

Iarskia-Smirnova, E. (1997) 'When there is a handicapped child in the family', *Russian Education and Society*, 39(10): 54–68.

Iarskia-Smirnova, E. (1999a) 'Social work in Russia: professional identity, culture and the state', in B. Lesnik (ed.) *International Perspectives on Social Work*, Pavilion Publishing, Brighton.

Iarskia-Smirnova, E. (1999b) ' "What the future will bring I do not know": mothering children with disabilities in Russia and the politics of exclusion', *Frontiers: a Journal for Women's Studies*, XX (2): 68–86.

Lamneck, S. (1988) *Qualitative Sozialforschung*, Psychologische-Verlags-Union, München, Germany.

Mairs, N. (1996) *Waist-high in the World: A Life Among the Nondisabled*, Beacon Press, Boston MA, USA.

Oliver, M. (1990) *The Politics of Disablement*, Macmillan, London.

Peters, S. (1999) 'Transforming disability identity through critical literacy and the cultural politics of language', in M. Corker and S. French (eds.) *Disability Discourse*, Open University Press, Milton Keynes.

Priestley, M. (1999) 'Discourse and identity: disabled children in mainstream high schools', in M. Corker and S. French (eds.) *Disability Discourse*, Open University Press, Milton Keynes.

Read, J. (1991) ' "There was never really any choice": the experience of mothers of disabled children in the United Kingdom', *Women's Studies International Forum*, 14(6): 568–69.

Riessman, C. (1993) *Narrative Analysis*, Sage, Thousand Oaks, CA, USA.

Silverman, D. (1993) *Interpreting Qualitative Data. Methods for Analysing Talk, Text and Interaction*, Sage, London.

Sutton, A. (1980) 'Backward children in the USSR: an unfamiliar approach to a familiar problem', in J. Brine, M. Perrie, and A. Sutton (eds.) *Home, School and Leisure in the Soviet Union*, Allen and Unwin, Boston MA, USA.

Thomas, C. (1999) 'Narrative identity and the disabled self', in M. Corker and S. French (eds.) *Disability Discourse*, Open University Press, Milton Keynes.

10   Lifting the Iron Curtain

Kaido Kikkas

I was born in September 1969 in Tallinn, the capital of Estonia and was immediately diagnosed as having a birth trauma. This diagnosis was soon formulated as cerebral palsy (some doctors have speculated that it might have been due to a rhesus conflict, others suspect the real cause to be carelessness by medical personnel). After the birth, the doctors did not leave my mother with much hope. At this time a young woman of 24, she was told that I would not live long and, at best, that I would remain a 'vegetable' for the rest of my life. Unofficially, she received a number of suggestions from the doctors (nowadays, perhaps best described as passive euthanasia). Many other disabled children have been, and continue to be, abandoned to the state at birth on the advice of doctors (*see* Human Rights Watch 1998).

The impact on my mother can only be imagined, particularly since I could have had an elder sister just three years earlier, who did not survive until birth. However, I decided to survive. Everyone except my parents dismissed my life in advance. Even many friends of the family shook their heads in disbelief. Faced with these circumstances, I can only assume that I owe my life to two really stubborn families, who came together to deny the critics and all those so-called realists. Many of the things that happened in those days are too traumatic to write about, or are too difficult to believe for readers from a Western culture. This was the USSR, a state that officially denied the very existence of disabled children. This was a state that insisted on universal content, anything 'different' was unwanted.

The Soviet definition of disability differed from the ones used in the West, being measured directly by a person's ability to work. Invalidity (disability) was defined as 'a permanent damage (lessening or loss) to a person's professional or general working abilities due to an illness or trauma' (Disability Affairs Council 1998). This definition meant that both young and elderly disabled people were excluded from the official statistics. The USSR first acknowledged the existence of disabled children as late as 1979 (*ibid.*) and before then families with disabled children were practically unsupported. The only available rehabilitation was strictly medical, and I remember that my mother was forced to run around from one hospital to another, taking me from Tartu to Leningrad (now St Petersburg). But whenever the medics examined me, they shook their heads and sent me away again.

During the Soviet regime, disabled people were considered to be a negative influence on the cultivated image of a 'state of happiness' and because of this, kept as much as possible out of public sight. They were acknowledged only as second-class citizens, forced to accept the line, 'be thankful that the state takes care of you'. For the ordinary citizen, contacts with disabled people were usually limited to relatives and acquaintances. Very often, disabled people were mistakenly pointed at as 'drunk' (especially people with CP or epilepsy) or 'lunatic'. I remember the countless twisted looks and innocent, but stupid, questions – even some medical professionals routinely asked, 'Are the parents alcoholics to have such a child?'. Segregation rather than integration was promoted, by establishing a network of special schools and nurseries for people with different impairments. While these facilities provided some degree of education and training, the result often proved useless, as society was unable to accept them. All of this resulted in a negative public image of disability, indirectly fuelled by the official 'Soviet people are happy people' rhetoric.

I took my first footsteps at the age of six. It was a kind of miracle for the doctors. Some of them could not understand it at all (impairment issues were treated very superficially in their training). But the real struggle was just beginning. At first, I used a walker that was made to special order. Things like this were unknown at that time but my father, being a construction engineer by training, designed it himself and ordered it from the workshop of the state firm that he worked for. I also used the walls for support, and then gradually gained enough balance to take some steps on my own. At first, even the short walks across the room were celebrated as great events.

Only much later did I understand my father's statement, 'Forget the word "impossible" – there is no such thing!'. At that time, it just meant trouble. Every evening, when Dad came home from work, I had to have done a hundred 'walkarounds' (going through all the rooms in our three-room apartment). To be honest, I did not understand the point at the time. In this way, my father became my first personal trainer and has continued in this role until the present day (at least with his occasional remarks on my way of sitting or walking). Both my parents became self-made rehabilitation therapists – the whole concept being totally unknown in our society at that time.

The next big period in my life was at the hospital for people with neurological impairments in Haapsalu, West Estonia. From the medical/ rehabilitation point of view, Haapsalu was the best option available in those days. The children who went there received the full range of rehabilitative interventions, including physiotherapy, massage, mud baths, medication and so on. The hospital was also linked to a school for children with mobility impairments, which most of the children could attend while they were in hospital. I first went there at the age of six, visiting eleven times in ten years, staying two months each time. My dad called it 'going to the army' and in some ways he was right. I had been raised at home, as a kind of hothouse flower and had little idea about 'real life' in all its colours. I had read the novels of James Fenimore Cooper and Alexandre Dumas (very early), but things like bullying and black eyes were totally unknown to me. I was raised in an atmosphere that was just too different from the reality of the world beyond. Although my parents did not spare me from difficulties and challenges, they did their best to spare me from evil.

So, it was at the hospital that I first received my first real life training. I have a wide range of memories from Haapsalu. There were better and worse people there, among both the staff and my pals. I survived being beaten up, robbed blind and even having a switchblade thrown at me! I also made friends who defended me (although I am only in touch with one of them now). From my last visits I have only good things to remember. I suppose that when you learn the hard way there are two options: to deal with people in the same way or to consciously choose not to do those things to others. I like to think that I chose the latter.

At seven, I reached the normal age for going to school. During the time of Russian-style Communism, no one even dreamed of the rights of disabled people, as they are understood today. Even though my mother was (and still is) a teacher who tried to help me into every activity, she did not manage to get me into school. At that time it was practically impossible for disabled children to attend school with their peers. All the schoolhouses were built according to a centralised set of Soviet rules and were totally inaccessible. The minds of the school staff were often even more inaccessible, and no school wanted to risk acquiring the label of a 'weirdoes' school'.

The first real attempts at special education in Estonia had come at the end of nineteenth century (Kõrgesaar and Veskiväli 1987) and during the first period of the Estonian Republic (1918–40) early pioneers, like Hans Valma (1921), made principled arguments for the education of 'mentally retarded' children. However, such principles were neglected in the years that followed and serious setbacks came with the 'race-health' ideas adopted from Western Europe at the end of the 1920s, culminating in the Sterilisation Law of 1936, which prescribed mandatory sterilisation of the 'mentally retarded, epileptics and deaf-and-dumb'.

The incorporation of Estonia into the Soviet Union meant replacement of the previous system by the unified 'Soviet pedagogics' (which evidently followed the same guidelines in all of the former Eastern block countries) and the development of the segregated school system. During the 1960s, a number of special schools were established. By 1980 there were thirty-four schools for children with sensory or mental impairments with 3290 Estonian-speaking and 801 Russian-speaking pupils. Today, Estonia is generally considered to have a Western-type education system, although deeply underfinanced. According to the United Nations (UNDP 1997), Estonia competes with Iran, Algeria, Surinam and Ecuador in terms of education, social conditions and wealth. Estonia's education system has retained at least some of the look and feel of Western Europe. However, in school enrolment, it lags quite seriously behind.

So, the first idea was that I should go to a special boarding school for children with mobility impairments in Haapsalu. However, this would have meant leaving home and I did not want to do that. Therefore, it was decided that I should be enrolled in a class at my mother's school, but that I should study at home. The class teacher used to visit me a couple of times every week, to check my work and to give me new tasks. But my real teacher lived with me every day. My mother, a music teacher by profession, decided to become a generalist. She became my sole teacher for the first seven grades of my school career (although there was also my official class teacher and a second teacher who came with the compulsory choice of foreign language).

At that time, only one additional language was taught besides Russian in grades 4 to 11, and the silently accepted policy was to teach it poorly (since the USSR treated every citizen able to communicate with the outer world as a potential hazard). My mother had learned German and insisted that I should do the same. But I was surprisingly stubborn in holding to my idea of learning English (even now, I cannot say where I got that from). My mother's only knowledge of English was 'I love you' and 'Kiss me' – not a bad choice, but unfortunately not enough to pass the grade.

Meanwhile, we had moved and both of us changed schools. We decided to try for a mainstream school and, to our surprise, I was accepted quickly and got on well. At the end of grade 7, I took the official exams and passed them at the first attempt. I remember that my father looked at the diploma and laughed: 'Very uninteresting! The highest marks only'.

Considering the general attitudes in society at that time, the attitude of my classmates and teachers was very much ahead of its time. Life can be rather like underwater swimming – sometimes you need to breathe in between. They gave me the space and the company to do that. As a nation, we Estonians are relatively well educated, by comparison with the USSR (where diplomas could be bought as well as earned in some places). Education does not guarantee more humane social relations but it can make a difference. Today there is still very little available data about disabled young people attending schools in Estonia but it seems that I was lucky. The number of registered disabled students in primary and secondary schools is disproportionately small for the size of our population, and I can only conclude that a great many disabled Estonian children are still not attending.

The school I attended was a basic 8-grader and so I had to leave to find a secondary school. I started to look around for a school, and this led to perhaps my most painful experience at the hands of 'professionals'. There was a facility called something like the Commission for Professional Choices, which had to approve all applications from people planning to continue their education (whether in secondary or vocational schools). This was one of the last times when my mother came with me – and we both received our share. 'Such a child, at secondary school? What, you must understand that these diplomas are not bought' – and so on. They were sure that we wanted to pass a bought diploma for a real, earned one.

In the end, we received the necessary stamp, but in terms of lost neural cells, it was probably the most expensive piece of cellulose and ink in the whole world. I decided to remember it, so that I could look this person up in the future and remind her of the whole thing. I still have the urge to do it, even today. She did not manage to bury me – but I often wonder how many lives she did ruin.

So, I was accepted through individual tests to the 44th Secondary School (the school did not have an open contest for vacant places that year). The school specialised in English, to the extent that it was even the language of tuition for some subjects. Considering the generally poor level of language teaching at that time, this was quite remarkable. Interestingly, this was the same class that I had enlisted in during the first grades (although I had studied at home). I enjoyed the time there, and public attitudes had developed a bit – the number of those staring at me twistedly, and yelling 'Lo, a freak!', had certainly diminished. My diplomas were still 'uninteresting' and I graduated *cum laude* (with gold medal).

Again, I faced a dilemma. On the one hand, I enjoyed English and would have had nothing against studying it further but this would have meant moving to the largest Estonian University in Tartu and, again, I did not want to leave home. On the other hand, I had already had my first experience with computers (having been the only survivor of a computer class with my peers). This raised the option of applying to Tallinn Technical University (in those days, the Tallinn Polytechnical Institute).

There were of course some obstacles – I could not apply to the Faculty of Automatics simply because I had an impairment (regardless of its type and seriousness). It was plainly stated that people with central nerve system impairments were not allowed to apply. So, I enrolled in the data processing department instead, at that time under the Faculty of Economics (a separate Faculty of Information Technology was formed later on).

As a group of students, we got on well from the start. Paradoxically, we owed a lot to a unique twist of Communist rule. At the beginning of the academic year, all new students were immediately deported to the countryside for a month to help in gathering the harvest. Strangers to each other, we were sent to the island of Saaremaa to help gather the potato crop. This kind of work, and living on our own for a month, turned out to be the best possible introduction and we became great friends from then on. These close relationships remained, at least until the fourth year, resulting in the frequent pre-exam sight of some twenty people in my small room, surrounded by coffee cups, cookies and murmuring. Life was interesting and most of my memories from that time are pleasant. I was surrounded by amazing people.

During this time, I also took part in the Lions' Youth Summer Camp for young disabled people in Grønolen, Norway. This camp was (and presumably still is) arranged annually, featuring two weeks amidst the fairytale Norwegian scenery and the fantastic company of young people from all over the world. I had the rare privilege to attend twice, and never forgot those two summers. Most of all, I learned how to overcome the obstacles raised by disability and got to know people who I will never forget.

Two more noteworthy events fall into the university period. The first was a spiritual journey. I have always liked to think about life, and this gradually led me to Christianity. I have always disliked 'Bible-whacking' and the process was step by step with me. I took part in local gospel music projects (playing keyboards, bass guitar or harmonica), which also contributed to my spiritual development. I was finally baptised in 1998.

The second event that occurred, interestingly enough in parallel, was when I became a member of the university's Shotokan Karate-do Club. It was something that would never have entered my wildest dreams just a couple of years earlier, and it is only possible to imagine the embarrassment of Sensei Alar Põllu when I went to meet him for the first time. Even he had a hard time imagining me in karate, but I was accepted and continue to progress today. Why karate? Perhaps because all boys need heroes and aspire to be like them – even boys whose bodies are disobedient.

Although many of the Western martial arts icons, like Bruce Lee or Chuck Norris, did not make it through the Iron Curtain, martial arts and especially karate had already reached Estonia by the 1960s. Some of the top competition karateka of the USSR were Estonians, until karate was officially outlawed at the beginning of the 1980s. The tradition was maintained underground, resulting in a boom when the ban was finally lifted in the last years of the USSR. Every youngster dreamed of being the invincible hero, putting the bad guys in place with his bare hands. However impossible it seemed, I secretly shared these dreams (although in reality I have never liked to hurt people, either physically or verbally). I have never had to 'try it out' and really hope that I will never need to.

At last, my studies were over. I was awarded my diploma and it was suggested that I should enter for a Master's degree, which I subsequently completed. Although my career to date had exceeded the most daring dreams of my early days, I pressed on. Choosing to study accessible technology meant pioneering a whole new field in Estonia (although my reasons for wanting to do so are no doubt evident in this story).

Somewhere during my university days, I had playfully set myself three life goals – a doctorate, a black belt in karate, and (less importantly) a Pontiac Firebird sports car. The first of those goals is now a reality. In August 1999, after a two-hour viva, I was awarded a Doctor of Philosophy in Engineering for my thesis on *Using the Internet in the Rehabilitation of People with Mobility Impairments* (Kikkas 1999). Another life goal, set right at the beginning, was also reached at that time – I finally got to live on my own. With my own savings and help from the family and relatives I was able to raise enough to buy a two-room apartment. I have lived there since then and although I retain very good relations with my family, I have a home of my own.

Conclusion

What to say for the conclusion? For me, life has always been about teamwork, be it with parents, relatives, friends or colleagues. I have received so much and can only hope to pass on a fraction of this to others. More generally, for disabled people in Estonia, the future remains uncertain.

After seven years of free access to data, there is still no complete overview of the population data for the Soviet period (Katus *et al.* 1997). According to data from the Estonian Board of Social Security and the Board of Pensions, the total number of registered disabled people in 1998 was 59,938, of whom 7428 (12.4 per cent) were employed. The Estonian Ministry of Social Affairs, estimate the employment rate for disabled people of working age (18–59) at around 18 per cent. Disabled people do receive monthly allowances, but these are far too limited to provide even a minimal standard of living.

During the last few years the social situation has improved. Modern ideas concerning the treatment of minorities, including people with mobility impairments, have found support in Estonia as in many other countries. Estonia is heading towards integration within a united European community (Lauristin *et al.* 1997) and this has given an extra boost to the development of all aspects of human and civil rights. However, while such ideas are accepted at the governmental level, they are rarely implemented in practice. Although the Constitution declares all citizens to be equal in employment and education, there is still no working mechanism to allow disabled people to become educated or employed on an equal basis. Real equity remains wishful thinking.

In May 1995, the government of Estonia officially accepted the United Nations *Standard Rules* concerning equal rights for disabled people. However, while in other countries it is supported by more specific acts, this has not been the case in Estonia – leading to a situation where everything seems to be in order at the governmental level, while at the real, grassroots level it is down to disabled people themselves and a few NGOs.

The rise of the Estonian national movement was reflected also in the rise of self-realisation and dignity amongst disabled people. It is probably no coincidence that the Estonian Union of Disabled People's Organisations, the first nationwide organisation in this field, was officially founded in 1988, during the days of the Estonian 'singing revolution' (Pillau 1989). Estonian organisations became members of international organisations, like Mobility International and, in August 1989, Tallinn hosted the International Meeting on Human Resources in the Field of Disability. This rise in activity was unfortunately short-lived, giving way to the post-revolution realities of everyday life, with its economic hardships and competition at all levels of society. Today, the disability movement in Estonia has not developed much and maintains a relatively low profile.

To summarise, the factors influencing disabled people's lives in Estonia are varied. On the one hand, there are positive factors. We have a future vision of Estonia as a part of Europe, with a Nordic (or West European) type of democratic government and basic guaranteed rights. We are a small country with up-to-date communication networks, including the rapid spread of the Internet. There is a long tradition (at least comparable to Western Europe) in special education and an existing network of non-governmental organisations of disabled people (although most are facing serious financial setbacks).

There are also negative factors, many of which are common to nearly all the former Communist countries. We lack information. The beginnings of more widespread disability research (beyond the medical or pedagogical) can only be traced back to the beginning of the 1990s. Academic co-operation between different facilities is still at an early stage. What is even harder to change is the old model of viewing disability, which is apparent in models of education involving segregation by physical or mental condition. Often, those facilities willing to make use of new ideas lack information and guidance. This situation is worsened by the fact that the disability statistics are still very unreliable.

Estonia has almost no legislation concerning the general rights, rehabilitation and integration of disabled people, and the Estonian social system is still largely based on care, rather than independence or integration. There is a lack of public knowledge, and many misconceptions about disability. Since the re-establishment of independence, the image of disabled people has been challenged and public acceptance has improved remarkably (e.g. a wheelchair user in the street is no longer viewed as out-of-place). However, previous attitudes still prevail in education and employment (e.g. 'I am not sure that she can handle it . . . she's using this chair'). While this is probably a natural development, the lack of supportive legislation to ensure positive changes may result in setbacks during the process.

There is also a low level of education among disabled people. This is perhaps one of the crucial problems in Estonia. There are problems with all levels of education – from the large numbers of disabled children who are excluded in primary level to the inaccessibility of university buildings. As a consequence, there is a low employment rate for disabled people. Low social status and lack of access to education provide an unfavourable starting position in the job market, and when there is no legal enforcement of employment rights, the outcome is predictable.

There are many similarities with the situation in other East European countries, and some of the social processes resemble those in the West ten to twenty years ago. However, the life experiences of disabled people in Estonia are quite different from those in Western Europe, and are influenced by many specific historical and cultural factors. Therefore, while it is possible to draw parallels, the situation is complex enough to demand our own original solutions.

REFERENCES

Disability Affairs Council (1998) *O polozhenii invalidov v Rossiiskoi Federatsii* [Of the status of disabled people in the Russian Federation], State Report by the Disability Affairs Council under the President of the Russian Federation, Moscow, Russia.

Human Rights Watch (1998) *Abandoned to the State: Cruelty and Neglect in Russian Orphanages*, Human Rights Watch, London.

Katus, K., Puur, A., Sakkeus, L. (1997) 'Population data and reorganisation of statistical system: case of Estonia', *Trames*, no. 3, vol. 1 (51/46), pp. 173–82.

Kikkas, K. (1999) *Using the Internet in the Rehabilitation of People with Mobility Impairments – Case Studies and Views from Estonia*, PhD thesis, Tallinn Technical University, Tallinn, Estonia.

Kõrgesaar, J. and Veskiväli, E. (1987) *Eripedagoogika Eestis: eripedagoogika tänapäevaküsimusi* [Special education in Estonia: today's questions in special education], Eripedagoogika kateeder, Tartu Ülikool, Estonia.

Lauristin, M., Vihalemm, P., Rosengren, K.E. and Weibull, L. (1997) *Return to the Western World: Cultural and Political Perspectives of the Estonian Post-Communist Transition*, Tartu University Press, Estonia.

Pillau, E. (1989) *Eestimaa kuum suvi 1988* [The hot summer of 1988], chronicles of press releases, Olion, Tallinn, Estonia.

Puur, A. (1997) Emergence of unemployment: evidence from Estonia 1989–1995, *Trames*, no. 3, vol. 1 (51/46): 253–55, 261.

United Nations Development Programme (1997) *Estonian Human Development Report*, UNDP, Tallin, Estonia.

Valma, H. (1921) *Mõnda nõdramõistuslikkude laste eest hoolekandes ja nende kaswatusest* [Of the care and upbringing of feeble-minded children], Lääne, Haapsalu, Estonia.

11 Revisiting deaf transitions

Mairian Corker

> Now if you'll only attend, Kitty, and not talk so much, I'll tell you all
> my ideas about Looking Glass House. First, there's the room you can
> see through the glass – that's just the same as our drawing-room,
> only the things go the other way. I can see all of it when I get upon a
> chair – all but the bit just behind the fireplace. Oh! I do so wish I
> could see *that* bit!
>
> (Lewis Carroll 1871, *Through the Looking Glass and What Alice Found There*)

All researchers, including those who research the life course, work in
theoretical practices whose concerns are different from the practical
concerns of people as participants in the research. The social relations of
research production bring researchers' theoretical preoccupations – and
categories – to bear on the process and outcome of the research, sometimes to the point of producing or re-producing particular subjectivities
(Corker 1999a, b). For example, Mike Oliver suggests that in his
research with Jane Campbell on the 'disability movement' (Campbell
and Oliver 1996) 'we were producing ourselves collectively as a coherent, strong and articulate political movement, and individually as
proud and committed political actors' (Oliver 1999: 188). By extension,
the researcher is increasingly acknowledged as an *active participant in*
rather than as an *objective observer of* the research process. *How* active she
can be may depend on how far she can penetrate the inside of the
communities in which she does research, which, in itself may depend on
whether she recognises that her own positions and interests are imposed
at all stages of the research process. When researching the life course, it
is particularly important to understand that the researcher's self, by
virtue of its own life story and life transitions, is located in different
places and at different times in relation to those with whom she does
research.

Writing from a feminist perspective, Harding (1986, 1987) suggests
that researchers are often compelled to impose a relatively stable,
enduring and safe 'configurational structure' (Ricouer 1981), or 'collective representation' (Oliver 1999) upon chaotic personal experiences. In

123

relation to life course research, I would further suggest that the unreflexive imposition of structures can lead to the privileging of particular idealised representations of lived experience, existing in a kind of parallel universe, which become bound up with a *narcissistic* pursuit of particular life trajectories. Indeed, this is more likely to happen when research seeks to emancipate people who are oppressed.

These contrasting perspectives on research seem to be particularly important for life course research because they suggest that, as researchers, we not only need to be prepared to have our often hard-won positions and interests questioned – we also need to understand ourselves as *maturing* human beings engaged in the process of knowledge production with the researched at different points in time and space. People's lives do not stand still and, as such, the forms of knowledge we produce in this relationship are often snapshots of where we are at particular moments in time and space. This raises Judith Butler's (1999, p. xvi) point that the question to ask, then, is not whether a particular theory is transposable onto disability, but what happens to the theory when it tries to come to grips with disability in different times and places.

We could examine this process in action with respect to life course theory, by contrasting theories that are underpinned by developmental psychology, for example Erikson's (1950) 'stage theories', with those that are founded on sociological approaches to development (see, for example, Clausen 1998).The aim of such a comparison would be to see whether particular ways of conceptualising the life course tend to predetermine generational and lifespan positions for those with whom we do research, and whether they re-produce or problematise social categories such as 'child', 'adult', 'youth', 'middle age', 'old age' and 'disability', *along with notions of 'time' and 'space'*. This suggests that, when doing research on disability and the life course, there are three *linked* theoretical positions to consider:

- What model of disability or impairment is assumed by the research and, in particular, what emphasis does it give to impairment, structure and/or agency, the individual and/or society and difference and/or sameness?
- With respect to issues of socialisation and development that underpin most theoretical approaches to understanding the life course, which form of understanding is central to analysis?
- What are the social contextual forces and processes that militate against but also for particular conceptions of life stages and life potentials, and how are they distributed in contemporary life?

In this chapter, I want to examine these questions with respect to one group of disabled people – deaf people – by 're-visiting' a qualitative research project that I carried out in 1995. My justification for concentrating on a single impairment is that deaf people have always had an uneasy relationship with disability studies (Corker 1998), which·continues to be controversial and the subject of largely unresolved debate. More importantly for the purposes of this chapter, deaf people epitomise some of the difficulties of contesting theoretical positions for the social relations of life course research, and of a 'social model' that 'does not deny the significance of impairment in people's lives, *but concentrates on* those social barriers which are constructed "on top of" impairment' [or] "socially created"' (Barnes, Mercer and Shakespeare 1999: 2, *italics added*).

Deaf Transitions

The project, which resulted in the book *Deaf Transitions* (Corker 1996), involved the retrospective, narrative study of the life transitions made by eight deaf people. Initially, *Deaf Transitions* was intended to be a companion volume to an earlier publication about counselling deaf people (Corker 1994). What that book lacked was a detailed description of actual examples of 'counselling' process, and so *Deaf Transitions* became an 'unravelling' of the 'life scripts' of deaf people from a variety of backgrounds in a way that made the scripts central to the book. This approach was taken, first, because narrative is the primary vehicle of counselling process (see, for example, McLeod 1997, and references therein) – it builds the relationship between the therapist and the client. Second, one of the foremost aims of therapy is to uncover the structure of the 'life-story' in a way that emphasises the social and cultural dimensions of narrative, and gives the person an opportunity to gain insight into it and control over its effects. In this way, story-telling is also an active way of affirming the basic beliefs of a socio-cultural group (Isenberg 1996). 'Stories are instructions, which go beyond simply recalling the past and teach about how one's life should be conducted and what must be valued' (Padden and Humphries 1988: 33).

Beyond the socio-cultural impact of story-telling, however, there is a political dimension – 'the credibility of a story may depend on issues of power, control and authority' (McLeod 1997: 108). In this context, *Deaf Transitions* was grounded in and had the intention of informing anti-discriminatory counselling practice. My main objective was to capture the integrity – the 'local' knowledge – of *these deaf people's* accounts, in particular their sense of how they perceived social relations, agency and identity over time, but in a way which acknowledged that they were filtering their past experience through their present circumstances. Indeed, in the introduction to the book, I am repeatedly critical of searches for 'universals' and their ability to diminish human experience because 'what we perceive is a function of *how* we see' (p. 4), and I emphasise different 'ways of seeing' (p. 2) as being 'symbolic of the need to move from simplistic, objectified and fixed ways of viewing people.' (p. 7). This was the main reason for the use of the term 'deaf' to refer to the community of people for whom deafness is an important and sometimes dominant ontological status. This usage was intended to be inclusive of the different identifiable meanings of 'community' used by deaf people, for example a linguistic minority, communities demarcated by disabling, gendered, 'racialised', and sexualised social structures and practices, and those deaf people whose dominant community affiliations are not clear.

From an analytical perspective, I therefore worked on two levels. First, the scripts are presented both in an unedited, relatively intact form and in an interpreted form to emphasise that, as the researcher, I was part of the construction of the scripts (McNamee and Gergen 1992) and experienced transitions in relation to the scripts. In that sense, then, *Deaf Transitions* was an organic account, only in part authored by me, which grew out of these scripts *and my interpretations of them*, but which also remained open to other interpretations in the life of the text. Second, I deliberately sought to create an encounter between a particular theoretical framework relating to the life course – one which takes 'age' or 'life stage' as an objectively factual departure point (Erikson 1950) – and accounts that emphasised deaf people's *diversity* and *difference*. I therefore hoped to show that 'lifespan change does not merely "happen". It is both experienced by and enacted by people' (Coupland, Nussbaum and Grossman 1993: xiii).

Re-visiting *Deaf Transitions*

In spite of my efforts to emphasise that the self is continually 're-authored' as its life and circumstances change (Bakhtin 1990), *Deaf Transitions* in many ways remains marked by the time and the context in which it was written. The life scripts were those of deaf people who were 'coming of age in the age of self-determination' (Ward 1996) that, for disabled people, emphasised the political goals of 'autonomy, integration and independence' (Barnes *et al.* 1999: 177). The Deaf advocacy movement, however, located self-determination at the community level and increasingly placed 'positive' premiums on the development of linguistic and ontological difference (Deaf identity), and social co-existence with mainstream society (Deaf community) as the primary goals of socialisation and development. This in turn posited a particular perspective on the life course. At this time, I was also primarily a Deaf studies scholar, and I did not have the theoretical knowledge to explain why taking a particular view of the community of deaf people, and of identity development and the life course, went against the grain of orthodox Deaf studies, *because such knowledge was not part of Deaf studies*. Five years later however, and writing from increasingly interdisciplinary territory, three main issues arise, which relate to epistemology (changing knowledge), particularly changing perspectives on the social practices that underpin the life course, and the impact of different research methodologies.

Changing knowledge

From my current vantage point, it has become clear, that change in the life of a text does not always follow the same trajectory over time. The orthodox 'frame' of Deaf studies in many ways remains central to the way in which the text's primary audience 'read' the narratives. For example, one reviewer of *Deaf Transitions* wrote:

I found the author's premise – that the interviewees' core issues were in the areas of gender, ethnicity and sexuality rather than the issue of being deaf – intriguing or, rather, faulty. I disagree with this *because their life stories began mostly with relationship problems* – not understanding what was happening to them at a very young age – *the exceptions to that were deaf children in deaf families*. Therefore, the core or first issue for them was one that dealt with being deaf persons in their families. Several deaf psychologists and mental health practitioners of stature have recognised that *there are developmental issues unique to deaf people*. They recognise that societal expectation does not necessarily agree *with our (deaf) views of healthy development and deaf individuals*. Similarly, the acceptance of *the deaf self* is a *precondition towards the resolution of other issues* leading to healthy and holistic living. (Weiner 1998: 273, *italics mine*)

This commentary provides helpful insight of how different theories impact upon our understanding of the life course. Weiner's view of development is characterised by an emphasis on stages, social difference, an essentialist view of personal identity, and what is perhaps a reductionist view of the family. From a *psychosocial* perspective on development, this seems to be 'normative' in the sense that it assumes that there are only *two* possible 'positive' outcomes of the developmental process – a Deaf identity *or* a hearing identity. This perspective doesn't take into account that the 'families' of the narrators are *not* all white, middle-class, Christian, straight and hearing, nor is it the case that Caroline, a deaf child from a *Deaf* family, was an exception. Rather, she encountered Weiner's 'core issues' later in life than, for example, Sam (who was a deaf child from a hearing family), when she gave birth to a hearing child.

From a *sociological* perspective on development, however, it appears that Weiner ignores the main theoretical premise of *Deaf Transitions*, explained at length in the first chapter of the book, that different ideological and institutional bases and social rituals predetermine generational and lifespan positions in different communities of social practice. This perspective locates deaf people's experiences in the context of the growing body of work that challenges the universality of life course stages, and suggests that stages may be different according to personal characteristics and life circumstances that vary by gender, race, ethnicity, class, and national origin. However, Weiner promotes *normative* community practice (Nancy 1991) – what he calls 'our deaf views' – in a way that places emphasis on social structure and yields oppositional (Deaf) patterns of socialisation, which attribute different social values to *particular* ontological resolutions of the developmental process. This perspective, as it is informed by theory, is then applied to the deaf people's narratives.

Deaf Transitions, on the other hand, takes a *constitutive* view of community practices (Nancy 1991) as the best possible 'theory' for representing the stories of human agency and struggle related by the narrators in resisting and conforming to 'traditional' community structures and socio-cultural expectations, stories that dominate the text. This constitutive view may be part of what Barnes *et al.* (1999: 185) mean when they write that 'identities are produced and regulated in and through consumption and conspicuous leisure practices'. However, their social creationist agenda would tend to stress that community practices are themselves organised within hegemonic social structure and ritual in a way that creates normative categories that act as barriers to the development of 'a positive disabled identity'. Removal of the barriers also resides in the creation of an oppositional 'social category' (disability), made visible (or made 'real', perhaps) in the disabled people's movement's struggles for political dominance over the oppressive social rituals that characterise 'traditional' life course practices.

Practising the life course

Nevertheless, it is pertinent to return to the comments at the start of the previous paragraph, and to ask whether Giddens' 'reflexive project of the self' (1991: 5) – which underpins his theory of the lifespan, and which is also an important basis for informed social struggle – is evenly distributed across all individuals of all ages? To attempt to answer this question, I would draw upon Carol Thomas' (1999) concept of 'impairment effects', which refers to the material fact, in this case, of being deaf. She suggests that they *may* become the medium of disability in particular social relational contexts' (1999: 43). Clearly, the material fact of being deaf prevents socialisation and knowledge consumption and production in mainstream society in ways that might influence the construction of autobiographical accounts of the self. There is therefore a sense in which, *at the level of ontology,* all deaf people experience temporal disjuncture as an impairment effect, whilst at the same time being disabled by society's figuring them as 'the past' (that is, 'primitive') as inherently 'childlike' and therefore as inferior (in Thomas' terms, a 'disability effect').

These different 'effects' are not always easy to distinguish, however. In *Deaf Transitions*, Andrew, who was once able to hear, observes: 'I watched my children growing up and somehow every change that happened seemed to catch me by surprise, because although I had been seeing the changes over time, I wasn't *aware* of what was happening because they were not communicated to me in a way that I had access to or understood. So I felt all the time I was missing out on my children growing up' (p. 132). Andrew gives a sense of feeling 'young' or 'behind the times' in relation to his peers, but he has an understanding that 'youth' and 'time' are socially constructed categories, which turns the developmental process *inwards*. He says 'I cannot look at myself as someone who is defined only in terms of how I relate to others – I can't dance with others, only with myself.' (p. 149), suggesting a life characterised by social conflict that is resisted through individual agency – what Hogan (1999: 79) calls 'carving out a space to act.' Laclau suggests that:

. . . if all social conflict were, necessarily, to provoke a certain destructuration of social identities . . . it would follow that any social identity would necessarily entail, as one of its dimensions, construction, and not simply recognition. The key term for understanding this process of construction is the psychoanalytic category of *identification*, with its explicit assertion of a lack at the root of any identity: one needs to identify with something because there is an originary and insurmountable lack of identity (1994: 3, author's italics).

When deaf people experience this temporal and spatial disjuncture collectively, this may create circumstances where a deaf world *comes to exist* in a different time and place. From a historical perspective, and at different points on the life course, in both a general and a specific sense, this world has assumed both a socially constructed and a socially created character. Though rudimentary sign languages have undoubtedly been in existence since Ancient times, Wrigley (1998) suggests that the physical warehousing of deaf people in institutions of education and work created the 'accidental' side effect of 'proper' Sign language and Deaf culture. Deaf children were not originally grouped together because of their language, but *because they were deaf* and therefore interesting and challenging objects of inquiry, and also because they were often from wealthy, influential families. It is therefore hard to say whether the use of Sign language is an impairment effect or a disability effect, because at that time, the primary reason for using Sign language was deafness.

Following Foucault's (1980) arguments about the social category 'homosexual', it could be argued that the social category 'Deafness' didn't exist before it was classified or legitimated by hearing benefactors – mainly linguists and psychologists – who were fascinated by Sign language and the processes through which it was learnt. However, social practices centred on deafness clearly did exist. This established a 'real', but in many ways 'parallel' world built on the foundations of the different time and place described earlier, and more importantly, on a language that itself exists in a different temporal and spatial dimension. Once recognised as such, this DEAF-WORLD increasingly privileged certain forms of knowledge and ways of being as 'truly' Deaf – the DEAF-WAY. These became 'natural' developmental targets and policy goals that were embedded in social practices of the life course such as the privileging of intergenerational Deafness, education in Deaf schools, Sign bilingualism, intermarriage and the creation of Deaf social spaces. The DEAF-WORLD grew, I would argue, because:

If agents were to have an always already defined location in the social structure, the problem of their identity, considered in a radical way, would not arise – or, at most, would be seen as a matter of *discovering or recognising* their own identity, not of *constructing* it (Laclau 1994: 2, *author's italics*).

However, by this formulation of how Deaf identity is 'achieved' the vast majority of deaf children begin life on the *outside* of the Deaf community because they are born to hearing parents, and have little hope of achieving the 'core identity' of a Deaf community that privileges intergenerational Deafness as a marker of 'purity' (Corker 1998). This is emphasised both by Deaf people like Krishna, Joseph and Peter, for whom the life course is characterised by a struggle between the Deaf 'centre' and the 'centres' of other races, cultures and religions, and by the experience of Fiona, who is a *hearing* child living in the DEAF-WORLD. She says: 'I remember asking myself why she (a Deaf cousin) went to a Deaf school and had hearing aids because every other aspect of the family dynamics seemed to be the same. I also remember wondering if I had been a bad girl and that is why these "privileges" had been withheld' (p. 68). Deaf forms of knowledge did not include an understanding of how she could develop as a hearing person and, in consequence, her acceptance in the DEAF-WORLD seems conditional on the hearing role she adopts. It is significant in this respect that the 'norm' for career development of hearing children in the Deaf community is that they become Sign language interpreters. But even before this, childhood is frequently characterised by learning (the Deaf version of) the hearing role in a way, as Fiona describes, that turns 'traditional' concepts of 'child' and 'parent' on their head. It is interesting that Caroline, when she has a hearing child, begins to feel uneasy about the social values of the Deaf community in relation to hearing children as contrasted with her own realisation that she is a 'parent' of a 'child'. These issues are discussed at length in the literature about hearing children of Deaf adults (Preston 1994).

There is no doubt that the DEAF-WORLD, whether we view it as socially constructed or created, is a world where the centre is different, and where outsiders are disabled by the social practices of insiders unless they meet the conditions of belonging that the DEAF-WORLD values. But the question I have is whether what may have been in the past a localised 'disability effect' remains so in the complex, industrial societies and 'real virtualities' of the present, given that Deaf people and their organisations increasingly demand that their parallel world and its incumbent practices of social reproduction are allowed to co-exist socially. And if, in the absence of 'disability effects', identity is not 'linked to impairment' (Barnes *et al.* 1999: 16), how is it produced?

Reviewing methodology

The final issue that arises on re-visiting the text is one of methodology, arising from a broadening of research practice, which has brought with it an added dimension to interpretation of the life scripts. At the level of practice, for example, I have since been involved in a research project with deaf young people that employed *prospective* methodology, albeit within a limited time scale (for further information see the *Lives of Disabled Children* project report 1999). There is not the space in this short chapter to examine the critique of retrospective and prospective methodology in life course research. But in general, life course researchers tend to favour prospective methodologies, and are critical of retrospective data largely on the grounds that data 'quality' and 'reliability' cannot be guaranteed because of 'changes and flaws of memory' (Scott and Alwin 1998: 123). That is, the past tends to be reviewed in terms that make it congruent with present circumstances. On the negative side, this creates a conflict with my understanding of recall *in the counselling context* and issues around the 'accuracy' of what the client recalls. My *modus operandi* as a counsellor has always been 'believe unconditionally and be alert for contradictory information', and so I feel uncomfortable with the assertion that retrospective data were somehow less valid or less reliable.

On the positive side, however, it is useful to note that in spite of different methodologies many of the issues uncovered were similar in both studies, though changing contexts and times appear to suggest that they manifest themselves in different ways. For example, in *Deaf Transitions*, Sam and Peter recalled periods of sustained abuse of all kinds and the prevalence of regimes of surveillance and physical discipline during childhood and adolescence, and there was anecdotal evidence at the time that these experiences were not uncommon. The young people in the current study also highlight surveillance and discipline, but the main mechanism is through self-discipline, encouraged by the maintenance of an environment where internalised oppression is allowed to prevail. This seems to support Foucault's (1978) view of changing patterns of power and how they are distributed through different forms of cultural transmission. Moreover, today's deaf young people are 'coming of age' in an age where multiple expressions of collective identity contest the globalisation of strategic economic activities, flexibility and instability of work, on behalf of cultural singularity (Castells 1997). Many older Deaf people are unable to comprehend why more and more young Deaf people are abandoning the Deaf clubs of 'past times' in favour of spaces where they can be like other young people today. Only time will tell what this means for *Deaf Transitions*.

Concluding remarks

Re-visiting *Deaf Transitions* has emphasised, for me, that research needs to build critical accounts of how we formulate the life course over time and space – either in general or in particular cases – and that those of us who 'do' research need to view life course research as an interdisciplinary project. However, pursuing this project can remove us further from the 'centres' of the worlds we seek to explain and liberate if we allow ourselves to be unreflexively led by narcissistic agendas that distort the richness of a lived experience that changes over time, and limit the range of interpretations and understandings that are possible in the interests of preserving epistemic orthodoxy. This becomes all too obvious when we examine the impact of different epistemological and methodological 'frames' – each with their constitutive ideologies and distributions of social value – on the outcomes of life course research.

Giddens (1991) believes that the constant questioning and reconstruction of the self in a lifetime project is a 'real' process and that the individual has a real control over his or her self. Others, for example Craib (1998), prefer to think of this process in terms of ideology, and I tend to echo his position. Craib significantly attributes this to the restructuring of capitalism, where the development of the market over the last thirty years has intensified a process of individualisation that intrudes into personal relationships. He points to the validity of modern feminism's commercialisation of relationships, where the self, identity, becomes a product to be re-constituted and re-presented at regular intervals. This perspective may go some way towards explaining the narcissistic pursuit of 'positive' identities and community boundary-marking through 'normative' processes of socialisation and development in the life course of different individuals and collectives.

But, in spite of the changing context of *Deaf Transitions,* I find it necessary to re-affirm the importance of a 'constitutive' worldview in life course research, which acknowledges the importance of a range of tenable trajectories and outcomes, if the life course is not to be a deterministic straitjacket that perpetuates 'traditional' perspectives of socialisation and development. As I wrote in *Deaf Transitions,* 'safety is fragile, and what is safe for one individual is not so safe for another. This is especially so when the family unit is founded on a particular difference, which means that all the wisdom of other families' experiences is in danger of being obsolete or inaccessible, all the family rules have to be renegotiated, and all the best laid plans go out the window' (p. 65). The real danger lies in the failure of researchers to acknowledge that research also takes place at different points in the life course, and this can lead us to ignore change and local 'realities' in the interests of 'idealiz[ing] certain expressions of [social identity]' and the processes of socialisation and development that underpin them, in a way that we 'produce new forms of hierarchy and exclusion.' (Butler 1999: vii).

REFERENCES

Bakhtin, M. (1990) *Art and Answerability: Early Philosophical Essays by M. M. Bakhtin,* M. Holquist and V. Liapunov (eds.). Translation and notes, V. Liapunov, University of Texas Press, Austin, TX, USA.

Barnes, C., Mercer, G. and Shakespeare, T. (1999) *Exploring Disability: A Sociological Introduction,* Polity, Cambridge.

Butler, J. ([1990] 1999) *Gender Trouble: Feminism and the Subversion of Identity,* Routledge, New York, USA.

Campbell, J. and Oliver, M. (1996) *Disability Politics: Understanding Out Past, Changing Our Future*, Routledge, London.

Castells, M. (1997) *The Information Age: Economy, Society and Culture*, Blackwell, Malden, MA, USA.

Clausen, J. A. (1998) 'Life reviews and life stories', in J. Giele and G. Elder (eds.) *Methods of Life Course Research: Qualitative and Quantitative Approaches*, Sage, Thousand Oaks, CA, USA.

Corker, M. (1994) *Counselling: The Deaf Challenge*, Jessica Kingsley, London.

Corker, M. (1996) *Deaf Transitions: Images and Origins of Deaf Families, Deaf Communities and Deaf Identities*, Jessica Kingsley, London.

Corker, M. (1998) *Deaf and Disabled or Deafness Disabled?*, Open University Press, Milton Keynes.

Corker, M. (1999a) 'New disability discourse, the principle of optimisation and social change', in M. Corker and S. French (eds.) *Disability Discourse*, Open University Press, Milton Keynes.

Corker, M. (1999b) 'Differences, conflations and foundations: the limits to "accurate" theoretical representation of disabled people's experience', *Disability & Society*, 14(5): 627–42.

Coupland, N., Nussbaum, J. F. and Grossman, A. (1993) 'Introduction: discourse, selfhood and the lifespan', in N. Coupland and J. F. Nussbaum (eds.) *Discourse and Lifespan Identity*, Sage, Newbury Park, CA, USA.

Craib, I. (1998) *Experiencing Identity*, Sage, London.

Erikson, E. (1950) *Childhood and Society*, Norton, New York, USA.

Foucault, M. ([1976] 1980) *The History of Sexuality, Volume 1: An Introduction*, [Translation, Robert Hurley], Vintage, New York, USA.

Foucault, M. ([1978] 1988) 'On power (interview with Pierre Boncenne)', in L. Kritzman (ed) *Michel Foucault, Politics, Philosophy and Culture: Interviews and Other Writings 1977–1984*, Routledge, London.

Giddens, A. (1991) *Modernity and Self-identity: Self and Society in the Late-Modern Age*, Polity, Cambridge.

Harding, S. (1986) *The Science Question in Feminism*, Cornell University Press, Ithaca, USA.

Harding, S. (1987) *Feminism and Methodology*, Indiana University Press, Bloomington, USA.

Hertz, R. (ed.) (1997) *Reflexivity and Voice*, Sage, Thousand Oaks, CA, USA.

Hogan, A. (1999) 'Carving out a space to act: acquired impairment and contested identity', in M. Corker and S. French (eds.) *Disability Discourse*, Open University Press, Milton Keynes.

Isenberg, G. (1996) 'Storytelling and the use of culturally appropriate metaphors in psychotherapy with deaf people', in N. Glickman and M. Harvey (eds.) *Culturally Affirmative Psychotherapy with Deaf Persons*, Lawrence Erlbaum Associates, Mahwah, NJ, USA.

Laclau, E. (ed.) (1994) *The Making of Political Identities*, Verso, London.

McLeod, J. (1997) *Narrative and Psychotherapy*, Sage, London.

McNamee, S. and Gergen, K. (1992) *Therapy as Social Construction*, Sage, London.

Nancy, J-L. (1991) *The Inoperative Community* [ed. P. Connor, trans. P. Connor, L. Garbus, M. Holland and S. Sawhney], University of Minnesota Press, Minneapolis, USA.

Oliver, M. (1999) 'Final accounts and the parasite people', in M. Corker and S. French (eds.) *Disability Discourse*, Open University Press, Milton Keynes.

Padden, C. and Humphries, T. (1988) *Deaf in America: Voices from a Culture*, Harvard University Press, Cambridge, MA, USA.

Preston, P. (1994) *Mother Father Deaf: Living Between Sound and Silence*, Harvard University Press Cambridge, MA, USA.

Ricouer, P. (1981) *Hermeneutics and the Human Sciences*, Cambridge University Press.

Scott, J. and Alwin, D. (1998) 'Retrospective versus prospective measurement of life histories in longitudinal research', in J. Giele and G. Elder (eds.) *Methods of Life Course Research: Qualitative and Quantitative Approaches*, Sage, Thousand Oaks, CA, USA.

Thomas, C. (1999) *Female Forms: Experiencing and Understanding Disability*, Open University Press, Milton Keynes.

Ward, M. (1996) 'Coming of age in the age of self-determination', in D. Sands and M. Wehmeyer (eds.) *Self-determination Across the Life Span: Independence and Choice for People with Disabilities*, Paul H. Brookes, Baltimore, USA.

Weiner, S. (1998) 'Review of deaf transitions', *Disability Studies Quarterly*, Fall 1998: 271–3.

Wrigley, O. (1998) *The Politics of Deafness*, Gallaudet University Press, Washington DC, USA.

12 The hidden injuries of 'a slight limp'

Devorah Kalekin-Fishman

With the title, I am fashioning a paradox. From the classic insight of Sennett and Cobb (1972) I take the 'hidden injuries' that imply suppression and gross injustice. The term 'slight limp', on the other hand, is to remind the reader and myself that although I am not 'normal', I am not 'really' disabled. In the long view, the fact that I am capable of writing this out means no less than that I am proclaiming emancipation, and furthermore, that at long last I am willing to cope with the issue of how normality is processed and structured on a personal level.

I will try to make my point of view clear by talking about how and where, in the course of my life, I have experienced normality, absorbed setbacks, and occasionally reversed them. My thesis is that normality and abnormality are experienced in on-going processes of situated sociality, mediated by macro-structured perceptions, awarenesses and discourse, and are irrationally embodied. The micro-processes and the macro-structures are interwoven according to differently proportioned models in different stages of the life span.

Agency and the self

If agency is the ability to make decisions on action, I am an agent. I am constantly making decisions about what I can and what I cannot do. I use the computer, I read books, I cook and bake, I play the piano, I lecture, I vote and eat, I shop and go 'out'. I judge many activities to be beyond the pale. I do not, nor have I ever, 'decided' to run a race, to ride a bicycle, to stand on my left foot without support. I have not 'decided' to do a high jump, to dance ballet, or to perfect the poses of T'ai Chi. Both what I do and what I do not do are classified according to an apparently well-ordered rationale of how I can use my body. So, before every action, there is a pause . . . and a beginning again. The pause is for description, for mulling over the requirements of balance, for comparing the proposed action with movements that are familiar and for explaining to myself why I can or cannot do what is at hand. This abstract guide ties together the succession of people and milieus, the jobs and the homes, the cars and the entertainment, the political framework, and the civil ambience – all pervaded with an unforgiving concern with that 'slight limp'.

In the course of daily living, the thinking is not observable; the behaviour just happens, part of what this person does naturally. The physiology of 'a slight limp' is part of the unmediated expression of what my 'I' is (Mead 1934). Continuity can be traced in the way I hold my body; in the way I stand up or lean against a wall; as in the way I sit down; in the crossing and uncrossing of my legs. And then, when I have nothing in mind but getting to where I really must go, and there is no possibility of pausing or planning the gait, the 'slight limp' takes over anyway. And, as Mead understood, the introspection is never cut off from an interpretation communicated by the surround. Every action is connected with a situation and the consequences that are engraved not merely in ephemeral memory, but in concrete acts. Not only do I hesitate over the performance; I worry about the possibility of negative vibes, the extent to which I am spoiling the party by 'not being able' to perform what seems to be on the agenda. What is embodied, moreover, is a worry about how long it will take me to make the decision and to what extent I am interrupting the natural rhythm of whatever episode is in progress. Natural rhythm is, of course, determined by the 'normals' in these circumstances.

My dawdling self has evolved both as a cumulative consciousness of what the slight limp means in terms of performance; and as an aggregate of conclusions from chronic interventions. At every age I have had to learn to what extent I can do what seems to be worth doing in my circles; and to assimilate opinions about my attainments from others whose opinions were of central importance at different times. There were the children who did not want to play with me because I wore a brace till the age of four and ran, if at all, in an odd way. There were the tap-dancing lessons 'everyone' on the block was taking. Much, much later, there was the woman at the kibbutz who, when I was pregnant with my first child, warned me that the limp would probably make it very difficult for me to have a natural birth. When I taught school, and gave marks strictly 'according to the book', a student who had not done too well stood on the corner as I went by and yelled – 'here's the cripple'. And again, at the university, there was the professor of sociology who assured me that he understood very well why I was trying so hard to be a good student. It was obvious to him that I was engaged in 'overcoming the disadvantage' that I was saddled with.

The bigger picture confirmed the messages transmitted face to face. For a person growing up in the United States, I had no choice but to understand that the lower limbs are crucial to a hope for normality. My left leg has always been thin and shapeless; my right leg fleshy and muscular. I had no place in the world of pin-ups, a world where curvaceous legs in sheer stockings were the *sine qua non* of feminine desirability. Good legs were a constant topic of adolescent conversation, and part of grown-up male jokes.

Contexts

It would be a mistake to reduce the macro to simulacra of the body. The matrix of class, ethnicity, religion and gender all come together in this story. In a nutshell, I was born: just about at the beginning of 'talking movies', a few months before the Great Depression, about a decade after my parents had immigrated to the United States from an impoverished village in Poland, six years after their wedding, eleven years after World War I and ten years before World War II.

I was born in New York and brought home to a three-room flat in the East Bronx, not very far from Crotona Park. This, I learned, was a better neighbourhood than the dreary brownstone houses of Williamsburg, where my grandparents and my uncles lived. Only several decades later did it turn into the 'bombed out Bronx' and the era of my childhood is commemorated today in a museum that celebrates the highlight of the borough's history. But even when we moved to the very respectable Grand Concourse, I had only one thing in mind: leaving the Bronx behind. The borough was clearly the locus of a configuration that was not normal.

Class

Lots of eminent people committed suicide in October 1929; they could not cope with the shock of Wall Street's fall and the shame of poverty. We were with those for whom the conditions were no novelty. We had had no money before the depression. The experience of class was simply being poor and not having a grocery store of one's own. Situationally, it was having my mother tell me that she did not have a penny to give me for candy.

Ethnicity

We were quintessential hyphenated Americans. Having immigrated to the US from a village with an unpronounceable name less than a decade before I was born, my mother liked to inform her acquaintances that she was from '*Russian* Poland'. We had a peculiar home language, and without realising it, we often mixed Yiddish words into our English sentences. Textbooks in primary school disclosed that this too was not normal. They made it clear that being an immigrant was excusable at best if you had been born in England, or at least had come from the northwestern side of the European continent.

Religion

Apart from that, we were observant Jews and religion governed our way of living. We followed eating habits that were 'different'; our holidays clashed with the practices of the public school. That raised doubts in my mind because we also knew that education was very important. There was great respect in the neighbourhood for those who had managed to go to school in the old country. From their conduct we learned that enlightenment meant being communists; and, furthermore, that religion, like Yiddish, was a ghetto appurtenance, neither approved nor recognised as normal.

Gender

Gender was mixed up with the other significant background variables. Role models were women with no marketable skills. Women were slaves to the household and to the male breadwinners. Women could pray, but had very little of importance to do at the synagogue. A woman came into her own when she produced a son. No doubt about it, as the first child, I should have been a boy. That would have given my mother a chance to queen it over a circumcision, and thirty days later, over a ceremony for 'redeeming' her first born from the fate of the priesthood, and the danger of the plague (of the Passover tales). Girl children are less than normal by fiat of the Almighty.

I must not forget that in my life I embody being a woman, a Jew, dark-skinned, born into a poor family of immigrants from East Europe to the 'golden country', the United States of America. The dominant majority of each category is a giant shadow. This is the stuff of radical disadvantage. Even before I had 'a slight limp' my life was being shaped by the vectors of critical sociology: the matrix of race, gender, religion and ethnicity. Still, these conceptualisations are statistically *a fortiori* and the place of an individual in the distributions is determined in the last analysis by peculiarities of life circumstances. The stuff of non-radical disadvantage entered my life when I was two years old.

Illness

When I was two, I was one of the children who became ill during a nation-wide epidemic of polio. The immediate experience of the illness has faded except for some stills. I have a poignant memory of wailing as I was put into an ambulance on a stretcher, and looked back at my mother who stood at the door with outstretched hands. The stay in the hospital was a nightmare of rustling white sheets, over-competent nurses and loneliness. I have vivid memories of going back and forth for treatment to the Hospital for Joint Diseases on 59th Street (for many years, I thought that the peculiar name meant that it was a hospital for an inexplicable combination of ills.) It was my mother who navigated the subway, and carried me up and down the staircases of the IRT. I remember myself immured in a cast from the waist down; I remember her putting me down, to rest and sigh on the landing between the two exhausting flights of stairs. At the hospital, doctors told her to make sure that I learnt how to swim. Frightened of the water, not knowing how to swim herself, she ignored the advice and shut that particular gate to normality. On her part, she was convinced that she had saved me from at least some of life's greatest hazards.

Residues

In the family, the limp was always centre stage. At the age of four, the hospital promoted me to a knee-high brace. But I was still living a melodrama. One Sunday, when we were on the way back from Brooklyn after visiting my grandmother, a woman with a pronounced limp entered the car of the elevated train, with her husband and two sons. My mother looked hard at the procession, and then, as if at a signal, burst into tears. She covered her eyes with her hands while her shoulders heaved. The young woman sitting across the aisle came to sit beside her, embraced her, and kept whispering something that sounded to me like, 'you see, it has all worked out . . .' But my mother was inconsolable until we left the train at 174th Street station. Very soon after that she communicated her dream. The best thing for me would be to marry my Uncle Ben, her youngest brother. She explained that a match between uncle and niece is not prohibited under Jewish law. Furthermore, he was the intellectual of the family – a teacher, and that was something to aspire to. The real point was that doctors in Vienna had somehow butchered his right leg, shortened it by about six inches when as a child he had broken it, and he limped very badly. I was made to realise that my world was to be one for 'those who limp'.

School days

School was a chronicle of learning what is normal and discovering the extent to which I deviated. Everything seemed to come together to prove that I was abnormal. By the time I was admitted to kindergarten, the brace was gone. My left ankle would not move; and that led to a drop foot and a thin leg. I was left with 'a slight limp' and a host of worries. As I advanced from grade to grade in primary school, I found that I needed glasses, and I was also 'a little' cross-eyed. In addition, my clothes were all wrong. My classmate, Elaine, a doctor's daughter, had the kind of moccasins, and the kinds of blouses that every child wanted. I did not. My classmate, Joan, could run races and I could not. My classmate, Doris, had beautiful dimples, lived with her divorced mother, and always had interesting stories to tell. The untidy mix of bodily failings and poverty meant I always had something to be ashamed of.

The 'slight limp' became a heavy burden in junior high school where I was overcome by confusion about the normal and the abnormal. For some reason I thought the girl, who wore a brace on her back, and managed to carry off a fake English accent, normal. I knew that Jessie who was nicely 'developed' and favoured by the much-admired English teacher, Mr. Okun, was normal. But I got a consolation prize. He did choose me to be editor of the school newspaper, with a feature column of my own. I was annointed quasi-normal, almost 'like everybody else'.

In high school, the drawbacks took another form: blatant demonstrations of class and ethnicity. Most of the girls at the select girls' school, Hunter College High, came from the Upper East and the Upper West sides of Manhattan. They had money; their fathers had cars; they regularly went to the theatre; and they just naturally knew everything I wanted to know. There were girls who went to Mexico with their parents during the summer vacation. There were girls who served on the student council and knew how to chair decision-making sessions. There were classes of girls who had already been attending the school in the ninth grade. We 'J's (graduates of junior high school) were latecomers. Some of 'us' were admirable, but I had a 'slight limp' and still another kind of abnormality. A teacher with an exotic first name, Evangeline, put me into a remedial group because I, like a lot of my classmates from the Bronx and Brooklyn, dentalised my 't's. Again it was clear that my birthplace – and I – could not measure up.

It was no help to recognise that other people were not intimidated. Jean with a bad case of acne and a really bad limp was bright, an officer of the student council, unafraid to pace the length of the assembly hall in order to walk up on the stage and address all the teachers and the girls in the auditorium. And she smiled while she did it! Looking at her, I automatically transferred into the comparative mode. It was clear that her limp was not 'slight'. Her 'bad' foot was much worse than mine. Instead of encouraging me, the contrast seemed to accent my own incapacity. I could never, I was certain, do the things Jean could do. When, in her senior year, she was accepted to Sarah Lawrence, I took that as an indubitable sign that my conclusion was valid. True, she was not Jewish, nor the daughter of immigrants, or from a working class family. Her disability was wiped out, while my 'slight limp' was, in my construal, forcing me to be an 'other'.

I am not outlining the full picture. As in the literature on alienation (*see* especially, Seeman 1967; Willis 1977), I resolutely used my otherness to what seemed like good purpose at the time. With downcast eyes, and a shamed heart, I acted to make sure that I gained all the boons. As a kid, I went to the movies instead of running around the block. My slight limp was a ready-made excuse that worked. In junior high school, I could ask the doctor for a note and escape the railings and ravings of what seemed to me to be a sadistic physical training teacher. She yelled at all the girls in the gym while I could sit at the piano patiently, prepared to hammer out a Chopin Mazurka as soon as she calmed down enough to ask them to do a march around the room. It never bothered me that the three-quarter rhythm did not suit the left-right of a march. Curiously, it did not seem to bother Mrs M. either. This was a mixed blessing because between yells, she taught the girls the steps of some important ballroom dances, and I never did get the hang of them.

Shifting contexts

Youth movement

Saturday afternoon activities in a Zionist youth movement marked the beginning of a long process of leaving the Bronx. The youth movement was the ideal place for 'others'. Here it all came together, and even my body fitted. We were all religious Jews. We could all dance because the steps were simple glides. Dancing meant singing loud, stamping hard and fast. Because of my slight limp I was allowed to choose not to go on long hikes that were de rigueur for a movement with pretensions to scouting, and thus I could hide my indifference to nature. Later, I was to use the movement, after I left it, as a lever to rebel against my parents. The goal it had imparted of becoming a pioneer in a 'new' country, Palestine, at least for a short time, suited my need to leave home. It was far more acceptable to religious parents than just moving out and taking an apartment in another part of the city.

Israel

In 1949, I came to a country that had recently been torn apart by war. Though the look and the conditions were incomprehensible to me, what was important was that from the first I felt that I belonged. On a Jerusalem street, somebody whistled, and they sometimes meant me. I worked hard at learning Hebrew, and was delighted when a storekeeper asked me if I had migrated from Bulgaria. My olive skin and my studiedly rolled 'r's helped me make it. I was no longer competing for inappropriate prizes. In the context of no longer being a statistical other, there was a surge of daring to be normal. When I decided to join a cooperative village, I found the man who was the nicest looking one of the bunch. I played the piano in the big mess hall at night because that was the only time it was free, and he loved music. So there we were. There are children, and like the woman on the elevated train in the Bronx, I could have said to my Mom, 'You see, it has all worked out'. But even when I think of telling her that, I know that that would be cheating.

During the many years of my life in Israel, there has been very little justification for concern with a slight limp, even though aesthetically normal is 'like America'. All the banalities of cheesecake, beauty queens, and paper-thin models have penetrated the shared imaginary of this country that is part of the realm of communications. But this is still slightly ambiguous. Historical complexities have made it possible for me to conduct situations of my adult life in denial, that is, in a mode of identifying with the normal. Ultimately this is where the personal melds with the political.

There are two niches for abnormality intertwined with the history of the state. A slight limp has no status in such a set-up. The one is the niche of the soldiers, injured in the wars that make up the official history of our country for the last fifty years. Another is the niche of the survivors of the Holocaust. Whereas the soldiers have been lavishly compensated for impairment, the survivors of the Holocaust have for the most part, been able only recently to attain recognition of the fact that they, too, are disabled. The chronology of making allowances for impairment is reversed, and that is part of the story. An explanation is necessary.

Wars and wounded soldiers

The very night after Israel proclaimed her independence (15 May 1948) with the backing of the United Nations, the first war broke out. And since then, there were wars in 1956, 1967, 1968–70, 1973, 1978, 1981, 1989, 1990, and off and on in the 1990s. Every war left hundreds of disabled young men incapacitated to different degrees. Disability as a result of military involvement is a badge of honour. Committees recognise a generous 'percentage' of disability, allot tax discounts the veteran soldier can enjoy, and decide on an overall amount of remuneration for the person and/or his (in almost all the cases) family. Success in making legitimate claims on government support, however, is not the same as enjoying an appropriate environment. Incapacitated veterans are not usually provided for in the construction of public buildings, at street crossings, in seating arrangements in an auditorium. Until very recently, the public arena was exclusively organised for the physically 'normal' and the sight of physical struggle among the disabled was interpreted as normal evidence of unconditional Spartan values. What is conveyed is the message that being wounded in a war is rare good luck. Furthermore, convenience is a luxury; and munificence should not turn into indulgence.

Survivors of the Holocaust

After World War II, survivors of the Holocaust and the war atrocities turned into displaced persons with literally no place to go except to a place where a relatively large Jewish community needed reinforcements to ensure her own survival, and was eager to have them. A simplistic myth considered part of the 'charter' asserts that Israel was recognised as an independent state because the member states of the UN were remorseful about letting the Nazis carry out their fiendish designs. In Israel, compensation of individuals for their suffering has consistently been an ambiguous issue. Since survivors were reticent about what had really happened, the entire Nazi era was translated into talk about money. On the individual level their injuries were for long unseen. Those who suffered most are, after all, not among the survivors. And those who are alive were understood to be living 'normal' lives. It is not by chance, apparently, that only in the 1990s, have the survivors come to occupy a niche that is unassailable. They are for the most part old; many of them are ill with diseases whose aetiology can be traced to those terrifying days. Perhaps the most important element is the fact that now more and more of them are telling their stories.

Those who could not be included in either of the above categories were, and are, at a financial disadvantage and do not attract any attention. This stricture includes members of minority groups no matter how or where they have been incapacitated. And of course, it refers to people whose disability was 'acquired' simply through illness or accident. It was, therefore, normative for a person with a limp to be normal. The injuries of a 'slight limp', if any, were fated to be relegated to denial. On the basis of early socialisation I had to repress a worry that soon there would be another woman with a prettier face and 'nice legs', and all the really important things I shared with my partner would pale into nullity. With the children, I pretended that I was just like all the other Moms – light-minded and light on my feet. Wearing shoes and sandals just like everybody else was part of the normal persona. I did not walk a lot and never learned to swim, but neither did I admit to limitations. It was normal, too, to be especially proud of my son who is an excellent swimmer and sprinter, and of my daughters who do athletics and dance – one professionally. I am deeply grateful for what I see as a miracle of perversity; their bodies seem to be acting out a mindless rebellion. Actions that I denied having an interest in, emerge as joyful doing in their lives.

Growing old has brought me face to face with an obstinate body. There is a difference. The ageing self is constrained to face the true state of things. With a weakening of the body, the 'I' is pushed to the background. Less spontaneity can help one get through the day. A new sensitivity to people's responses helps the 'me' plan more, though not better. My tools – my perceptions of what skills I command and my theorised construals of the situations that I can be involved in – have taken on different forms. I make a case I never wanted to formulate before and apply for an invalid's tag so that I can park in convenient spots. I no longer pretend that I can drive as easily as anybody else, or that I can walk no matter what distance from the parking area. When 'seriously' disabled people demonstrate in order to get better support from the National Health System, I no longer conceive of them as different or place them in my mind among those to be pitied. In terms of what one might imagine as the normal community, their situation is like mine in many ways – and that is now something I see as normal.

Socially sanctioned signs of age are constant pains in my hip, and weakness in my back. The slight limp has affected my 'healthy' leg, causing incontrovertible difficulties in mobility. After a lifetime of escaping into a slight limp, I have for several years had to have shoes made even though they cannot totally alleviate the discomfort. Some time ago, an orthopaedist told me, that there is no such thing as a 'slight' weakness in the ankle as the result of polio. The muscles of a person who has been through polio weaken earlier than do the muscles of normals. The parts of the body that take over for the sick limb pay the price of the mobilisation. The limp, no longer hiding under a bushel of youthful spirits, family responsibilities, and the prospect of a long future; is with me every moment of the day as a twinge, a jolt, a burning sensation, out and out pain. This is not mysterious, and definitely not abnormal. At my age, 'normal' means having aches and pains.

Summing up

In the writing, I have discovered that for a person with what she tries to construe as a slight disability; ethnicity, religion, poverty and style of life all fit together as in a jigsaw puzzle. But the physical inadequacy stays at the core. I could move out of the neighbourhood; out of religious practices; out of a career in peripheral schools; out of the country of my birth. I discovered as I did this that there is no place to go except into a new constellation of associations, beliefs, and 'charter myths' (Moore 1962, 1958). Every new context has a name, or a place, for it; and in the small, every situation begins with an examination of the extent to which the 'slight limp' affects events.

My story is one of taking up shifting positions between poles of normality and abnormality with a differential relationship to the physical and to the socially structured at different ages. The overall frame is the structured discourse of normality throughout the life span. Although it caused almost no physical discomfort in my childhood, the slight limp cast a shadow of abnormality over every kind of activity that is formulated as important to children and was important to me then. The shadow accompanied me to every situation as it emerged. Mediated by the public discourse, my relationship to the limp in adolescence and early adulthood was determined by the normative evaluation of the extent to which it constituted an aesthetic (and sexual) blemish. Awareness of the normativity I could not achieve, because of the slight limp, polluted situations of making an appearance in school functions, campaigning for a place of leadership, finding a mate, the theme and substance of those years. With the pain and discomfort of advanced age, the slight limp finally fits me nicely into a socially approved place. At this point in the life trajectory, it is normal to have a slight limp with adjunct inconvenience. The configuration is on the list of troubles legitimately to be expected and allowed for in the third age. Coping with collateral physical impairment is officially part of the normal course of ageing. All the books agree, as do the ads, the doctors, and the laws of quasi-welfare states: struggles with the physical are normative. No question but that the social structuration of normality is echoed in the embodied irrational and rational.

Abstractions

Discussions of identity are a highly popular pastime. Etymologically, we are talking about what makes me 'the same' today as I was yesterday, even though locating that sameness is problematic. How can we explain continuities of self when there is not only palpable evidence of change, but also an established ideology of valuing novelty? Attempts to deal with this question are many – a few of them sociologically convincing.

Mead's (1934) conceptualisation of identity as a dynamic dualism proffers a useful theoretical hook. In his construction, sameness lies in process. Initially, the physiologically driven, unthinking 'I' produces activity that is unplanned and unpredictable. The responses of the surround inform the 'me' what the summary actions mean to the environment. This information governs the planning of the next activity. But even in carrying out planned action, the 'I' continues to influence performance infusing it with unforeseen elements. The perpetual dialectic of the 'I' and the 'me', of blind physiology and the assessment of social input, is the invention of the self, the heart of what it means to be a living human being. Continuity is sealed into the inter-relations of 'I' and 'me' and can be observed in the persistence of unanticipated instinctual initiatives. Continuity is seen in the impact of the person on her milieu and the impact of those in the surround on her.

Striving to illuminate the moral challenges of our age, Bauman (1995) honours the individual-society dialectic as a meeting ground of 'identity' and 'culture'. Like Mead's self, Bauman's 'identity' is the vehicle for construing situations and deciding on action. Because of the self-other encounter, identity, or 'compressed culture' demonstrates and generates culture through 'action infused with theory'. In this definition, Bauman preserves the insight that culture is not something that people 'have', but rather something they do; and the Meadian dialectic is hereby re-read as a process of reciprocal emergence on still another level. What is not accounted for in the descriptions of the dynamic is the issue of how we can become aware of our 'self' and of our 'identity'.

But there is still another plane of meaningfulness. James'(1890) intuition that thoughts connected as we think they ought to be connected, are our personal selves, encourages us to find out the sense of it all by setting out ideas in writing. His notion is extended in the framework of positioning theory suggested by Harre and van Langenhove (1999). In their view, the self is made manifest in discourse through the display of a unique point of view, through assertions of agency, and through illustrative reference to events in one's biography (Harre and van Langenhove 1999: 24). Moreover, the mode of manifesting the self depends on the choice of a relational 'persona' for performing the discourse with those one construes as the partner or partners. I have written this chapter in an effort to unpack elements that have shaped an identity in a lifetime with a slight limp. So much is left out. I wonder about the theory that infuses the things that I do, the culture that folds into the identity of disability, and unfolds in turn as creation and re-creation.

I would hope that my self-presentation in this chapter has accomplished two normative goals. My tale could, perhaps, be an exemplification of a large group of people, perhaps a statistically significant portion of the population in which each individual has something 'slight' and shameful and not worth talking about, but is the core of her being, a constant companion, a rude daily awakening. The potency of this particular kind of incapacity – its tenacity, its obstinacy, its illusory mildness and unobtrusiveness can be debilitating. In the final analysis, this self that I have sketched here presents itself in what Harre and van Langenhove call the 'mode of supplication'. For all of us with persistent and inescapable limitations, and that is all of us, the political challenge is to define normativity with a range of inclusiveness that enables disabled people to engage in sociation – being with people – with an assumption that discomfort is normal. Normative emancipation enjoins a configuration we have little experience with: the ultimate, of consideration for one another mixed with complete indifference. Let us invoke the emblem of weakness and save ourselves: Salvemus nos!

REFERENCES

Bauman, Z. (1995) *Life in Fragments: Essays in Postmodern Morality*, Blackwell, Oxford.

Harre, R. and van Langenhove, L. (eds.) (1999) *Positioning Theory*, Blackwell, Oxford.

James, W. (1890) *Principles of Psychology*, Holt, New York, USA.

Mead, G. H. (1934) *On Social Psychology*, University of Chicago Press, USA.

Moore, B. (1958, 1962) *Political Power and Social Theory*, Harper & Row, New York, USA.

Seeman, M. (1967) 'On the personal consequences of alienation in work', *American Sociological Review*, 32 (2): 273–85.

Sennett, R. and Cobb, J. (1972) *The Hidden Injuries of Class*, Knopf, New York, USA.

Willis, P. (1977) *Learning to Labour: How Working Class Kids Get Working Class Jobs*, Saxon House, Farnborough.

III

The politics of transition

13   Disabled children: an emergency submerged

Sue Philpott and Washeila Sait

Noluthando is a strapping 16-year-old girl with severe cognitive impairments. She attends a day care centre in an informal settlement, where her mother cares for other children with similar impairments. Noluthando has been repeatedly raped within her community, but her perpetrators have never received any punishment for the crimes that they have committed against her. The reason for this is that she is perceived to be unable to give evidence in her defence. To a large extent, children like Noluthando have little access to the justice system, as they are regarded as unreliable witnesses.

Lisa was a six-year-old physically disabled child who used a wheelchair. She lived in an informal settlement, consisting of cardboard homes under one of the many bridges that form part of the busy highways in Cape Town. A fire broke out within the settlement, and Lisa, forgotten in the pandemonium, was burnt to death because she could not escape in time, and because no one helped her.

Noluthando and Lisa are but two examples of the life experiences of disabled children living in South Africa, yet their particular situation resonates with the life experiences of many of their peers on the African continent. It is important to ask how disabled children's lives and life course pathways are influenced by changes in the society in which they live. Many things are changing in South Africa, yet Noluthando and Lisa's stories remind us that the lives of disabled children may not be changing so quickly.

This chapter arises from the recognition that, since the inception of the International Day of Disabled Persons in 1981, most of the issues pertaining to disability have centred on adults, and that very little has been done to improve the situation of disabled children. At the same time, international children's aid agencies have tended to focus on non-disabled children, taking little account of the needs and aspirations of disabled children. Thus, disabled children have been largely excluded from *both* disability *and* children's programmes. In addition, issues pertaining to disabled children have most often been seen within the domain of health and welfare, and thought of as the responsibility of the state. The state for its part has tried to submerge the issue, and to prevent it from becoming a priority, preferring instead to allow donor agencies and non-governmental organisations to assist as best they can.

The first part of the chapter explores the present realities for disabled children in South Africa. The second section focuses on some of the key interventions which may be required if the ideals of 'equal rights for all' (from the disability sector) and 'first call for children' (from the children's rights sector) are to become a reality for disabled children in this country.

Disabled children in South Africa

South Africa is situated on the southern tip of Africa, bounded by the Atlantic Ocean to the west, and the Indian Ocean to the east. The new democracy is constituted of nine provinces, and has a population of 39 million. Of these, there are 17 million children younger than 18 years old – a staggering 44.24 per cent of the country's population (Statistics South Africa 1998). In light of this, it is a tragedy that children also bear the largest impact of poverty in South Africa. They find themselves in a society where past policies have left a legacy of severe regional and racial disparity. Many South African families still live in conditions that do not allow them to meet the most basic or developmental needs of their children (Robinson and Sadan 1999).

Disabled children experience the difficulties faced by all children in South Africa even more acutely. Even the limited education, health and social services are often inaccessible to them – and, as in Noluthando's case, they may have no access to the justice system. Indeed, the link between poverty and disability is well documented, with the recognition that poverty is both a cause and a consequence of disability (Elwan 1999).

Since coming to office in 1994, the new government of South Africa has made a number of specific attempts to address the many difficulties facing children in the country. It has promised children a 'better life', and has prioritised children's needs in its efforts to address poverty (the first democratically-elected president even established the Nelson Mandela Children's Fund, to which he contributed a significant proportion of his salary for the years in which he was in office). Non-governmental organisations, such as the Disabled Children's Action Group (DICAG), the Down's Syndrome Association and the Deaf Federation of South Africa (DEAFSA) have also been active in campaigning for the protection and promotion of the rights of disabled children. While these initiatives are commendable, and a great deal has been achieved to date, the challenge remains to bridge the gap between the rhetoric of progressive policies and the reality faced by disabled children in their day-to-day lives.

The urgency of the situation cannot be over-emphasised. Every day of delay in decision-making, every postponement of budget allocation is a day lost for a disabled child. Early identification of difficulties and barriers, and prompt action in response, has long-term implications, not only for the individual disabled child and their family but also for the socio-economic status of the country.

The policy context

When South Africa celebrated the achievement of 'the long walk to freedom' and entered a new post-apartheid era in 1994, its citizens had high expectations of what the new democracy would bring. These expectations are embodied in the Constitution, which declares the new democratic state to be founded on the principles of human dignity, the achievement of equality, the advancement of human rights and freedoms, non-racialism and non-sexism. In addition, it proclaims that 'All citizens are equally entitled to the rights, privileges and benefits of citizenship' (RSA 1996: 3). In working towards these ideals, South Africa as a nation has faced the challenging task of shedding a history of separation, exclusion and discrimination on the basis of race. The task of building a new society is ongoing, and draws on the strength, endurance and spirit of all South African citizens in fighting for equality and recognition. However, the reputation of 'the rainbow nation' is still conceptualised primarily in terms of *racial* diversity. On a practical level, disabled people, and particularly disabled children, face another 'long walk' to achieve the same rights and opportunities as others in the country. Indeed, the present process of transformation raises unique challenges (as well as opportunities) for disabled children in South Africa.

The political transformation within South Africa has led to the development of new policies and legislation, based on the recognition of equal rights, privileges and benefits for every citizen, and promoting the vision of a 'society for all' (RSA 1997: v). Indeed, the Bill of Rights in the Constitution (1996: 13) gives recognition to the fact that every child has the right to family or parental care, and to basic nutrition, education, shelter, health care services and social services; every child has the right to be protected from maltreatment, neglect or abuse.

In 1995, the South African government ratified the United Nations Convention on the Rights of the Child (UN 1980), and by so doing made a commitment to undertake specific actions 'to the maximum extent of available resources', in order to realise children's economic, social and cultural rights. The National Plan of Action for Children was launched in 1996, outlining the government's programme of implementing the Convention.

The Integrated National Disability Strategy was adopted as a White Paper in 1997, after widespread consultation within the country (and based on the United Nations Standard Rules on the Equalisation of Opportunities for Disabled Persons). In addition, the government has set up the Office on the Status of Disabled Persons, and the Children's Desk, both of which are located in the President's Office. There have also been a number of specific initiatives in different sectors – such as education, where a Commission was established to examine the possibility of providing 'quality education for all, overcoming barriers to learning and development' (DoE 1997).

The intentions within each of these documents are admirable – indeed, the country boasts some of the most progressive disability policies in the world. However, the transformation that has begun to take place remains by-and-large at the level of rhetoric. Its implementation remains a constant struggle. Implementation of the UN Convention is subject to available resources, and 'lack of resources' has become the rationale for ignoring, or failing to implement, policies for disabled children. For example, government schools have a teacher-pupil ratio of 1 to 40. Education authorities and many teachers argue that it is impossible to give individual attention to disabled students in this context (Muthukrishna 2000). However, if parents are aware and have access to information on the rights of disabled children (i.e. if this is taken up as an issue by disabled children, their families, and organisations) then government service providers are obliged to accommodate them. Non-governmental organisations, like DICAG, have also played an important role in lobbying for change (for example, in forcing wider entitlements under the Social Assistance Act).

A great deal of work remains to be done, in fostering the will and commitment to ensure that aspirational policies become a reality for all disabled children in South Africa. The underlying value of justice needs to be upheld, and a culture of respect for the human rights of all people, young and old, cultivated.

Poverty and access to resources

Among the symptoms of a society in transition is a general sense of insecurity, and a high level of crime. At one time, South Africa was quoted in the media as having the second highest murder rate in the world. Other problems linked to poverty and criminality, are the crises of HIV/AIDS, child abuse and child prostitution, to which disabled children are particularly vulnerable.

Poverty in South Africa is such that one in three households has an available income of less than R1000 per month (£90 or US$130), and two-thirds survive on less than R3000 per month. It is estimated that some three million children should qualify for a child support grant, due to their dire financial circumstances. However, of these, only one per cent are currently receiving such grants (DICAG 1998).

Deprivation, violence, malnutrition, poor health, inferior education and discriminatory social security systems have created and entrenched severe disparities in access to social security for children of different racial groups and genders. Children often suffer from the break-up of family as their parents and siblings move to urban areas in search of work. Migration to urban areas exacerbates poverty for children living in densely populated urban squatter settlements and for children who remain behind in poorly serviced rural areas. (Robinson and Sadan 1999).

There is a strong relationship between disability and poverty: poverty makes people more vulnerable to disability, and disability reinforces and deepens poverty. In this context, disabled children are among the most vulnerable, subject to a vicious cycle of deprivation, which often brings with it a sense of worthlessness and despair. This problem is compounded by the fact that many of the primary caregivers of disabled children are single women, who are neither economically independent nor literate.

A report on *Poverty and Inequality in South Africa* (1998) recognises that *absence of power* is an important dimension of poverty, and that poverty is characterised by poverty traps and poverty of opportunity. It is this that leads to the marginalisation and exclusion of certain groups. Such exclusion can have profound psychological effects, including an 'internalised oppression', in which low self-image and a sense of disempowerment may be transmitted from parent to disabled child (and to other siblings). De-humanising attitudes foster a culture in which acts of violence and abuse towards disabled children become acceptable, as too do crime, social marginalisation and the systematic breakdown of family support systems. The irony is that, while the primary focus of the Department of Welfare is on poverty alleviation, there is very limited access to welfare services for those who really need them. The legacy of apartheid means that rural black women (and particularly those with disabled children) remain amongst the poorest and most marginalised in society.

Access to basic services and resources, like health and education, is essential if the lives of disabled children, especially poor children, are to change. The government's new approach to Primary Health Care (RSA 1997) has meant that access to basic health services is much improved for disabled children. They too benefit from health services, which are now free for all children under the age of six years, and from protection against preventable diseases, through more effective immunisation programmes. Disabled children in primary schools have access to improved nutrition, through the school nutrition programme. Some disabled children have also benefited from the policy of compulsory school education for all children aged five to 15 years. However, a survey by the National Commission on Special Needs in Education and Training (1997) estimated that approximately 270,000 disabled children are still outside of the formal school system. The reasons for this include inaccessible school buildings, the reluctance of authorities to accept disabled children, the negative attitudes of teachers, and access to transport. There are still very few early childhood development facilities for disabled children.

The vulnerability of disabled children is a function both of their generational status, of being young in a society dominated by adults, and of being disabled in a society that erects many barriers to exclude and marginalise those with impairments. This vulnerability manifests itself in many ways. For example, disabled children may be particularly vulnerable to physical and sexual abuse when they are dependent on one or many adults for their physical needs. Disabled children may not be able to speak out about what is happening to them due to communication difficulties, and may not be believed when they do so. Family members may not always use Care Dependency Grants directly for the benefit of the disabled child who qualifies for it. Social attitudes often undermine the value of children, and particularly disabled children. As a result they may not be given priority in terms of access to basic services such as health and education.

Attitudes leading to segregation and exclusion

South African society still regards disabled children as incapable, incompetent, sick, a burden to society and a 'problem' that should be dealt with separately from other children's issues. Disabled children fear, and experience, exclusion from a very young age. Separation from family, friends and peers is common. Deaf children in particular are often removed from the family environment as young as two years old, due to a lack of early intervention programmes within the community (professionals justify this, as being 'in the best interest of the child'). Non-disabled children, in turn, learn to accept the exclusion of disabled children as the norm.

In other instances, parents experience shame at having a disabled child, and the child is often sent to live with extended family (mainly grandmothers) in distant rural areas, or simply hidden from the community. These early experiences undermine the capacity of disabled children for inclusion in society, and reinforce an acceptance of segregation in later life. The danger that disabled children will internalise such attitudes is illustrated in the response of one young girl attending a special school.

I long to be in a school for 'normal' children. I do believe that I can cope with the workload. But I am so deformed, and my disability might turn other children away from me. It is best to be with children just like me.

Disabled children often suffer more from social barriers than from their impairment. They and their parents, usually the mother, are held responsible for their impairment, which may be viewed as punishment for violating ancestral taboo, or looked upon as an inherited family curse. It may be seen as a curse or punishment for something that the mother has done wrong. She, in turn, may then be ostracised and even deserted at a time when she needs the most support. It is this lack of support, *not a lack of love*, which often leads mothers to lock their disabled children in shacks, so that they can go to look for employment. It is this lack of support that results in confusion between the benefits of protection for vulnerable children and over-protection (which in the long-term increases vulnerability).

Such perceptions and stigmatisation are linked to, and perpetuate, many specific beliefs and practices – for example, that a child with epilepsy or seizures is bewitched; that the rape of a young disabled virgin will cure the perpetrator of HIV/AIDS; that disabled children cannot be educated within an inclusive environment, and that their presence within the classroom could be disruptive. Such beliefs and associated attitudes are in themselves barriers that perpetuate the exclusion and marginalisation of disabled children in society, further limiting the children's meaningful integration and participation within the family and the wider community.

One mother recently related the story of her struggle to get her nine-year-old son educated. The child is now in his second school, as the first school labeled him 'incapable of learning'. Knowing that her son might be in need of remedial support, she sought and found a school that offered this particular service. On relating her request, she was told that *she* had no right to label her child, and he was promptly placed in a classroom of forty children with no support from the teacher. A year later the child has not only been held back, but has been placed in the very remedial class that the parent requested in the first instance. His current situation is worse, in that he has been placed together with children much older than him, where he is constantly being bullied.

I requested remedial teaching because I knew that he has a problem in reading and spelling, he cannot even write his own name, but they would not listen to me . . . They are currently not teaching my child, and he is so unhappy. Soon he will be a teenager, and sooner still a man. How will he ever be able to provide for himself economically? I fear for the future of my son, I feel so helpless.

The assumption that disabled children are helpless and dependent has meant that responses to them have been based on a charity approach. Disabled children and their families have been regarded as passive recipients who need to be looked after and cared for. Much of the 'help' given has focused on immediate physical needs, such as food and clothing. However, this approach has reinforced an expectation to *receive*, rather than to *develop*. It has focused on short-term charity or relief, rather than long-term empowerment. Within the disability sector, it is adult issues that take precedence, with few (if any) avenues for the participation of disabled children. The voices of disabled children remain largely unheard. Their cries are submerged in a quagmire of ignorance, fear, and extreme negative attitudes, while politicians and policy makers hide behind the contingencies of Article 23 of the Convention on the Rights of the Child, that enforcement of the rights of disabled children is 'subject to available resources' (UN 1980: 6).

What makes a difference?

What makes a difference in disabled children's lives? How influential are the attitudes of others, the economics of the society in which they live, the policies and services of the state, their parents, or their personalities? How can we promote the inclusion of disabled children at all levels and within all sectors of society, and recognition of their rights as children.

Lungi is a six-year-old girl who has been blind since birth. She lives with her extended family in a rural household of three huts. Their home is approximately 100 kilometres from the closest town, and the roads are extremely poor. The surrounding terrain is steep and rocky, and un-conducive to agriculture. Lungi stays most of the time in one of the huts, where family members look after her; she is very fearful of moving

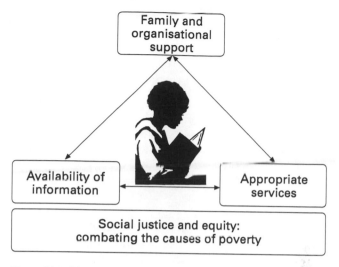

Figure 13.1 Significant factors to be addressed if the rights of disabled children are to be protected, and their full potential realised

around, even within the homestead. Recently, a Community Based Rehabilitation (CBR) worker has been visiting Lungi and her family. One of the major areas of focus has been to help her develop the basic skills of independence, such as dressing and washing, and to build her skills and confidence with mobility. Acquisition of these skills, as well as the support and information provided by the CBR worker, has helped Lungi's family to begin to recognise, and to affirm, her potential. As a result they have now submitted an application for her to be enrolled in school.

Figure 13.1 illustrates how family and organisational support interacts with the availability of information and provision of appropriate services to support children's rights. However, this interaction must also rest upon a firm foundation of social justice and equality, including strategies to combat the underlying structural causes of poverty.

Rights of disabled children

The Integrated National Disability Strategy (RSA 1997) in South Africa has challenged the view that disability is primarily an issue to be dealt with by the health and welfare sectors. Instead, it strongly asserts that disability must be addressed as a development issue, including every sector of government, as well as NGOs. The Constitution provides the basis of this strategy, that every citizen is equal under the law and entitled to a life without discrimination on the basis of age, disability, gender, language or culture (RSA 1996: 7).

The challenge is to ensure that these basic principles permeate and underpin both planning and service provision at all levels in society. The establishment of the Disability Forum in KwaZulu Natal (one of the nine provinces of South Africa) provides an example of how this can be achieved on a provincial level. Every government department is represented in the forum, including transport, correctional services, and education, and the disability sector. The forum provides a mechanism to hold each department accountable for planning and implementing the Integrated National Disability Strategy (ensuring that even the jails are accessible!).

There is a need to ensure that *every one* of the Articles of the Convention on the Rights of the Child applies to disabled children. One way of doing so is to create mechanisms for monitoring and reporting violations of disabled children's rights (such as the South African Human Rights Commission), and for documenting examples of good practice. Evaluation of the impact of the implementation of the Convention on the Rights of the Child over the past ten years indicates a *lack of participation* of disabled children in programmes that are intended to benefit them. One of the reasons for this is the assumption that disabled children are passive and dependent, leading adults to make decisions on their behalf without appropriate opportunities to express their opinions (Woll 1999, Philpott and Mdunyelwa 2000).

Participation by disabled children is critical if their exclusion and marginalisation by society is to be reversed. Their feedback is essential in assessing the impact of different programmes and policies. For example, a programme may proclaim 'success' in ensuring acceptance of a certain number of disabled children into a mainstream school. However, unless this data is accompanied by documentation of children's experiences within the school (e.g. the level of acceptance they experience) it may be misleading. Admittance without acceptance is not inclusion.

The affirmation of the rights of disabled children to equal participation in socio-economic development (both as recipients and future contributors) requires the fulfilment of three basic areas of development that impact on disabled children's lives (DICAG 1998). First, there are economic policies that impact directly on the basic needs of the child (those dealing with primary health care, education, early childhood development, access to assistive devices); second, there are economic policies that impact on the family and therefore on the child (such as

housing, social security, poverty alleviation, access to water, transport
and roads, employment and job creation); third, economic policies that
have an indirect impact on the child and on the family (such as
monetary and exchange rate policies, which determine budget alloca-
tions for government programmes).

Parents and peers

As with any child, the mother of a disabled child has hopes for what that
child may become and who they will grow up to be. It is here that
disabled children often experience, at the most basic level, contradictory
feelings of acceptance, love, rejection, or realisation that they are the
objects of bitter disappointment.

Felicity has been going through a difficult time recently, and has been
missing her family a great deal, as she attends a boarding school. She
has been tearful, waiting for her mother to fetch her at the end of the
week (see Figure 13.2).

Parents have a central role in nurturing and encouraging the development of their children, in building a sense of trust and in early learning.
But they need support in this role, from other family members and from
the community as a whole.

Experience has shown that the role of parents is critical in determining
whether a disabled child has hope, expectations of life, and the resilience
to cope with the many barriers they may have to face. In order to
perform this role, parents need support as individuals, and support to
work collectively. Organisations of parents of disabled children, like
DICAG, have played a significant role in direct service provision (e.g.
running centres for early childhood development), peer counselling, and
lobbying for the provision and improvement of basic services (Philpott
and McLaren 1999; PMRG 1998).

As a child grows up, other children become increasingly important.
Langalihle's picture (see Figure 13.3) shows how happy everyone can be
when children feel included within a circle of family and friends.

Disabled children experience feelings of acceptance or rejection,
based to a large extent on the way they are treated by their siblings or
peers. The Child-to-Child approach has been used in a number of
different contexts in Africa to encourage children to work together
constructively, and to build healthy relationships with one another. This
is one area that needs to be further encouraged and developed in South
Africa.

Figure 13.2 Felicity's picture

Figure 13.3 Langalihle's picture

Appropriate services

Another significant factor in the lives of disabled children is that of accessibility and appropriateness of services they receive. This includes all levels and sectors, from basic health care to nutrition, education and the justice system.

Too often in the past, segregated 'special' schools have contributed to the marginalisation and exclusion of disabled children and have failed to give them tools for living healthy and creative lives as contributors to the broader community. Instead, such schools need to be seen as centres of expertise, as resources for the training and support of teachers, disabled children and community groups. In addition, specific resources need to be allocated to support the expansion of integrated education (e.g. through teacher skills development and greater access of school buildings).

Community Based Rehabilitation programmes have the potential to provide more appropriate and accessible rehabilitation to disabled children, and to do so in a way that involves the local community in addressing barriers to their participation. Where mothers of disabled children are involved as CBR workers their status is often enhanced, as they become 'experts', and as their wealth of experience and knowledge is recognised and affirmed. In this way they become contributors and a resource to the community.

It remains a challenge for services in all sectors to become accessible and to address the barriers to development for disabled children. In education, teachers need the attitudes and skills to cope with diversity in the classroom, and community schools need to be more accessible. We need better co-ordination and referral between different sectors, and recognition of the important role that can be played by disabled children themselves, not only their parents and families. We need to develop child-focused indicators for the evaluation and monitoring of services, which reveal the ultimate impact of programmes on the protection of the rights of disabled children.

Availability of information

To make informed decisions that affect their lives, parents and children need accurate and 'understandable' information. Information should come from a variety of sources, including other disabled people. This is one way in which parents and children become empowered and can take responsibility for their lives. For example, in making a decision about whether a Deaf child should receive a cochlear implant, parents need to have technical information from rehabilitation professionals, as well as counselling and advice from members of the Deaf community.

Conclusion

Among the yardsticks by which to measure a society's respect for human rights, to evaluate the level of its maturity and its generosity of spirit is by looking at the status it accords to those members of society who are most vulnerable: disabled people . . . and its children. (TM Mbeki, quoted in RSA 1997: i).

Disabled children have not yet been accorded the same status as other citizens, even other children, in the new South Africa. They continue to bear the brunt of poverty and inadequate service provision. However, it must be acknowledged that great strides have been made towards the protection and promotion of disabled children's rights since the democratic government of South Africa was elected in 1994. Significant and far-reaching policy documents have been ratified and developed, both in the children's rights sector and in the disability sector. The challenge is to determine how these rights will be translated into reality in the daily lives of disabled children and their families – how they will receive the necessary support, gain better access to information, and receive more appropriate education, health and other necessary services.

The urgent needs of disabled children cannot be addressed through a welfare-charity approach, nor can their fulfilment be dependent upon foreign funders, whose agendas and concerns differ from year to year. Instead, there must be recognition within South African society of the rights of disabled children to live lives of dignity with equal access to opportunities for development.

REFERENCES

Department of Education (1997) *Quality Education For All: Overcoming Barriers to Learning and Development*, Report of the National Commission in Education and Training and the National Committee on Education Support Services, Pretoria, South Africa.

Disabled Children's Action Group (DICAG) (1998) *Understanding the Links Between Economic Policies, the Convention on the Rights of the Child, and the Rights of Children with Disabilities: A DICAG User-Friendly Guide on Economic Policies*, DICAG internal publication, Cape Town, South Africa.

Elwan, A. (1999) *Poverty and Disability: A Survey of the Literature*, paper prepared as background for WDR 2000/2001 and as part of the Social Protection Unit's research on the economic consequences of disability, World Bank.

Muthukrishna, N. (2000) *Personal communication*, unpublished paper, Department of Education, University of Natal, Durban, South Africa.

Office of the Executive Deputy President (1998) *Poverty and Inequality in South Africa*, report prepared for the Inter-Ministerial Committee for Poverty and Inequality, South Africa.

Parent Mobilisation Resource Group (1998) *Annual Report*, PMRG, Zimbabwe.

Philpott, S. and Mdunyelwa, M. (2000) *Evaluation of the Amaoti Disabled People's Association*, funded by Save the Children Fund (UK), Disability Action Research Team (DART), Howick, South Africa.

Philpott, S. and McLaren, P. (1999) *Evaluation of the Disabled Children's Action Group (DICAG)*, Disability Action Research Team (DART), Howick, South Africa.

Republic of South Africa (1996) *The Constitution of the Republic of South Africa*, Act 108 of 1996.

Republic of South Africa (1997) White Paper for the Transformation of the Health System in South Africa, *Government Gazette*, 382(17910).

Republic of South Africa (1997) *White Paper on an Integrated National Disability Strategy*, Office of the Deputy President T.M. Mbeki, South Africa.

Robinson, S. and Sadan, M. (1999) *Where Poverty Hits Hardest: Children and the Budget in South Africa*, IDASA, Cape Town.

United Nations (1980) *Convention on the Rights of the Child*, UN, New York, USA.

Woll, L. (1999) The Convention on the Rights of the Child Impact Study, *Child Rights Information Network*, 11November 1999.

14 Failing to make the transition? Theorising the 'transition to adulthood' for young disabled people

Kay Tisdall

In 1978, the vastly influential Warnock Report (1978) on special educational needs in Britain recognised the difficulties that many young disabled people faced when they left school. And it is within the special needs literature that discussions of the 'transitional problem' have tended to remain.

While the disability studies literature in the UK has increasingly applied its 'social model' (and its modifications) to children's education, the social model has far less frequently been applied to policies and theories around the life course (with some exceptions: e.g. Priestley 1999, 2000) and particularly to young people in transition. Similarly, the rich theorisation and research on the transition for young disabled people has been virtually ignored in the literature on young people more generally (again, with some exceptions: e.g., Coles 1995). For example, only recently has the youth field moved from a preoccupation with the transition from school to work – with little recognition of the decades of intense and extensive debates about what should constitute 'adulthood' in the transition literature for disabled people. Those in the youth field who have moved beyond the straight transition from school to work tend to present a transition from dependence to independence. Scant consideration is paid to the debate around 'dependency' in the disability studies literature or the ever-growing literature on children's rights and the sociology of childhood.

What can be learnt by breaking down these divisions and juxtaposing these three literatures – disability studies, youth transition in the life course, and the sociology of childhood? How can these lessons reframe the 'transitional problem' for young disabled people? In this chapter I will look at the recent history of 'youth transition' theorisation, first with attention to its development in the UK for young disabled people. I will then consider the disjunctions and connections with other theorisations of 'transition' and (in)dependence, and conclude with

167

future possibilities for this particular stage in the life course for young disabled people.

Theorising the transitional 'problem'

Sparked by the Warnock Report's revelations on the (un)employment careers of young disabled people, research has extensively charted the difficulties many young disabled people face when they leave school. The list of difficulties typically contains high unemployment, a continuous loop of training, young people's extended dependence on their parents well past their teens, scarcity of suitable and affordable housing, inaccessibility of community and buildings, and inadequate access to health and other services (e.g. *see* May and Hughes 1985; Morris 1999; Thomas *et al.* 1989; Thomson and Ward 1994; Riddell *et al.* 1999). In 1994, Hirst and Baldwin produced *Unequal Opportunities: Growing Up Disabled*, which reported on interviews with 591 disabled young people (age 14–22) and a comparison group of 726 other young people. The findings were unfortunately familiar: 'a sizeable minority of disabled young people, we estimate between 30 and 40 per cent, would find great difficulty in attaining a degree of independence in adult life comparable to that of young people in the general population' (p. 110). Young people who were 'severely and multiply disabled' were identified as particularly disadvantaged.

While this accumulation of research clearly identifies that many young disabled people are facing considerable difficulties, questions were increasingly asked about the indicators of 'successful' transitions – and particularly the place of paid employment. Writers who looked at transition more abstractly wished to de-emphasise paid employment for young disabled people (e.g. CERI 1991). Paid employment was not a possibility, said the argument, considering the high unemployment rates worldwide, especially amongst young people. Furthermore, contribution and status in the community was wrongly connected to a work ethic and to a false idea of independence, went the rationale: voluntary activity was also needed for our society to function, and independence should not be defined as physical independence (for after all, in modern society, were we not all interdependent?). Rather, independence should mean control over our own lives. Paid employment, therefore, was an unsuitable goal of transition, according to some; yet, paid employment was the stated goal of many disabled advocacy groups and government services (CERI 1983, 1991; Pearson 1993). McGinty and Fish (1992) discuss the change of thinking in the international ten-year project by the Centre for Educational Research and Innovation:

At first it was thought that alternatives to paid employment should be sought. However, the demand from individuals for equal opportunities and raised expectations led to an acceptance that the transition goals for young people with disabilities should be the same as those of their age groups (p. 7).

The influence of civil rights' demands, spearheaded by disabled adults, could be seen weaving its way into transitional research. McGinty and Fish (1992) explained the rationale for their book: 'This book is about the rights of all young people with disabilities and learning difficulties to an adult life with the same opportunities as their contemporaries' (p. 3) and demanded that ' . . . it is young people themselves who should decide how they wish to prepare for their futures' (*ibid.*). While recognising this rights approach, McGinty and Fish also buttressed the policy trends of promoting inter-agency collaboration and focusing on improved planning for individual young people: 'Successful transition depends on inter-agency co-operation, collaboration and planning . . . Professionals working in education, social services, health, employment and voluntary organisations can make an effective contribution to transition only by working with other professionals, with parents and with the young people themselves.' (p. i).

Arguments against such individualisation, no doubt influenced by the 'social model' of disability, could be found creeping into the literature to a lesser extent. Corbett and Barton (1992: 27), for example, wrote: 'An individualized model avoids acknowledging the political context in which change has to occur'. But whether the full power of this approach has been incorporated into research is more questionable. UK research on transition for young disabled people often does investigate and discuss the range of environmental and social barriers and opportunities that individual young disabled people face (e.g. Beattie Committee 1999). Yet, research has tended not to take a locality approach, such as undertaken by the Economic and Social Research Council's (ESRC) 16–19 Initiative in the 1980s, which directly linked environmental and social barriers, and opportunities for individual young people, and *then* investigated the very same young people's experiences of transition (but *see also* Riddell *et al.* 1999). The focus has usually remained on young disabled people and their individual and collective experiences of transition, while the context is described more globally.

In summary, the transitional literature for young disabled people shows strong trends and patterns in the UK. It has moved from focusing strongly on the transition from 'school to work' to considering other transitions from school for young disabled people, and taking a more 'holistic' approach. For the most part, it has retained an individualised focus and calls for improved inter-agency co-operation and planning, while to some extent raising the profile of young people's involvement and their rights.

'Youth' and 'childhood'

Structure, individual agency – and something in-between?

The youth literature on transition more generally has a very different history and tradition than that of the transition literature for young disabled people. Rather than taking an individualistic approach, research in the 1980s focused on 'transitions' and then 'trajectories': 'the use of the term trajectory implying that labour market destinations were largely determined by social forces and transitions largely outside the control of individual social actors' (Evans and Furlong 1997: 1–2). Structural factors such as social class, educational attainment and labour market conditions were the focus in such research programmes as the ESRC 16–19 Initiative. Disability was rarely addressed directly as a variable, perhaps because of its statistical smallness.

The structural approach became unpopular in the 1990s, with the influence of 'post-structuralist' and 'post-modernist' thinking. Theorisation around young people's individual agency, and the ways that individuals assess risk and negotiate opportunities, predominated (e.g. Beck 1992; Giddens 1991). Some recent youth academics have seen such theorisation as exaggerating individualisation and now seek to bring the theoretical advantages of both types of theory together into an idea of 'structured individualisation':

... while traditional sources of inequality continue to ensure the reproduction of advantage and disadvantage among the younger generation, various social changes have meant that these social cleavages have become obscure. Moreover, young people increasingly perceive themselves as living in a society characterized by risk and insecurity which they expect to have to negotiate on an individual level. (Furlong and Cartmel 1997: 10).

What is different for young people today, according to Evans and Furlong (1997), is the balance between structure and agency. 'Manufactured uncertainty' has increased, due to the acceleration of information, knowledge and technology, plus the increase and diversity of individual risk situations.

If Hirst and Baldwin's findings were compared to such theorisation (recognising that their survey was situated in the transitional literature for young disabled people), it would appear that for many young disabled people structural factors continue to outweigh individual agency. Rather than becoming more obscure, structural factors have become less obscure to disabled people in general due to the disability rights movement. Having an impairment – and society's (re)action to this – seems to create a 'collective biographical pattern' (Evans and Furlong 1997), particularly for those seen as having 'learning difficulties' or a range of impairments. Rather than being faced by an array of confusing choices, young disabled people can find themselves on a 'conveyor belt' (Tisdall 1996), with a very limited number of options indeed.

The youth literature challenges the transitional literature for young disabled people to consider a collection of 'risks' that it has not always considered. If the youth literature could be criticised for seeing disabled people as statistically, and thus theoretically, insignificant, the transitional literature for young disabled people could be criticised for failing to bring in class, gender and ethnicity satisfactorily. The combination of qualitative interviews with more traditional quantitative methods (e.g. Riddell 1998; Thomson and Ward 1994; Ward et al. 1991) – not only in fieldwork but also in resulting dissemination – allows for more exploration of young disabled people's individual agency than has previously been reported.

Reflections on such studies would suggest a further development of the debate between 'structure' and 'individualisation'. Families, and other key relationships, are key mediating factors in the transitional choices and barriers for young disabled people – and ones often ignored by the youth literature (Allatt 1997). Such family negotiations and patterns may be even more salient for young disabled people in certain situations, when one considers to what extent families limit or enhance young disabled people's self-efficacy, desire and practice to take charge of their lives and life course decisions (e.g. see Cavet 1998; Hirst and Baldwin 1994).

Dependence and independence

The youth literature has shifted its focus from concentrating almost exclusively on work, to recognising a range of transitions that interact for young people. Jones, a leading youth academic, offers the taxonomy outlined in Table 14.1.

The table is not only of theoretical interest, but also of practical importance. For example, it was used to underpin the Joseph Rowntree Fund's 1997 call for research and practice initiatives on youth. Jones (1997) seeks to head off at least two potential criticisms of her use of 'dependence':

As a working definition let us think of childhood as a period of economic dependence (on parents or other carers) and adulthood as the achievement of

Table 14.1. *Extended transition to adulthood (Jones 1997)*

Childhood	Youth	Adulthood
Dependence < 16 years	Semi-dependence 16–18; 18–21; 21–25 years	Independence > 25 years
School	College or training scheme	Labour market
Parental home	Intermediate household Transitional housing	Independent home
Child in family	Various statuses inc. single parenthood	Partner-Parent
Citizenship through parents	Semi-citizenship	Adult citizenship

economic independence, though we all know that these are simplifications. There are children who have an important social and economic role in their families as earners or carers, and independence is not 'automatically' achieved with adulthood. (1997: 4)

If Jones' first row was supposed to refer solely to *financial* in(dependence), then her table does seem to be a reasonable simplification in the UK. But Jones states that the move from 'the period of childlike dependence on parents to adult independence (and subsequent responsibility for the next generation)' is the main dynamic in youth (1997: 6) – and thus appears to place dependence–independence as the fundamental transition, of more than descriptive value.

The disability literature suggest that Jones should further elaborate and explore her definitions of in(dependence). Writers such as Oliver (1990) have argued for some time for the recognition of people's mutual interdependence. Research on caring demonstrates how caring and (in)dependence exist on a continuum, with disabled people taking on roles both of caring and being cared for (Morris 1993; Walmsley 1993). The focus on 'physical' (in)dependence has also been challenged, with advocates for independent living arguing that independence is about making one's own choices and decisions, and not whether the person can enact them him/herself (e.g. Morris 1993). Whether Jones' use of (in)dependence is theoretically useful can thus be disputed: perhaps concepts such as control, self-efficacy and command over resources and decision-making would be more helpful.

The question of young people's power (or lack thereof) is brought to the fore by recent theorisations of 'childhood' within sociology and related fields. A five-year international research programme (1987–92) resulted in several defining statements about children that resounded around the academic field under the term the 'new sociology of child-hood' (Qvortrup 1994):

- children are marginalised, both in terms of place and nature
- marginalisation is often coupled with children's need for protection
- while marginalisation may be protective it can also, or alternatively, be paternalistic
- children are the quintessential minority group, which is defined by its subordinate relationship to a dominant group (adults)
- children are in practice being individualised and institutionalised while ideologically they remain within the family (familialisation)
- while hidden from the public gaze by familialisation, children are actors and are an integrated structural form of society (e.g. children labour in school)
- childhood is a permanent category in society, although for individuals it may be a transient phase.

The defining features of (Western) childhood bear a noticeable similarity to certain patterns for disabled people. Disabled people of all ages have (at least in the past) been marginalised, and physical and social space continues to be inaccessible to many. Disabled people have been institutionalised and individualised within the educational system, protectively or paternalistically placed in segregated or 'integrated' schools. Disabled people have in the past been subordinated to the 'norms' and assumptions of 'non-disabled' people. Yet disabled people have always been an integral structural part of society, as actors and contributors. Similarities also extend across criticisms of the past disability and 'childhood' literature. In their search to establish theoretical features, both literatures have been accused of presuming commonalty across all disabled people and all children, ignoring the diversity caused by gender, ethnicity, class etc. Indeed, Prout and James (1990: 4) argue that such variables cannot be entirely separated from the study of childhood.

On the theoretical side, certain writers see 'childhood' irretrievably connected with the idea of 'dependence' on adulthood: ' . . . without the dependency of children on adults, the social construct of childhood cannot exist. However, this does not eliminate the possibility of some modification in the boundaries of childhood, the 'rights' and 'obligations' of children, the rewards for children's investment in determining their own destiny etc" (Shamgar-Handelman 1994: 265). Increased attention has been given to disabled children's relationships with their peers – and not just with adults (e.g. Watson *et al.* 1999; Closs *et al.* 1999). There are those who promote children's rights who feel that the boundaries of childhood should indeed be moved, to recognise children's rights not only to provision and protection but also to participation (e.g. Franklin 1995; Willow 1997).

Such advocates of children's rights would be highly critical of Jones' presumption that children are not already citizens. Writing in a Council of Europe publication (1996), Knutsson states three reasons why children should be recognised as citizens: (1) a moral argument, that children have the right to a basic standard of living; (2) an 'end result' argument, that children contribute significantly to society, in its 'biological, organisational and cultural reproduction'; and (3) the 'utilitarian' argument that childhood is an integral part of society and its division of labour (interestingly, arguments quite similar to those made by Oliver 1990 and 1996, within the disability studies literature). Under the European Union's Maastricht Treaty, for example, children are now officially included within the definition of 'citizens'.

The citizenship of children is more than an abstract point, as citizenship is a powerful concept in policy and practice. Thus the idea that children can be 'indirect citizens' is potentially important, as shown by Jones and also by Lister: 'Although they are members of the community, children are not full citizens in the sense of political and legal rights which pertain to citizenship; the social rights of citizenship come to them indirectly through the adults responsible for their care' (1990a: 62). Whether one believes that the foundations of citizenship are political rights (e.g. Frazer and Emler 1997) or economic rights (e.g. Lister 1990b), or whether one perceives citizenship as a relationship between an individual and the state (e.g. Prior *et al.* 1995) or an individual living with others (Donati 1995), the concept of 'indirect' citizenship mediated through other people is arguably foreign and antithetical to theorisations of citizenship. Such a position, 'dependent' on adults, belies the very advantages that 'rights' and 'citizenship' can have in practice for children. It hides children in the 'black box' of family life and fails to recognise them as individuals, thus replicating the very criticisms Lister (1990b, 1997) herself makes against the traditional male-dominated presumptions of citizenship. The United Nations (UN) Convention on the Rights of the Child, ratified by the UK Government in 1991, established that children are people in their own right. To announce that children are 'indirect' citizens or 'to be' citizens (Lister 1997) can be seen as a retrograde step indeed.

Concluding thoughts: a learning process

Theoretically, the transitional literatures on young disabled people, youth and the 'sociology of childhood' have grown and developed with a notable lack of cross-fertilisation. Yet they have much to learn from each other. For example, the transitional literature on young disabled people benefits from considering 'risks' and 'biographies' that allow for a combination of structure and individual agency. The youth literature on transition has now moved beyond merely considering the 'school to work' transition but does appear to retain simplistic concepts of dependence-independence, questioned by both the disability studies and 'childhood' literature. The 'childhood' literature would suggest attention be paid to adult surveillance and the structuring of young people's lives. While the youth literature is criticised for having in the past focused on too narrow an age range in its considerations of transition (Bynner *et al.* 1997), the transition literature for young disabled people has long considered young people's transitions into their twenties. As Coles (1995) recognises, the youth and childhood literatures can benefit from considering those who 'test' the general assumptions – who illuminate or challenge theoretical concepts and patterns.

Practically, cross-fertilisation could lead to a substantial re-thinking of transitional policy for young disabled people. The present approach for young disabled people relies on individual assessment and incessant calls for improved inter-agency collaboration; without a structural perspective. This (expensive) assessment and collaboration lacks purpose when decisions are being made between, at best, a handful of options. Policy reviews in further education demonstrate steps towards a more structural approach (e.g. Beattie Committee 1999), although continuing to contain recommendations on inter-agency collaboration etc.

Educational legislation and policy is based on the 'indirect citizenship' of children, with parents rather than children having rights (until the child is aged 16). The youth literature illuminates this confusion, as young people gain rights at different ages in different areas of their lives (e.g. able to get married at age 16 but not able to vote until age 18); the 'childhood' literature would point out the illogicality of using age to determine such changes in the first place. The childhood literature would also highlight children's lack of power, and the failure to see them as part of, yet separate from, their families. It would suggest both small and large changes in practice: for example, ensuring that children and parents are both, but separately, consulted and reported to in assessments.

Both theoretically and practically, young disabled people risk being marginalised for at least three reasons: because they are disabled, because they are young and because they are in 'transition'. Those who seek to influence through writing and thinking need to consider all three risks, whether they are writing in the disability studies, youth or child-hood literature. Those who are involved in policy and practice also need to consider them: for example, so that disability advocacy groups do not (intentionally or unintentionally) exclude young people from participation and support; so that youth work and youth policies do not promote unhelpful concepts of (in)dependence and do consider the inter-connections between society, families and individual agency; and so that children's rights advocates and children's policy makers address the need to connect with those for youth and for adults.

REFERENCES

Allatt, P. (1997) 'Conceptualising youth: transitions, risks and the public and the private', in Bynner, J., Chisholm, L., Furlong, A. (eds.) *Youth, Citizenship and Social Change in a European Context*, Avebury, Aldershot.

Beattie Committee (1999) *Implementing Inclusiveness, Realising Potential*, The Scottish Executive, Edinburgh.

Beck, U. (1992) *The Risk Society: Towards a New Modernity*, Sage, London.

Bynner, J., Chisholm, L. and Furlong, A. (1997) 'A new agenda for youth research', in Bynner, J., Chisholm, L., Furlong, A. (eds.) *Youth, Citizenship and Social Change in a European Context*, Avebury, Aldershot.

Cavet, J. (1998) 'Leisure and friendship', in Robinson, C. and Stalker, K. (eds.) *Growing Up with Disability*, Jessica Kingsley Publishers, London.

Centre for Educational Research and Innovation (CERI) (1983) *The Education of the Handicapped Adolescent: The Transition from School to Working Life*, Organisation for Economic Co-operation and Development, Paris, France.

Centre for Educational Research and Innovation (CERI) (1991) *Disabled Youth: From School to Work*, Organisation for Economic Co-operation and Development, Paris, France.

Closs, A., Stead, J., Arshad, R. and Norris, C. (1999) *School Peer Relationship of Children 'At the Edge' of Mainstream Education*, Paper at BERA Conference, University of Edinburgh.

Coles, B. (1995) *Youth and Social Policy: Youth Citizenship and Young Careers*, UCL Press, London.

Corbett, J. and Barton, L. (1992) *A Struggle for Choice: Students with Special Needs in Transition to Adulthood*, Routledge, London.

Donati, P. (1995) 'Identity and solidarity in the complex of citizenship: the relational approach', *International Sociology*, 10(3): 299–314.

Evans, K. and Furlong, A. (1997) 'Metaphors of youth transitions: niches, pathways, trajectories or navigations', in Bynner, J., Chisholm, L., Furlong, A. (eds.) *Youth, Citizenship and Social Change in a European Context*, Avebury, Aldershot.

Franklin, B. (1995) 'Children's rights: an overview' in Franklin, B. (ed.) *The Handbook of Children's Rights. Comparative Policy and Practice*, Routledge, London.

Frazer, E. and Emler, N. (1997) 'Participation and citizenship: a new agenda for youth politics research?' in Bynner, J., Chisholm, L., Furlong, A. (eds.) *Youth, Citizenship and Social Change in a European Context*, Avebury, Aldershot.

Furlong, A. and Cartmel, F. (1997) *Young People and Social Change*, Open University Press, Milton Keynes.

Giddens, A. (1991) *Modernity and Self Identity: Self and Society in the Late Modern Age*, Polity Press, Oxford.

Hirst, M. and Baldwin, S. (1994) *Unequal Opportunities: Growing Up Disabled*, HMSO, London.

Jones, G. (1997) 'Barriers to adulthood: dependency and resistance in youth' Paper given at *Families and the State: Conflicts and Contradictions*, Third Annual Colloquium, 23–24 May 1997, International Social Sciences Institute, University of Edinburgh.

Knutsson, K.E. (1996) 'A new vision of childhood' in Jeleff, S. (ed.) *The Child as Citizen*, Council of Europe Publishing, Belgium.

Lister, R. (1990a) *The Exclusive Society: Citizenship and the Poor*, CPAG, London.

Lister, R. (1990b) 'Women, economic dependency and citizenship', *Journal of Social Policy* 19(4): 445–67.

Lister, R. (1997) *Citizenship: Feminist Perspectives*, Macmillan Press, London.

May, D. and Hughes, D. (1985) 'The prospects on leaving school for the mildly mentally handicapped', *British Journal of Special Education*, 12(3), Research Supplement: 151–8.

McGinty, J. and Fish, J. (1992) *Learning Support for Young People in Transition: Leaving School for Further Education and Work*, Open University Press, Milton Keynes.

Morris, J. (1993) *Independent Lives: Community Care and Disabled People*, Macmillan, London.

Morris, J. (1999) *Transition to Adulthood For Young People with 'Complex Health and Support Needs*, JRF Finding 919, http://www.jrf.org.uk (13.1.00)

Oliver, M. (1990) *The Politics of Disablement*, Macmillan Education, London.

Oliver, M. (1996) *Understanding Disability: From Theory to Practice*, Macmillan, Basingstoke.

Pearson, S. (1993) *Baking Cakes at 60: Young Disabled People in Transition*, Access Ability Lothian, Edinburgh.

Priestley, M. (1999) *Disability Politics and Community Care*, Jessica Kingsley, London.

Priestley, M. (2000) 'Adults only: disability, social policy and the life course', *Journal of Social Policy*, 29(3): 421–39.

Prior, D., Stewart, J. and Walsh, K. (1995) *Citizenship: Rights, Community and Participation*, Pitman Publishing, London.

Prout, A. and James, A. (1990) 'A new paradigm for the sociology of childhood? provenance, promise and problems', in A. James and A. Prout (eds.) *Constructing and Reconstructing Childhood: Contemporary Issues in the Sociological Study of Childhood*, The Falmer Press, London.

Qvortrup, J. (1994) 'Childhood matters: an introduction', in Qvortrup, J., Bardy, M., Sgritta, G., Wintersberger, H. (eds.) *Childhood Matters. Social Theory, Practice and Politics*, European Centre, Vienna, Austria.

Riddell, S. (1998) 'Transitions to adulthood for young disabled people', in

Robinson, C. and Stalker, K. (eds.) *Growing Up With Disability*, Jessica Kingsley, London.

Riddell, S., Wilson, A. and Baron, S. (1999) 'Capture customers: people with learning difficulties in the social market', *British Educational Research Journal* 25(4): 445–61.

Shamgar-Handelman, L. (1994) 'To whom does childhood belong?' in Qvortrup, J., Bardy, M., Sgritta, G., Wintersberger, H. (eds.) *Childhood Matters. Social Theory, Practice and Politics*, European Centre, Vienna, Austria.

Thomas, A.P., Bax, M.C.O. and Smyth, D.P.L. (1989) *The Health and Social Needs of Young Adults with Physical Disabilities*, MacKeith Press, London.

Thomson, G.O.B. and Ward, K. (1994) *Patterns and Pathways: Individuals With Disabilities in Transition to Adulthood*, Edinburgh: Department of Education, University of Edinburgh.

Tisdall, E.K.M. (1996) 'Are young disabled people being sufficiently involved in their post-school planning?', *European Journal of Special Educational Needs* 11(1): 17–31.

Walmsley, J. (1993) 'Contradictions in caring: reciprocity and interdependence', *Disability, Handicap and Society*, 8: 129–41.

Ward, K., Riddell, S., Dyer, M. and Thomson, G. (1991) *The Transition to Adulthood of Young People with Recorded Special Educational Needs*, Final Report to the Scottish Office Education Department, The Departments of Education of the University of Edinburgh and Stirling.

Warnock Report – Report of the Committee of Enquiry into the Education of Handicapped Children and Young People (1978) *Special Educational Needs*, Cmnd. 7212, HMSO, London.

Watson, N., Shakespeare, T., Cunningham-Burley, S., Barnes, C., Corker, M., Davis, J. and Priestley, M. (1999) *Life as a Disabled Child: A Qualitative Study of Young People's Experiences and Perspectives*, ESRC Research Report, University of Edinburgh.

Willow, C. (1997) *Hear! Hear! Promoting Children and Young People's Democratic Participation in Local Government*, Local Government Information Unit, London.

15   Breaking my head in the prime of my life: acquired disability in young adulthood

Allison Rowlands

Peter is a young single man. He owns his own home, which he shares with his parents, living in a detached flat in the backyard. He sustained a traumatic brain injury in a motor vehicle accident when he was 19, which has resulted in a range of cognitive impairments that severely compromise his capacity to relate independently in the social world, as well as manage his own care. Prior to his injury, Peter was an apprentice fitter and turner. He now receives a disability support pension and purchased his home from his insurance settlement. A financial adviser manages his funds. He is unable to drive a car, so he relies on his mother to drive him or uses taxis, as public transport is not available in the semi-rural area where he lives. He describes himself as lonely; his dream is to find 'that special person'.

I think I had a dream of a you beaut champion friend . . . You know someone that could be with me all the time . . . and I've got that once a week so I can't ask anything more.

Peter has not made friends through the community access service, which provides him some support, although for many others the service is their major source of friends. He rarely attends the actual premises. From Peter's perspective, and despite having brain injury in common, he finds little to share with the other consumers. Because of his settlement, Peter can afford to pay for support workers, or respite breaks away from home. However, these relationships do not replace genuine friendships as far as he is concerned:

. . . yeah I'm buying a friend . . . why should I have to . . . if I've got to pay for it then don't worry about it . . . I haven't got people that will be a friend to me you know they're only coming out here because they're getting paid . . . I need friends . . . if I want that type of friend I can go and buy friends . . .

Introduction

In this chapter I discuss the experience of severe traumatic brain injury acquired in young adulthood. The personal and social implications of these sudden changes are considered from the young adult's perspective. At this stage of the life course, young adults are usually focusing on their careers, friendships, an intimate relationship with a long term partner, and perhaps creating a family. Traumatic brain injury interrupts personal development and life plans, interfering with career goals, relationships and identity. Recently achieved separation from parents, and the establishment of independence, is often reversed as the young adult comes to depend on care and supervision from family for an indefinite period after discharge from hospital.

While strategies can be learned and equipment used to accommodate a range of physical, sensory and cognitive impairments, genuine community participation, and the enjoyment of a web of caring, reciprocal relationships, often elude young people struggling with the effects of brain injury. Yet Peter has as much claim as any other citizen to be included and valued. How he presents to the world around him, with slurred speech, arm tremor, an unusual gait, memory and concentration problems, an irascible temperament and a disfigured face, ought not be a barrier to his full participation in community life. Stunning advances in neurosurgical care and patient, intensive rehabilitation, delivered Peter to his parents, but these interventions were not able to address quality of life issues in his terms – how he was to make friends again without buying them. As Peter's father said: 'Quality of life's another thing. Keeping the body alive but for what? It puts a big load on the family and community'.

Peter was one of the participants in a study conducted between 1996 and 1999 in the Hunter Valley in regional Australia. This chapter draws on the data from that study. The study examined the social networks and friendships of young adults with traumatic brain injury. The finding that prevailed above all others was the loneliness experienced by young men and women as a result of this injury. Friendships that predated the accident were not able to sustain the radical changes wrought by the combination of impairments sustained. New friendships were difficult to form and maintain and most participants socialised with fellow peers from the local community access service. These friendships were valued, as they shared common difficulties and understanding, yet they were also somehow insufficient. A worker commented:

I mean it's fine, they're friends and that's great, but you could just suddenly see it dawn on the person and then he said, I really don't have anyone in my life that I haven't met through the service, or that I knew before my injury, or that I've met myself.

The effects of traumatic brain injury

Traumatic brain injury from a blow to the head can produce diminished or altered states of consciousness, and often results in impaired cognitive abilities and/or physical functioning (Ponsford, Sloan and Snow 1995). Each year 25,000 people in Australia sustain a traumatic brain injury, mostly as a result of road accidents. Of these 25,000 people, 5,000 will sustain a severe brain injury, usually resulting in some form of permanent impairment (Cuff 1987). For some, the level of disability leads to permanent institutional care. Traumatic brain injury is the greatest cause of impairment for people under 40 years of age in Australia. Over 70 per cent of those who experience a brain injury are aged between 16 and twenty-five years, with males at three times greater risk than females. The 'modern era' of brain injury rehabilitation, commencing approximately twenty years ago (Rosenthal 1996: 88) has meant that increasingly people are surviving brain injuries due to improvements in emergency medical services and acute care.

There are significant personal and social costs accruing from traumatic brain injury: in individual self-respect and dignity, autonomy, and participation in the community (Elsass 1991). The majority of people with a severe injury are not able to return to work (Ponsford *et al.* 1995) and many remain financially and socially dependent (Tate, Lulham, Broe, Strettles and Pfaff 1989). 'Many persons with brain injuries are friendless, dependent on their families, uninvolved in productive community activities and lack a sense of social identity' (Kosciulek 1997: 821).

Cognitive and behavioural impairments most compromise quality of life (Olver 1995). Central to the difficulties experienced by people with traumatic brain injury in resuming interpersonal relationships is personality change, which occurs in all but a minority of cases and increases over time (Bond 1984). Whereas physical recovery can be good, the changes to personality are not as amenable to treatment and are considered to be permanent (Thomsen 1984).

With time elapsing since injury social networks decrease and density increases, leading to the complaint of loneliness as the greatest subjective burden (Kozloff 1987; Rowlands 1995; Willer, Allen, Durnan and Ferry 1990). New relationships are often transient, lacking many of the features of durable, supportive relationships. Opportunities to develop new relationships are limited. Social skills, already compromised by the injury, are further reduced and self-esteem suffers, thus compounding the sense of isolation, as well as depression. The interaction of unemployment, motor/sensory impairment and behaviour change all contribute to the poverty of social relationships. The effects of traumatic brain injury also influence intimate relationships and sexuality, with losses experienced in the area of intimate relationships and sexual dysfunction, including breakdown of relationships/marriages (Lezak 1978; Ponsford *et al.* 1995; Prigitano 1988; Zeigler 1989).

Most people with traumatic brain injury live with their families. Caring for a family member with traumatic brain injury is stressful, is perceived as an increasing burden with time, affects all relationships in the family, and causes most disruption and distress through the cognitive and behavioural impairments (Lezak 1988; Perlesz, Furlong and McLachlan 1992; Resnick 1993; Serio, Kreutzer and Witol 1997).

The experiences of young adults in the Hunter

The young adults interviewed in the Hunter study all described the loss of friends after their accident. For most, their networks were limited to socialising only with others with brain injury. Otherwise, they relied on relatives or service providers for social interaction. It was a telling indication of the paucity of their networks that the people they identified in whom they could confide were parents, health/support workers, and shop assistants. These relationships were not described as reciprocal. Social outings were often with parents and parents' friends. Young adults did not often have a group of friends of their own age, relying instead on the parental friendship network for a social life. This contradicts the usual desires of young adults at this point in their life course.

A range of interventions have been undertaken to facilitate friendship making for disabled people, including matching a volunteer to befriend the person; harnessing local community leaders to assist in making connections in the neighbourhood; support workers assisting in identifying interests and locating local groups to join; and constructing networks or circles of friends around the person, using both people known to him/her and volunteers. The difficulty with many of these approaches is the artifice involved and the threat to spontaneity and reciprocity from something that is contrived. The young adults in the study were very sensitive to the issue of people being paid to befriend them – is it friendship if you are paid? Volunteers were unclear and uncomfortable about whether they were recruited to be 'friends', how this might come about, and whether the young person wanted their friendship. Some volunteers regarded their being there in an unpaid capacity as a demonstration of caring.

Workers interviewed in the Hunter study considered that the ultimate success of friendship interventions was the expansion of social networks beyond the intervention itself, leading to the development of natural networks beyond the worker's or volunteer's involvement. Increasing confidence and skills for the young adults with brain injury were seen as essential for this process. Re-establishing a social network presents a persistent challenge to workers seeking genuine community integration of people with traumatic brain injury. How to engage the community in the life of this person and how to generate a sustainable natural support network for people with 'special needs', are persistent questions.

Workers discussed the dilemma of intervening in the friendship-making process:

. . . one person was really into power lifting so we talked about how do you look for volunteers? Maybe you need to advertise at gyms for people who are interested in establishing a friendship with somebody who likes power lifting, who wouldn't mind having a buddy but also wants to go out and do stuff and this person is a bit this way inclined . . . and it sounds like a bloody ad in the personal papers.

The process of intervening in the young person's networks was cause for reflection for the workers on how they made their own friends.

. . . community integration – that idea of connecting people who don't know each other . . . I look at how I meet other people . . . I meet people through friends or I meet people through social situations . . . you know, it's networks.

Volunteers were not confident that the young adult with brain injury would reciprocate their offer of friendship:

I think I'd be more inclined to call him a friend than him call me a friend . . . not 'cause he wouldn't want to be, I think he just might be the type of person that would have to get to know you first . . . you know, I might be a better friend than I think I am! (sounds surprised) . . . so I don't know.

Parents were desperate to find friends for their adult children. One mother was very tentative about the strength of some of her daughter's friendships and how long lasting they might be. She stated: 'Deep down you don't really know . . . I don't really know whether they feel sorry for her'. She described the lives of young people with traumatic brain injury in very negative terms, while at the same time maintaining that she was a positive person. This was an example of an extreme ambivalence that I noted in these parents. They were able to articulate the huge losses sustained by the young person and family, while demonstrating resilience in continuing to hope for better outcomes and supporting their adult children's and their families' futures. This mother described the loss of her daughter who was 19 when she was injured:

I went through the mourning of Hope, that first year was such a hard year and I knew that I had really lost my daughter, and so I went through that mourning, and she had no recollection of that year at all . . . the picture was painted very very dimly for Hope . . . that's why we grieved that first year, and then we were kind of, mending after that . . . The one thing that I just prayed and prayed and prayed for was for her to get her speech back . . . not to have speech is just a horrible horrible thing you know . . . and when I imagined it, it was just horrific.

Combined with parents' desperation and sadness was gratitude for any interest at all that was shown in their adult child by others, again an atypical response in a parent whose child has become a young adult. There was a sense of amazement in some of their responses, for example Hope's mother describing some people coming to her daughter's Circle of Friends for two years:

We've got some people that've come along the whole time, and have been very supportive and have been doing it for two years . . . which is fabulous . . . Really really really good Really good (with emphasis, quietly). And they're still coming . . .

The friendships of these young adults appeared to need structure, or a form of 'scaffolding' (Sutherland 1996), to maintain them. Some friends stated that when people are very busy, it is hard to maintain contact, and the Circle of Friends provided a structure and regular time to spend with the person. In their view, the Circle did not ask a lot of their time. Regular attendance required three hours per month, which was time that some had been unable to find previously, despite intending to maintain contact with him or her. This structure assisted in maintaining contact so that these members could regularly attend Circle meetings despite their busy lives. However, scheduling monthly meetings in diaries is not a common way for young people to maintain their friendships, and it is likely that the young adult with brain injury is the only friend in these people's networks for whom contact was as regimented as this. It is interesting to speculate what cumulative impact such systematisation might eventually have on relationships that are usually understood to have a degree of spontaneity. It also means that these special friendships were treated differently, compared with other friendships, highlighting what was different, rather than what was similar. This would not be a desired outcome from the perspective of minimising difference and promoting acceptance (Bogdan and Taylor 1987, 1989).

In some ways we're probably much the same, we tend to keep to the same group of people . . . but his is always contrived . . . organised for him. (friend of Chris)

Some of the friends interviewed argued that it is usual to develop friendships with others who are similar, posing a contrast with their relationship with the person who was injured. They were explicit about the differences between themselves and him or her, and felt that it was the responsibility of school contemporaries to maintain their friendships, for example even to the extent of bringing total strangers to a picnic for Hope.

I thought if we can organise something . . . have a picnic or something, can you come along, and if you know any of your friends bring them, you know I don't think they care even if they don't know Hope. I think it's having a few people there is what counts and that's what helps.

The converse of this scaffolding of friendships is that the demands placed on the friendship network could become excessive. Could friendship interventions ask too much of people? Both family members and workers expressed this concern but the friends who were involved did not express it themselves. Peter demonstrated sensitivity to his friend, who already spent time with him regularly, and was adamant that he would not ask any more of him, despite the urgings of workers. The potential within the community to reach out to, include and support its members was not exhausted in the experience of this particular study, although it remains a consideration in any community building exercise. As I have argued, commitment to the ideals of community, notions of altruism and volunteerism remain buoyant despite the rapid social change in recent decades (Ife 1995, 1997b).

Isn't he doing enough? You know I'm lucky that I've got him . . . so we're like that . . . (knotted fingers) (Peter)

Supporting friendships also can reduce the load on family and carers. Friends and workers noticed this, for example this worker:

Now is the time that those guys can really offer something, that their friendship can really offer something, because it's friends that really, you know, help you through those times? I guess . . . actually relieves the burden on Mary. It actually provides some support from somewhere else, she's not plugging along on her own. That she gets that, that Maureen can get that from somewhere else.

Mary herself commented obliquely on the demands on parents:

I was thinking oh gee you know just another thing, with these other groups what do we need that for, but then when you get down there and see the other people it makes you appreciate the difficulties and I see all these other young mothers and fathers with their children and think you poor thing you know, what's ahead of you. (Mary)

Making friends, however, takes time. Possibly due to their lived experience of the loss of friends after traumatic brain injury, the young people and their family members were the most emphatic about the need to intervene as soon as possible in the recovery period, before friendship networks become depleted. It was also acknowledged by all the participants that friends naturally come and go (Antonucci 1985).

Your friends drift away. It's part of life – part of life that friends come and go. You don't always see them often – they've got other interests and so on. May go separate ways and may still remain friends.

The friends of these young adults were explicit about what they gained from their friendship: satisfaction, expanded horizons, feedback, a warming experience, valuing being part of the person's life, feeling flattered to be wanted and involved, and a social outlet.

Seeing them progress in their life. It helps me too sort of – when I'm not working – gets me out; a bit of a social life. Lots of my interests are the same as theirs – both David and Chris. Like photography.

Locating friendship building interventions within a theoretical discourse

The social model of disability, through its structural analysis of the broader social context (Abberley 1997; Finkelstein 1993; Oliver 1996) provides explanations for the difficulties encountered by workers adopting any of these strategies. A conceptual framework developed by Ife (1997a), discussed below, provides a template for understanding the limits of such interventions, explaining why sustainable improvements in the social inclusion of people with traumatic brain injury are unlikely without more fundamental social change.

Critical or empowerment approaches to intervention, aiming to foster community integration through building friendships, sit uneasily within a rehabilitation model. The reason for this is the tension between two different paradigms, as critical postmodernism confronts positivism. The dominance of the medical model influences many health professionals working with people with traumatic brain injury, especially with regard to cognitive impairment (Condeluci 1992). Such a consideration poses additional dilemmas regarding this person's self determination and judgements about his/her capacity to behave autonomously and take charge of his/her life, undoubtedly making mistakes in the process. When people with brain injury are consulted about preferred approaches to treatment and service delivery, their views are in accord with the perspective articulated by a social model of disability (Hill 1999). The balance between caring for and empowering people, and controlling them is determined by ideological and theoretical positions (Dominelli 1998).

Ife's framework, describing the competing discourses in human services, is a valuable tool in considering rehabilitation and disability

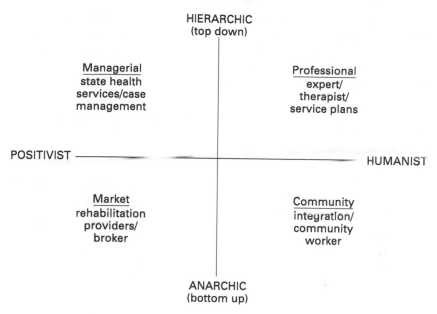

Figure 15.1 Competing discourses of human services

service provision. These discourses 'construct the boundaries of practice
. . . and define and legitimise relationships of power between the various
actors' (Ife 1997a: 40). The framework is located in the managerial and
economic rationalism of the 1990s, and demonstrates the tensions in the
environment in which practitioners operate and in which consumers
obtain services.

The framework represents two dimensions: power (hierarchic/anar-
chic; top-down/bottom-up) and knowledge (positivist [neutral, value
free]/humanist, including interpretivist). By constructing vectors of the
power and knowledge dimensions, Ife locates four major discourses:
managerial, market, professional and community. Applying this framework to rehabilitation and disability service provision yields the descriptions of context and worker role suggested in Figure 15.1. Community
integration interventions, built on a critical analysis, can be located in
the community quadrant of this framework. Community development
and empowerment are theories of practice that inform intervention and
guide the worker. Community building, consumer participation, valuing
of process and consumer wisdom, are all facets of this approach.
Practice located in the community discourse is therefore consistent with
a critical postmodern approach.

The conclusion that can be drawn from Ife's analysis, as applied here to rehabilitation and disability services used by young adults with traumatic brain injury, is that while the trend in these services is towards increasing managerialism and brokering/privatisation, the most effective interventions to engender social inclusion, the prime need of these young adults, come from the community discourse. It is from this theoretical base that interventions capable of addressing the structural problems at issue will come. Effective social inclusion for people with brain injury requires the community discourse to be dominant.

A dominant community discourse will reduce oppression, and empower citizens through full inclusion in society. It will promote community building, sharing of skills and resources, and facilitate members taking action to redress inequity. The community discourse can inform the other discourses through the sharing of skills and the equalising power differentials between clinicians and clients, influencing management approaches and organisational structures.

Conclusion

Young adults with traumatic brain injury seek inclusion in their community, a range of friendships with others, and an intimate relationship with a long-term partner. They seek to be autonomous individuals, directing their lives, participating in and contributing to the community. With the support of a group of concerned and committed acquaintances and friends, these dreams can be realised. Through this support, young people can be assisted to reach their desired objectives, learn skills and grow in confidence and self-esteem. Family and members of their network also benefit directly through their inclusion in society. As I have demonstrated, members of the community are concerned and motivated to involve themselves in the lives of disabled people. The community as a whole benefits, as previously disenfranchised members participate and share their skills. From a broader perspective, the building process strengthens the community, and the genuine inclusion of disabled members begins to break down the barriers that previously obstructed their full participation. Social justice is enhanced and oppression begins to be dismantled as the human rights of disabled community members are accorded full attention. For young adults with traumatic brain injury to be included in their community, a community-based discourse of empowerment is required as the over-arching framework for the delivery and shared management of services. Such services need to be premised on the values and principles of a critical theory approach. Under these conditions, the human rights of all citizens, regardless of individual differences, are assured.

It could be argued that I have not achieved what I set out to do in this chapter. I wanted to communicate the experiences of living with brain injury from the young persons' perspective. Despite this aim, much of the content reflects the voices of others in their lives: parents, workers, friends. Almost in contradiction of the issue being explored, I have put distance between myself, and my readers, and the young people concerned, yet it is exactly this social distance that they are finding hard to breach. Nevertheless, through this imperfect representation I have attempted to give voice to their concerns. I have learned, through the writing of this chapter, how truly difficult it is to present faithfully the voices of young disabled people without obscuring them in the more powerful professional discourses that continue to define the reality of their everyday lives.

REFERENCES

Abberley, P. (1997) 'The concept of oppression and the development of a social theory of disability', in L. Barton and M. Oliver (eds.) *Disability Studies: Past, Present and Future*, The Disability Press, Leeds.

Antonucci, T. (1985) 'Social support: theoretical advances, recent findings and pressing issues', in I. Sarason and B. Sarason (eds.) *Social Support: Theory, Research and Applications*, Martinus Nijhoff Publishers, Dordrecht, The Netherlands.

Bogdan, R. and Taylor, S. (1987) 'Towards a sociology of acceptance: the other side of the study of deviance', *Social Policy*, Fall 1987: 34–9.

Bogdan, R. and Taylor, S. (1989) 'Relationships with severely disabled people: the social construction of humanness', *Social Problems* 36(2): 135–48.

Bond, M. (1984) 'The psychiatry of closed head injury', in N. Brooks (ed.) *Closed Head Injury: Psychological, Social and Family Consequences*, Oxford University Press.

Condeluci, A. (1992) 'Brain injury rehabilitation: the need to bridge paradigms', *Brain Injury*, 6(6): 543–51.

Cuff, C. (1987) *Brain Injury Program for New South Wales: GIO's Commitment under Transcover*, Cuff Consultants Pty. Ltd., Sydney, Australia.

Dominelli, L. (1998) 'Anti-oppressive practice in context', in R. Adams, L. Dominelli and M. Payne (eds.) *Social Work: Themes, Issues and Critical Debates*, Macmillan, Basingstoke.

Elsass, L. (1991) *Behaviour Following Traumatic Head Injury: A Prospective Study*, unpublished doctoral dissertation in psychology, La Trobe University, Melbourne, Australia.

Finkelstein, V. (1993) 'Disability: a social challenge or an administrative responsibility?', in J. Swain, V. Finkelstein, S. French and M. Oliver (eds.) *Disabling Barriers: Enabling Environments*, Sage, London.

Hill, H. (1999) 'Traumatic brain injury: the view from the inside', *Brain Injury*, 13(11): 839–44.

Ife, J. (1995) *Community Development: Creating Community Alternatives – Vision, Analysis and Practice*. Longman, South Melbourne, Australia.

Ife, J. (1997a) *Rethinking Social Work: Towards Critical Practice*, Longman, South Melbourne, Australia.

Ife, J. (1997b) *Realising the Purpose of Social Work for Stakeholders: Maintaining the Vision and Making a Difference in a World of Change*, paper presented to the 25th AASW National Conference, Canberra, Australia.

Kosciulek, J. (1997) 'Relationship of family schema to family adaptation to brain injury', *Brain Injury* 11(11): 821–30.

Kozloff, R. (1987) 'Networks of social support and the outcome from severe head injury', *Journal of Head Trauma Rehabilitation*, 2(3): 14–23.

Lezak, M. (1978) 'Living with the characterologically altered brain injured patient', *Journal of Clinical Psychiatry*, 39(7): 592–98.

Lezak, M. (1988) 'Brain damage is a family affair', *Journal of Clinical and Experimental Neuropsychology*, 10(1): 111–23.

Oliver, M. (1996). *Understanding Disability: From Theory to Practice*, Macmillan, Basingstoke.

Olver, J. (1995) 'Brain injury: the need to assess outcome', *Current Opinion in Neurology*, 8: 443–46.

Perlesz, A., Furlong, M. and McLachlan, D. (1992) 'Family work and acquired brain damage', *ANZ Journal of Family Therapy*, 13(3): 145–53.

Ponsford, J., Sloan, S. and Snow, P. (1995) *Traumatic Brain Injury: Rehabilitation for Everyday Adaptive Living*, Lawrence Erlbaum Associates, Hove, Sussex.

Prigitano, G. (1988) *Work, Love, and Play after Brain Injury: Observations From the Neurosciences, Art and Literature*, paper presented to the 13th Annual Conference of the Australian Society for the Study of Brain Impairment, Melbourne, Australia.

Resnick, C. (1993) 'The effect of head injury on family and marital stability', *Social Work in Health Care*, 18(2): 49–62.

Rosenthal, M. (1996) 'The ethics and efficacy of traumatic brain injury rehabilitation – myths, measurements, and meaning', *Journal of Head Trauma Rehabilitation*, 11(4): 88–95.

Rowlands, A. (1995) *What iI It Really Like to Live With Acquired Brain Injury?*, paper presented to the 12th World Congress of International Federation of Physical Medicine and Rehabilitation, Sydney, Australia.

Serio, C., Kreutzer J. and Witol, A. (1997) 'Family needs after traumatic brain injury: a factor analytic study of the Family Needs Questionnaire', *Brain Injury* 11(1): 1–9.

Sutherland, D. (1996) *From Unconscious to Self-conscious: Cognitive Rehabilitation from the Perspective of Symbolic Interactionism*, unpublished doctoral dissertation in Social Work, Massey University, Palmerston North, New Zealand.

Tate, R., Lulham, J., Broe, G., Strettles, B. and Pfaff, A. (1989) 'Psychosocial outcome for the survivors of severe blunt head injury: the results from a consecutive series of 100 patients', *Journal of Neurology, Neurosurgery, and Psychiatry*, 52: 1128–34.

Thomsen, I. (1984) 'Late outcome of very severe blunt head trauma: a 10–15 year second follow-up', *Journal of Neurology, Neurosurgery, and Psychiatry,* 47: 260–68.

Willer, B., Allen, K., Durnan, M., and Ferry, A. (1990) 'Problems and coping strategies of mothers, siblings, and young adult males with traumatic brain injury', *Canadian Journal of Rehabilitation* 2(3): 167–73.

Zeigler, E. (1989) 'The importance of mutual support for spouses of head injury survivors', *Cognitive Rehabilitation,* 7(3): 34–7.

16 Work and adulthood: economic survival in the majority world

Majid Turmusani

Economically remunerated employment is a significant marker of adulthood in most societies. Yet many disabled people are denied access to employment and the adult status attached to it. In the majority world, employment is also a matter of economic survival for disabled people and their families. Based on research in Jordan (Turmusani 1999a), this chapter highlights the economic needs and strategies of disabled adults in the majority world from a social model perspective. Here disability is regarded as a social issue rather than an individual one, requiring solutions at the societal level.

In almost all societies, work and the kind of work people do, confers status and personal identity. For example, if someone has work and generates income then they are also more able to support a family. However, many disabled people have been unable to work within disabling environments, although this is generally explained in terms of their perceived functional limitations (Oliver 1990; Barton 1989). This is true both in the West, where the nature of work is fundamental to the way in which status is conferred, and in the majority world, where paid work is fundamental to economic survival. Access to paid work greatly affects disabled people's lives; including their relationships, self-autonomy and participation in society.

Exclusion from work affects the whole of people's lives (Brian and Layzell 1994) and this is central to the exclusion of disabled people in Western society (Stone 1984; Lunt and Thornton 1994). The same applies to people in many developing countries, now witnessing a transition to higher levels of economic development. Perceived impairments do not always exclude people from work in these countries, and disabled people are often more integrated into the life of the community than in the West (Albrecht 1992; Ingstad 1995). However, they are frequently excluded from the more developed economic activities (such as factory work) and looked down upon by other members of society (Tugnell 1992).

The transition to adulthood is critical for survival in the majority world, and entering the labour market is one of the main obstacles facing disabled people in this transition. Instead of taking a productive role within the family and becoming a breadwinner, many disabled people become adjunct to family resources – often with more demands than before. Perceived failure to perform expected roles places extra pressure on disabled people and their families. This may lead to a crisis of identity for the disabled person about their adult role, and result in social and economic problems for the whole family (Jayasooria et al. 1997).

Impairment aside, there are many barriers to employment, including inaccessible transport and buildings, non-adapted tools, and employers' prejudices and fears (DAA/UNESCO 1995). In addition, there is little provision to assist disabled people in developing countries to become economically active (Ingstad 1995; Coleridge 1993; Turmusani 1999a).This suggests not only a lack of awareness about disability but also a lack of coherent disability policy making.

Disabled people and economic needs

Worldwide, disabled people have experienced social and economic discrimination, segregation and exclusion. Disabled people are especially vulnerable to unequal opportunities in their economic life (Doyle 1995). In majority world societies, disabled people are highly over-represented among the poor and unemployed (Coleridge 1993; Ingstad and Whyte 1995; UNICEF 1993; Doyle 1995; ESCWA 1992, 1994; DAA/UNESCO 1995). Their needs, including their most basic needs, remain largely unmet.

The International Covenant on Economic, Social and Culture Rights (ESCR 1976) defines basic needs to include both the core material requirements (for food, water, health, education and shelter) and non-material requirements (such as access to paid work and participation in decisions pertaining to their lives). The basic need for economic participation through employment is particularly important where no welfare system exists to support those who have no work, as is the case for many disabled people in the majority world (ESCR 1976; ILO 1994).

Disabled people's needs vary across cultures and particularly between developed and developing countries. Although basic needs are constructed as universal, their satisfaction is very variable (Wetherly 1996), depending on available welfare resources. While disabled people in the West emphasise the need for equality and anti-discrimination legislation, disabled people in the developing world are still calling for their basic human survival needs to be met.

In the United Kingdom, disabled people involved with the Derbyshire Coalition of Disabled People (DCDP) identified seven areas of need: information, housing, technical aids and equipment, personal assistance, transport and physical access. Other needs (i.e. education, employment and leisure) were considered to be secondary, to be met through mainstream facilities (Davis 1990). It is interesting that a source of income does not feature on this list. This is possibly because income needs are often met by the welfare system in rich countries. By contrast, Helander's list of needs, based on the rights of disabled people set out by DPI (1982), includes: self-care, mobility, communication, education, income generation activities, social integration, participation and representation and legal security (DPI 1982; Helander 1993).

The needs and priorities identified by disabled people themselves in developing countries are often quite different from those on either of these lists. In particular, disabled people often place the need for income at the top of their list of priorities, followed by housing, transport, sex, and rehabilitation (Coleridge 1993). In my own research in Jordan, disabled people identified a source of income (especially paid employment) as primary to their lives (Turmusani 1999b). This is not surprising, given that many developing countries do not have a welfare system to support disabled people without work. This reflects the desperate problem of poverty in these communities and points to the importance of establishing welfare systems and employment opportunities across all societies.

Poverty, disability and employment

The issue of poverty has dominated the discourse on disabled people's needs in developing countries until recently. The causal relationship between poverty (the inability to meet basic needs) and disability is a vicious circle. There are two main arguments here. The first is that poverty is an important cause of impairment and disability, especially in the majority world. The second argument is that disabled people are more likely to experience higher levels of social and economic deprivation than non-disabled people, due to their exclusion from employment (UPIAS 1976; Rock 1981; Mercer and Barnes 1995).

Poverty and inequality exist throughout the world and many who are poor, even in developed societies, suffer greatly. For example, in the UK there are poor people without homes who live in the street. In developing countries, however, the extent of poverty is far greater and its implications more severe. The report of the United Nations Economic, Social and Cultural Committee for Western Asia (ESCWA) shows that the most significant socio-economic and environmental factor related to impairment in developing countries is poverty (ESCWA 1994). Poverty can lead to impairment in a number of ways. Among the most important is the lack of sufficient nutrition (Coleridge 1993; Helander 1993; Harris-White 1994; Doyle 1995; Acton 1983; Beresford 1996).

In the USA, UK and Canada about two thirds of disabled people live below the poverty line (DAA/UNESCO 1995). In many developing countries, the proportion is much greater and the poverty line itself far lower (Coleridge 1993). States often lack the fiscal resources to provide welfare services for disabled people, as they are subject to huge external debts. Disabled people, and disabled women in particular, are often doubly disadvantaged within this context (Beresford 1996). Disability can lead to poverty not only for disabled people but also for those close to them.

Disabled people are more likely to experience financial, social and economic deprivation, especially in the developed world, because work and society is organised around the needs of the non-disabled majority. Disability imposes a multitude of extra and hidden costs on those who have impairments, so that they may easily fall into severe financial difficulty (Rock 1981; Berthoud 1991; Berthoud et al. 1993). In this sense, poverty, along with the other consequences of institutional discrimination, restricts disabled people's rights and undermines their ability to fulfil the private and social obligations of adulthood.

Whether poverty causes impairment or is the outcome of disability, it should be emphasised that breaking the chain of disabled people's economic dependence helps to alleviate problems of impairment, the extra costs of living with impairment, unemployment, limited access to services and information, and negative attitudes. One of the most important ways to address this is to enhance economic participation through access to work for disabled adults, as a means to meet basic needs and to place disabled people in a better position to realise their own long-term life projects. The priority should therefore be to re-organise the workplace and work processes so that they are more accessible to disabled people.

In the West, the exclusion of disabled people from work stems from the very origins of the industrial revolution (Oliver 1990). Disabled people came to be seen as having little to offer to their communities as a result of their perceived 'inability' to work (Burgdorf and Burgdorf 1975; Doyle 1995; and Williams 1991). However, the exclusion of disabled people from the labour market is not universal and there is evidence that in some developing countries, especially in rural communities, disabled people are expected to participate in economic community life (Albrecht 1992; Ingstad and Whyte 1995). Having said that, it should be noted that disabled people in such circumstances are often excluded from the more developed and well-remunerated economic activities such as factory-based work.

A report for the International Labour Organization estimates that the level of unemployment worldwide among disabled people is two to three times higher than for non-disabled people. In addition, many work places are inaccessible, either physically or attitudinally (ILO 1994). High unemployment among disabled people is a central problem because income is the key to financial adult independence, as well as a source of satisfaction and self-esteem. Across the globe, including many developing societies, work is an essential part of economic and social life. It is central in providing the commodities for survival, and influential in personal relationships and interactions, both within and beyond the family. It provides a sense of identity and self-esteem (DAA/UNESCO 1995; Brian and Layzell 1994).

In developing countries, the unemployment rate among disabled people is much higher than that in the developed world. For example, in Tunisia 85 per cent of disabled people are unemployed, whereas in Zimbabwe the rate reaches 99 per cent (DAA/UNESCO 1995). In developing countries disabled people are highly represented among the poor and they are the last among disadvantaged groups to receive assistance when the benefits of development do begin to filter down (Acton 1983). The high percentage of unemployed disabled people in these countries means that they are often forced to beg to survive (Coleridge 1993; DAA/UNESCO 1995). In this context, Medawar (1983) argues that disability, particularly in the 'third' world, is a social, political and economic problem, resulting in injustice and inequality.

Work and adulthood

Access to remunerated employment affects the life course pathways and life chances of disabled people. Across cultures, access to work has a great impact on disabled people's lives, especially on self-identity in the transition to adulthood. In majority world countries, where economic and social inequality is more obvious, paid work is often a determinant factor in social identity. My research on the economic needs of disabled people in Jordan showed that work was central to the lives of disabled adults and largely determined the level of their inclusion into society (Turmusani 1999a, b).

The fieldwork for this research was carried out between 1996 and

1997, and completed in 1999. It concerned 181 disabled women and men from the central region of Jordan who were involved in economic activities through vocational training, sheltered workshop and self-employment schemes. The research used a participatory approach, emphasising the involvement of disabled people in the research process. The results suggest four main areas of adult life (amongst others) that are affected by access to paid work. These include sexuality and relationships, higher education, mobility and autonomy, and political participation.

Personal relationships

Close personal relationships are essential for everybody, including disabled people. At times of social isolation and marginalisation the need for such relationships becomes vitally important. Maslow included this need in the second level of his pyramid of human needs (Maslow 1970). The need for social relationships and the expression of sexuality has been identified as important to disabled people across the globe (Helander 1993). In developing countries disabled people included this need among their vital needs, alongside income, education and medical care (Coleridge 1993).

The ability to establish and sustain relationships – social, sexual or professional – is often determined by a person's financial independence. Disabled people, excluded from the labour market, may depend financially on others for their income and survival, and may therefore have less control over their relationships (Stone 1999). In a male dominated society, as is the case in many countries of the majority world, disabled men face extra difficulties in starting sexual relationships due to the values placed upon male economic productivity and financial independence. When men do succeed in developing sexual relationships and families they may face particular hardship in meeting the needs of their relatives and partners (Turmusani 1999a). It should be pointed out that the situation of disabled women is no better, since they are often denied the right to start such relationships in the first place (Turmusani 1999c; Habibi 1997).

The research in Jordan showed that the majority of disabled people had great difficulty forming relationships and sustaining them. This was especially true for women, who reported a general lack of control over their lives. Difficulty in establishing relationships was often attributed to financial dependency on others, especially by those with more severe impairments. Equally important were negative public perceptions of people's abilities, and negative public attitudes towards sexual rights and claims. For example, several participants in the study felt that their need to establish a family was often denied by society, because they were perceived as sexually impotent. For example, one physically impaired young man in sheltered employment said:

People think we are unable to function sexually. They think a physically impaired man not only lacks mobility, but he lacks also the ability to function sexually in a normal way.

More generally, these results are in line with Oliver's (1983) observations about the difficulties faced by young disabled people forming relationships and participating in social activities in the West. In my study, as in Oliver's, it was not only the rejection and prejudices of other people that inhibited the socialisation of disabled people, but also the practical barriers raised by inaccessible work environments and the over-protective attitudes of some parents.

Higher education

Higher education is something that greatly affects access to employment. Secondary and higher education are increasingly becoming an essential requirement for gaining paid employment in developing countries as well as in the West. Conversely, being in employment, and having an adequate income, can help people to further their education. Yet disabled people have been excluded from mainstream education at all levels and there are few opportunities for either higher education or employment training, leading to enforced dependency on others (Coleridge 1993). In the majority world, access to further education for disabled people remains particularly restricted. Funding and resources, peer and teacher attitudes and education policies all raise barriers to disabled people who wish to pursue lifelong learning through higher education (UNESCO/DAA 1995). Evidence from Jordan shows that disabled people's access to education was restricted largely by lack of financial autonomy. As one disabled person put it:

You simply cannot think of any future plans about education . . . since you're totally dependent on others and do not have financial power to make your own decisions.

Even when disabled people do have the opportunity for further education, they are more likely to be unemployed after completing their course, when compared to non-disabled people. In Jordan, disabled people had free access to higher education until relatively recently. However, the Law of 1993 introduced charges and, coupled with the extra expenditure by disabled students on additional materials, equipment and personal assistance, this has had a negative impact.

Mobility and autonomy

These are important needs in relation to employment and adulthood for disabled people, especially in the developed world (Davis 1990; Helander 1993; ESCR 1976). Being mobile is a pre-requisite to gaining more control over one's life in a modernising world. It also helps in finding and sustaining paid employment, which often takes place outside the home. Once in employment, mobility and autonomy may increase as a result of increased income. In the majority world, mobility is less often reported as an essential need, even by disabled people themselves. Indeed, Coleridge (1993) notes that disabled people in developing countries identified other needs, such as income, housing, education, medical care and sexuality, as more pressing.

In Jordan, the majority of disabled people did report a significant lack of mobility and personal autonomy, due to access barriers and public attitudes. As one man said:

You can't do anything outdoors without reasonable mobility such as accessible buses, traffic lights, etc let alone negative public attitudes towards disabled people.

Disabled women in particular experienced an additional restriction on their mobility, due to male-dominated values in society and family restrictions on their general public activities. This is best explained by a blind woman who said:

I went for an interview and on my way, the taxi driver pitied me and wondered how can I manage to move around while I'm a blind female. He even advised me to stay at home. The result of the interview, however, was not better since the headmaster could not believe I can manage to teach kids a subject of my speciality.

Political involvement

When in remunerated employment, or having a source of income, disabled people can more often afford to take part in other activities, including political activities compared with when being without income or paid employment at all. When a source of income is secured, whether from employment or welfare provision, disabled people are in a better position to think of needs other than income, including their need to participate in the life of society and in political representation. Participation in civil society and policy making gives disabled people an opportunity to influence decisions pertaining to their lives, including the creation of wider opportunities for employment. Despite the international recognition of disabled people's rights for political participation (Despouy 1993; UN 1994), disabled people remain poorly involved in formulating the political agenda (Drake 1994; Oliver 1990; Beresford and Harding 1990).

In Jordan for example, disabled people were represented in policy making bodies, but were not allowed any real participation in the decision making process. Their influence over decisions pertaining to economic participation in Jordanian society was therefore minimal. In fact, disabled people's voices and views were not incorporated in the policy formulation process concerning economic participation in society. As a consequence, subsequent economic provisions made for disabled people were very limited indeed in range and quality let alone being responsive to their survival needs.

Strategies for survival

In employment policy terms, most countries can be classified into three broad types. The first includes those, like Germany, where disability policy is associated with specific government departments (dealing with quotas, reserved employment etc.). The second includes countries such as the USA, Canada, Australia and the UK, which have general anti-discrimination legislation. The third includes states where there is no legislation at all. In developing countries, disability employment policy usually falls into the first or the third category (Harris-White 1994). In Jordan, the Law for the Welfare of Disabled People (number 12 1993) was the first legal document relating to disabled people's employment policy. Under this Law, the employment of disabled people is now dealt with by a specific department through a quota scheme (NCWDP 1993).

Various measures may be considered as useful in reducing discrimination against disabled people and enhancing equal opportunities through employment. These include anti-discrimination legislation, employment quota policies, welfare programmes, job creation schemes and self-employment. Quota schemes have been a common approach in the West, although they have not proved the most efficient mechanism (Lunt and Thornton 1994). Another common response is to integrate disabled people into the workforce through various employment schemes, including subsidised open employment. However, evidence from Jordan showed that sheltered employment and self-employment were the most common means of integration in the labour market (Turmusani 1999b).

In Jordan, supported employment schemes offer little integration with non-disabled people. Only a limited range and number of jobs were available to the thirty-three participants employed in the three sheltered workshops in the country. The majority of disabled people who were involved in sheltered workshops (twenty-seven) worked in skilled manual jobs. A smaller number (four) were involved in medical equipment production and the remaining two people worked as interpreters. These sheltered workshops were generally characterised by poor working conditions and many of those working within them complained of poor wages.

Sheltered employment remains a widespread approach in the majority world (ILO 1989). In many developed countries, especially North America and Australia, there has been a recent shift from sheltered to supported employment in the labour market (Thornton and Lunt 1997). Because disabled people are collected in one place, and employed in marginal settings, many believe that sheltered employment segregates disabled people and encourages a negative, medical model view of their needs. Having said that, it should be noted that the same medical model has been responsible for the creation of much existing provision in majority world countries. These programmes are often financed by external agencies, primarily international NGOs, and may also lack the endorsement of the state.

In Jordan, the limited employment opportunities available for disabled people (i.e. sheltered employment and on occasion quota employment) led many to look for self-employment. Walker (1982), Barnes (1991), and Lunt and Thornton (1994) argue that self-employment is important for disabled people, especially in a discriminatory society, as it offers a more flexible method of working, self-employment. Yet, it can also be a way of marginalising disabled people from the mainstream of society. Existing self-employment schemes in Jordan were limited in number and in their range of activities. They assisted twenty-seven disabled people in running their own business, mainly in trading, manual repair and crafts. Two people were also doing electronic repair work.

Disabled women in general, even when highly educated (i.e. several blind women) preferred to have their own businesses at home, due to the restrictive attitudes towards working women. Disabled women in the study felt isolated from social and economic life. Women are often expected and encouraged to be dependent on family members in male-dominated Jordanian society. Constraints exist to limit the social activities of many women, and this situation may be further compounded when a woman is disabled.

The exclusion of disabled people from paid employment, including self-employment, in Jordan meant that disabled people suffered from obvious social and economic deprivation and that their basic needs remained unmet due to lack of income. Hence, their financial dependency on others had been further perpetuated and their ability to pursue plans to establish a family, continue education or even to be socially mobile remained restricted.

Welfare programmes are an alternative strategy. In the West, especially in Europe, disabled people are entitled to certain benefits covering some of the extra costs associated with their impairment and helping to break the link between poverty, unemployment and disability (Walker and Walker 1991). Nearly three quarters of disabled adults in the UK rely on state social security benefits as their main source of income, although these benefits are considered very low (Martin and White 1988). In many developing countries, however, the absence of a developed welfare system for disabled adults perpetuates their financial dependency on families and exposes them to a circle of poverty (Ingstad 1995; Coleridge 1993).

Concluding remarks

Understanding the way that disability and adulthood are constructed is essential in explaining the disadvantaged position of disabled people in relation to their economic needs. How the problem is framed will influence the measures taken to eliminate it. In this chapter, I have viewed disability as a socially constructed outcome of capitalist development (Oliver 1990). The implication of this model is that disabled people's needs should be met through policies that focus on restructuring society, with a particular emphasis on the economy (i.e. through the creation of employment opportunities and access to work).

Access to employment in the majority world is not only a marker of adulthood but also a matter of economic survival. Yet, in many countries, disabled people's needs for economic participation are barely recognised. This situation makes the transition to adulthood particularly difficult, and strengthens the link between poverty, impairment and disability. Although there are a variety of different policy approaches, disabled people's economic needs in the majority world have not been adequately addressed by the state and its agencies. Disabled adults are denied equal opportunities to compete in the labour market and to determine their own employment needs.

From a social model perspective, these concerns should be incorporated into macro, socio-economic planning processes to ensure that disabled people's rights are taken into account, and that they benefit from the overall process of development in society. For far too long disabled people have had to accept a passive role in all stages of their lives. As consumers and citizens, in line with the international policy rhetoric of full participation and equality, disabled people have a right to be consulted and involved in policies and decisions pertaining to their lives, especially in economic matters.

REFERENCES

Acton, N. (1983) 'World disability: the need for a new approach: a cry for health', in O. Shirley (ed.) *Poverty and Disability in the Third World*, Third World Group and AHRTAG, Fromme, London.

Albrecht, G. (1992) *The Disability Business: Rehabilitation in America*, Sage, London.

Barnes, C. (1991) 'Institutional discrimination against disabled people and the campaign for anti-discrimination legislation', *Critical Social Policy*, 12 (1): 5–22.

Barton, L. (1989) *Disability and Dependence*, The Falmer Press, Lewes, Sussex.

Beresford, P. (1996) 'Poverty and disabled people: challenging dominant debates and policies', *Disability & Society*, 11(4): 553–67.

Beresford, P. and Harding, T. (1990) 'Involving services users', *NCVO News*, October 1990.

Berthoud, R. (1991) 'Meeting the costs of disability', in G. Dalley (ed.) *Disability and Social Policy*, Policy Studies Institute, London.

Berthoud, R., Lakey, J. and Mckay, S. (1993) *The Economic Problems of Disabled People*, Policy Studies Institute, London.

Brian, L. and Layzell, S. (1994) *Disabled in Britain: A World Apart*, SCOPE, London.

Burgdorf, R. and Burgdorf, M. (1975) *A History of Unequal Treatment: The Qualification of Handicapped Persons as a Suspect Class Under the Equal Protection Clause*, Brooks Baltimore, USA.

Coleridge, P. (1993) *Disability, Liberation and Development*, Oxfam Publications, Oxford.

Disability Awareness in Action/UNESCO (1995) *Overcoming Obstacles to the Integrating of Disabled People*, Disability Awareness in Action: London.

Davis, K. (1990) *Activating the Social Model of Disability: The Emergence of the Seven Needs*, Derbyshire Coalition of Disabled People, Derby.

Despouy, L. (1993) *Human Rights and Disabled Persons*, United Nations Centre for Human Rights, Geneva, Switzerland.

DPI (1982) *Disabled People's International: Proceedings of the First World Congress Singapore*, Disabled People's International, Singapore.

Doyle, B. (1995) *Disability Discrimination and Equal Opportunities: A Comparative Study of the Employment Rights of Disabled Persons*, Mansell Ltd., London.

Drake, R. (1994) 'The exclusion of disabled people from positions of power in British voluntary organisations', *Disability & Society*, 9(4): 461–80.

ESCR (1976) *International Covenant on Economic, Social and Cultural Rights (ESCR)*, Geneva, Switzerland.

ESCWA (1992) *The Impact of Socio-economic Changes on the Arab Family: Pilot Study*, Economic and Social Committee for Western Asia (ESCWA), Amman, Jordan.

ESCWA (1994) *The Situation of Disabled Women and Their Social Integration in the ESCWA Region*, working paper presented in ESCWA regional conference in Amman, Jordan.

Habibi, L. (1998) *Gender and Disability: Women's Experience in the Middle East*, Oxfam, UK and Ireland.

Harris-White, B. (1994) *The Political Economy of Disability and Development: With Special Reference to India. Economic Restructuring and New Social Politics.* Draft paper.

Helander, E. (1993) *Prejudice and Dignity: An Introduction to Community Based Rehabilitation*, UNDP, New York, USA.

Ingstad, B. (1995) 'Mpho Ya Modimo – a gift from God: perspectives on attitudes towards disabled people', in B. Ingstad and S. Whyte (eds.) *Disability and Culture*, University of California Press, Berkeley, USA.

Ingstad, B. and Whyte, S. (1995) *Disability and Culture*, University of California Press, Berkeley, USA.

International Labour Organisation (1989) *Vocational Rehabilitation and Employment of the Disabled People in ESCWA Region*, working paper presented to the ESCWA regional conference in Amman, Jordan.

International Labour Organisation (1994) *Assessment of Business Skills Training and Loans for Disabled Micro-entrepreneurs in Kenya*, ILO, Geneva, Switzerland.

IYDP (1981) *The International Year of Disabled Persons*, New York, UN.

Jayasooria, D., Krishnan, B., and Ooi, G. (1997) 'Disabled people in a newly industrialised economy: opportunities and challenges in Malaysia', *Disability & Society*, 12(3): 455–63.

Lunt, N. and Thornton, P. (1993) *Employment Policies for Disabled People: A Review of Legislation and Services in Fifteen Countries*, ED Research Series, Na 16, Sheffield Employment Department.

Lunt, N. and Thornton, P. (1994) 'Disability and employment: towards an understanding of discourse and policy', *Disability & Society*, 9(2): 223–38.

Martin, J. and White, A. (1988) *The Financial Circumstances of Disabled Adults in Private Households*, OPCS Surveys of Disability in Great Britain: Report 2, HMSO, London.

Maslow, A. (1970) *Motivation and Personality*, Harper Brothers, New York, USA.

Medawar, C. (1983) 'The disabled consumer: how multinational corporations affected the Third World', in O. Shirley (ed.) *A Cry for Health: Poverty and Disability in the Third World*, Fromme: Third World Group and AHRTAG, London.

Mercer, G. and Barnes, C. (1995) 'Disability: emancipation, community participation and disabled people', in M. Magi and G. Graig (eds.), *Community Empowerment: A Reader in Participation and Development*, Zed Books, London.

National Council for the Welfare of Disabled People (1993) Law for Welfare of Disabled People no 12 for the year 1993, NCWDP, Amman, Jordan.

Oliver, M. (1983) *Social Work with Disabled People*, Macmillan, Basingstoke.

Oliver, M. (1990) *The Politics of Disablement*, Macmillan, Basingstoke.

Rock, P. (1981) 'The extra and hidden cost of disability', in J. Campling (ed.) *The Handicapped Person: A New Perspective for Social Workers?*, RADAR, London.

Stone, D. (1985) *The Disabled State*, Macmillan, Basingstoke.

Stone, E. (ed.) (1999) *Disability and Development: Learning from Action and Research on Disability in the Majority World*, Disability Press, Leeds.

Tugnell, I. (1992) 'Enhancing the integration of persons with disabilities: opportunities and challenges development and managing the social impact of industrialisation', Institute of Strategic and International Studies (ISIS), Kuala Lampur, Malaysia.

Turmusani, M. (1999a) 'The economic needs of disabled people in Jordan: from the personal to the political perspective', *Disability Studies Quarterly* 19 (1) 32–42.

Turmusani, M. (1999b) 'Disability rehabilitation policies in Jordan: a critical perspective', in E. Stone (ed.) *Disability and Development: Learning From Action and Research in the Majority World*, Disability Press, Leeds.

Turmusani, M. (1999c) 'Some cultural representation of disabled people in Jordan', in Holzer, B., Vreede, A. and Weight, G. (eds.) *Disability in Different Cultures: reflections on local concepts*, Verlag Muhlenstraße, Bielefeld, Germany.

UNICEF (1993) *Priorities for Childhood Disability Program in Jordan*, UNICEF, Amman, Jordan.

Union of Physically Impaired Against Segregation/Disability Alliance (1976) *Fundamental Principles of Disability*, UPIAS, London.

United Nations (1992) *The Universal Declaration Of Human Rights*. UN, Geneva, Switzerland.

United Nations (1994) *Standard Rules on the Equalisation of Opportunities for Persons With Disabilities*, New York, USA.

Walker, A. (1982) *Unqualified and Underemployed: Handicapped Young People and the Labour Market*, Macmillan, Basingstoke.

Walker, L. and Walker, A. (1991) 'Disability and financial need – the failure of the social security system', in Dalley, G. (ed.) *Disability and Social Policy*, Policy Studies Institute, London.

Wetherly, P. (1996) 'Basic needs and social policies', *Critical Social Policy*, 16(46): 45–63.

Williams, G. (1991) 'Disablement and the ideological crisis in health care', *Social Science and Medicine*, 32: 517–24.

17   The possibility of choice: women with intellectual disabilities talk about having children

Kelley Johnson, Rannveig Traustadóttir, Lyn Harrison,
Lynne Hillier and Hanna Björg Sigurjónsdóttir

> Until very recently, the choice to be or not to be a mother was essentially unavailable to most women, even today, the possibility of choice remains everywhere in jeopardy. This elemental loss of control over her body affects every woman's right to shape the imagery and insights of her own being.   (Rich 1979a: 196)

As feminist researchers who have been working with women with intellectual disabilities, we found Adrienne Rich's quotation to be particularly poignant and ironic in relation to our recent work. Rich argues that a dominant traditional discourse in our societies has positioned women unquestioningly as mothers. Indeed she argues that 'a woman's status as child bearer has been the test of her womanhood' (Rich 1979b: 261). Women with disabilities have in the past been excluded from this societal expectation and their womanhood has been a problematic issue for those around them (Asch and Fine 1992; Johnson 1998a). This has been particularly the case for women with intellectual disabilities who were constituted by the eugenics movement early this century as a threat to the very structure of society because of their child bearing capacity (Brantlinger 1995; Rose 1979; Scheerenberger 1983).

Consequently, many women with intellectual disabilities were subject to sterilisation, constant surveillance and institutionalisation (Johnson 1998a; Potts and Fido 1991; Trent 1994) to prevent them from becoming mothers. For women with intellectual disabilities, then, the dominant discourse historically has situated them as women who are unfit to have children or to be mothers. This issue raised questions for us about the lives of women with intellectual disabilities now: What effect has the explicit exclusion from child bearing and mothering had on the way women with intellectual disabilities see themselves? How far does this historical view of women with intellectual disabilities as 'non child bearers and non mothers' still impact on their lives?

As a feminist, Rich challenges the traditional discourse equating womanhood and motherhood. She advocates a position that will free motherhood and child bearing from traditional societal expectations. Indeed in our lifetimes we have seen how the availability of contraception, changes to the economic and social structures and the rise of feminism have led to increased choices about how women live their lives. The traditional view of motherhood has been challenged.

Women now choose not to have children at all, to have them outside traditional family structures and to have them at particular times in their lives. As Rich notes, such choices are not made without a struggle. In this chapter we argue that for women with intellectual disabilities the challenge to the prevailing discourse and their struggle have had a different form. Feminism, deinstitutionalisation and the impact of self advocacy and rights discourses on the lives of people with intellectual disabilities have challenged some of the old stereotypes, including the view that women with intellectual disabilities cannot and should not be mothers or bear children (Johnson 1998b; Walmsley and Downer 1997). The contested nature of these issues is shown in the number of research studies carried out over the past fifteen years about people with intellectual disabilities and parenting (Andron and Tymchuk 1987; Booth and Booth 1994, 1998; Feldman 1986; 1994; Keltner, Wise and Taylor 1999; Llewellyn 1993, 1994; Pixa-Kettner 1999). Much of this research appears to have been directed at proving the capability of people with intellectual disabilities to be satisfactory parents. Some of it has sought to explore how such people themselves see these issues (Booth and Booth 1994; Llewellyn 1995). However while the research covers many aspects of parenting, we found that it did not really explore how women came to decisions about whether or not they would have children. This raised questions for us in our own research: How do women with intellectual disability make decisions about having children? What factors affect these decisions? What effects has the new rights discourse had for women in relation to having children?

The importance of women's choices and voices

Rich argues strongly for the importance of choice as an issue for women for it is by choice that women can become empowered and take control of their bodies and their lives. For women with intellectual disabilities however, choice remains a difficult issue particularly in relation to child bearing and parenting. In spite of evidence that some women with intellectual disabilities have always taken on caring roles, there remains a view that they are 'child like and dependent' (Walmsley 2000). In relation to their sexual lives there is evidence that they often feel they have limited choices about whether or not to engage in sex (McCarthy 1999) or in the development of relationships. The questions that these issues raise for us are: What, if any, choices do women with intellectual disabilities have in deciding whether or not to have children? What do they see as the issues that affect this decision-making?

We have found little discussion of our questions in the literature, particularly from the perspective of women themselves. Some women, not labelled as having disabilities, have written about the complex motivations that may lead to their decisions about whether or not to have a child (Dowrick and Grundberg 1980; Oakley 1980). And more recently women with physical disabilities have explored their experiences of life, including parenthood (Browne, Connors and Stern 1985; Keith 1994; Morris 1991; Wates and Jade 1999). But women with intellectual disabilities are only peripherally included in these works. For example, a collection of stories told by couples with intellectual disabilities discusses only superficially their views about child bearing (Melberg Schwier 1994). However, the recently published stories of two women with intellectual disabilities provide a more detailed account of their decision-making about having children.

It [sterilisation] was made a joint decision and that decision was made by me and my husband. I had the tubal ligation in 1983 and soon after I had that I felt this tremendous . . . I still can't describe it even today. I had a great big burden off my shoulders. And I still think, looking back today, I still made the right decision. That's allowed me to do the things I've been doing since then. It's freed me up and I haven't been tied down or anything like that. (Millear 2000: 245)

Millear's decision was informed by her knowledge of the law and her rights and by a desire to live a life without children. In contrast Janice Slattery (2000), writes movingly of a decision not to have a much wanted child. She describes the decision made in consultation with professionals, family and her husband as difficult and painful.

It was a very hard decision for us. And we came to the decision that we didn't want to put our child at risk of being teased at school like I was. I was teased about my balance and that and my speech and we didn't want our child to have that. And also we didn't want to put my health at risk because of my age. And if we did have a child with a disability I would have difficulty raising it. Like I wouldn't know what to do. I wouldn't know how to get him speech therapy or where to go to school and that. (Slattery 2000: 99)

For Slattery the issues had to do with her painful experiences of being 'disabled', her concerns about her ability to care for a child (perhaps with disabilities) and her age. These two women chose not to have children, one with a sense of relief and the other with great sadness. For both of them the decision was a momentous one, taken after a lot of thought and consultation. It was a decision in which they were active participants. How do other women with intellectual disabilities make this decision? How do they feel about the decisions they have made or been forced to make?

Women talking about having children: in Iceland and Australia

This chapter explores how some women with intellectual disabilities view the issue of child bearing in our two countries, Iceland and Australia, and seeks to explore the questions raised for us by Adrienne Rich's statement. The chapter is based on separate studies which we have undertaken with women with intellectual disabilities in Iceland and Australia over the past few years.[1]

The Icelandic study

The research with Icelandic women with intellectual disabilities started in 1994 with a small project, focusing on a woman with an intellectual disability who was a leader in the Icelandic self-advocacy movement. During interviews with this woman, whom we have named Stella, we learned that it was not her leadership career that she was most interested in talking about. Instead, her major concern was with motherhood, the recent abortion her family had forced her to have, her fight against sterilisation and her strong desire to have a child. When we started a larger study of women with intellectual disabilities in 1996, we placed a strong emphasis on motherhood and family life (Sigurjónsdóttir and Traustadóttir 2000; Traustadóttir and Sigurjónsdóttir 1998). Over a period of three years we have spent time with about thirty women with intellectual disabilities. Ten of the women are mothers. They comprise a diverse group and their living situations varied. The oldest woman was 83 years old and the youngest was 25 years of age. The wide age range in the group of mothers helped us understand how changing ideas, attitudes, policies and services over the years have influenced the possibility of motherhood for women with intellectual disabilities. Many of the twenty women who did not have children had been sterilised, some of them had a strong desire to have children and some did not want to become mothers.

The research was conducted using ethnographic methods (Hammersley and Atkinson 1994; Taylor and Bogdan 1998). We have spent a long time with each of the women and taken part in their daily lives and talked to them about their interests, including motherhood and family life. We wanted to gain in-depth knowledge of their lives and attempt to understand things from their perspective. We have kept in touch with most of the women over a period of a few months and up to three years. We still keep in touch with Stella, who participated in our initial study in 1994.

The Australian study

Thirteen women have contributed their life histories, with a particular focus on sexuality and relationships as part of a two-year study titled *Living Safer Sexual Lives* (Johnson, Hillier and Harrison 1999). The women ranged in age from their early twenties to their late fifties. Some had spent part of their lives in institutions and others had lived all their lives in the wider community. Women researchers spent a minimum of three occasions with each person in a free flowing discussion, which ranged across life choices and experiences. The stories were taped, then written up and returned to the contributors for change and corrections. The resulting stories are powerful and cover a wide range of issues that the women are concerned about in their lives. Eleven women expressed some view about child bearing or motherhood in their interviews and for some this issue was a central and important part of their lives. The women differed in their views of the issues and also in the degree to which they believed that they had some control over the decision-making.

Our work with the women in these studies suggests that their experiences are very similar across our two societies and that they raise important issues for us as women, and in our work with people with disabilities. In this chapter we draw on the stories to explore the diversity of women's experiences and to examine how they are affected by the changing discourses about women and intellectual disability. The women's names are changed to protect their confidentiality.

Women with intellectual disabilities talk about having children

The women who participated in our studies conveyed a wide range of issues in relation to discussions about having children. Here, we explore two major themes that directly address our questions: the challenges to the legitimacy of their desire for a child; and the variety of factors that influenced a woman's decision about having children.

The challenges to desire

None of the women who had been involved in decisions about having children, or the desire to have them, had found the processes easy or simple. They were trapped between two opposing discourses: one which focused on their own perceived desire and right to bear a child and to be a mother, and the other which has excluded them from the possibility of motherhood. Some women had internalised the societal discourse and did not see child bearing as a possibility for them.

Helga Jónsdóttir, has a large collection of children's photographs she has taken over the years. She treasures these pictures and goes through the albums frequently. Most of the pictures are of her sibling's children when they were babies, some are children of staff she encountered in service programs, and some of the pictures are of young children she has met in parks and playgrounds. 'I love children', Helga's face lights up when she talks about children. But she has internalised society's views about her possibilities to have a child of her own and believes it would be inappropriate for her to become a mother.

Other women, however, struggled against the societal restrictions. Often they were unsuccessful. Elaine, now 44, reflects back on an ongoing struggle to attain marriage and parenthood, a struggle which she lost.

I would have liked children. I'm getting too old. I would have liked to have a child. I said to mum. I said, 'Janet's [sister] married and got children. Bill's [brother] got a girl pregnant and didn't marry her now and Simon [brother] he's got three and he's married'. And I said, 'What about me?' I said, 'how do you think I feel mum? I feel horrible mum'. I said, 'You and dad don't even give me a chance'. You know. And I got really pissed off with mum and dad at one stage you know. I said, 'One of these days I'm going to run away from home. And get meself pregnant and then you might have something to moan about. Mum said, 'Over my dead body young lady'. She said, 'I've been through that, I don't want to bring any more up'. Mum and dad treated me like a little child. When I got older they changed a little bit.

Elaine believed that if she had got pregnant she would have been forced by her family to have an abortion. She comments:

I didn't want to bring a baby into the world and not have her. And you know when I had sex with James I went to the doctors because mum thought I might have got meself pregnant and I said, 'What about if I did?' I said, 'What would you do?' She said, 'I wouldn't own you'. I said, 'Yeah I thought so'. I said, 'your own daughter'. I said, 'You wouldn't own her'. I said, 'You're not my mother'. And then mum went home bawling her eyes out. 'Cause mum was hurt.

Elaine mourns her lost opportunities as both wife and mother:

Well in me I think back and I have a little cry now and then you know that I wasn't married and had children. I would have liked it. I am an auntie. Anyway that's the way it was. It didn't turn out. What can you do? Mum and dad wasn't that hard on me. Only about getting married. I couldn't have children. Mum thought if I had a baby it would have been like me. Mum was scared if I got pregnant and had a baby it would have polio too. That's what mum was thinking in her mind. And dad was thinking too. I thought mum was a little bit hard on me. You know mum and dad the way they brought me up. It was different the way they raised me and the way they raised Bill and Janet and Simon. They can do a lot more things than me.

Her account of her parent's anxieties about her possible decision to have a child contains not only a rejection of her as a woman and a mother unable to care for her baby or to be a wife but also a rejection of her as a daughter in that her parents did not want another child like her. This was a repeated theme in the stories that the women told us. Further, Elaine felt strongly that she was treated differently to her brothers and sisters in relation to marriage and children. This sense of being differentiated from siblings was common among the women. Molly described how her parents supported her sister when she became pregnant at 18, but also describes how when she was 23 and became pregnant they insisted that she have an abortion.

Parental reactions to the possibility of their daughter having a child seemed to reflect the view that they should not be mothers because they would not be able to cope, because the child might be disabled or because they might be required to become primary care givers. But for the women in our studies these reactions were seen as oppressive, life constraining and agonising.

Sometimes family intervention went beyond verbal discouragement. For example, when Elaine became involved with someone in a long term sexual relationship her mother suggested sterilisation.

And then mum said, 'What about having your tubes cut and tied?' Mum wanted me to have it done. The doctor said, 'you want to make your mum happy?' And I said, 'Yes. Of course. I love me mother'. 'Cause you've only got one mum. And I said, 'Yes I want to make mum happy'. 'Well what about it?' I didn't really have a choice. But there was nothing I could do about it. 'Cause I only had me tubes cut and tried to make me mum happy.

The power of societal or family pressure against women with intellectual disabilities becoming mothers can be extremely strong in spite of legislation which aims to protect them against discrimination on the basis of disability and which restricts sterilisation. A woman's love for her parents, manipulation, her distress or coercion can lead women to agree to either sterilisation as in the case of Elaine, or abortion in Stella's case.

From childhood on, Stella had watched friends undergo sterilisation and was relieved that this had not happened to her. When she was in her 20s, however, she learned that her family was strongly opposed to her having a child. She was in a long-term relationship with a man and they were planning to establish a home together. Stella's family was afraid she would become pregnant. She was on the pill but they wanted her to be sterilised. Stella had not realised her family was so strongly against her having a child but this did not stop her from wanting to become a mother. She became pregnant.

No one congratulated her or was happy for her. Everyone reacted negatively. Her family put an enormous pressure on her to have an abortion. In particular, her oldest sister insisted that she have an abortion and be sterilised at the same time. 'She forced me to have the abortion', Stella recalls. The sister threatened that Stella would be locked up in an institution if she didn't have the abortion. The fear of being institutionalised made Stella go with her sister to a social worker where she signed a paper that she would undergo both procedures. Stella was devastated and felt desperate. She could not bear the thought of never being able to have a child. Without her sister's knowledge Stella went back to the social worker later that same day and told her that she would have to go through with the abortion because of her sister, but she did not want to be sterilised. She had the abortion the next day.

Both of these women were strong self-advocates and plainly both struggled against their family's opposition. Yet both found it difficult to stand out against the pressure from family members.

Women making decisions about having children

There is a tendency among workers and families to see women with intellectual disabilities as passive and non-participative in decision-making. Certainly some of the women in the studies appeared to have little say in what happened to them. But many of the women thought seriously about their possible choices in relation to children. The reasons they gave for decisions they had taken about this issue were varied and often demonstrated powerful internal struggles between competing desires and needs. They also often demonstrated care and concern for others, particularly towards those with whom they were involved in relationships and for their possible children. Their responses were consistent with Gilligan's view that for women 'the moral imperative . . . is an injunction to care, a responsibility to discern and alleviate the 'real and recognisable trouble' of this world'. (Gilligan 1993: 100). While the 'womanhood' of these women may have been challenged by societal proscriptions they demonstrated that they were speaking with women's voices in their decision-making.

For example, Ruth has recently left an abusive relationship with a man with whom she became pregnant.

I had a termination last year. I wanted to have the child but because my fiancé was too intellectually disabled and because of his temper I just didn't go through with it. I just couldn't let him bring up a child knowing that he could hurt it. That was a decision I made because he was too pig headed. He wanted a baby and that was it. That was final. Too bad what I wanted. He wanted it so bad luck what I wanted. He wanted the baby and he couldn't see my point of view. He couldn't see why I couldn't bring it up. I was still living at home and I didn't want my mum to help me even though she would have. She's already brought up four kids.

They were really the main reasons [for the abortion]. It worried me a lot. I didn't want to bring up a child in that environment. I could have a child in the future if I wanted to. It is possible that the baby would end up with the same thing [as me] but other than that there's no reason not to have a child.

I should have waited you know but at the time I guess I wanted a baby really because I wanted to prove to myself that I can care about a child better than what my father did when he left me. I wanted to prove to my child that I can do that. I could stay with the situation. I also wanted a kid because I love children. I wanted a child because I wanted someone to love me I guess, 'cos at the time I was feeling that nobody wanted me. I was in the relationship with George and it was not going as well as I would have liked but I still wanted a child.

Ruth has given a great deal of thought to her decision to have an abortion. Concerns about her unborn child's safety, a violent partner and the possible extra work for her mother are issues weighed against her desire to have someone who will love her and whom she can love.

Other women commented that their health made it difficult or impossible for them to have children or that they felt they couldn't manage to care for a child.

So Alicia, who is married to Rob, comments:

I can't have kids . . . because my ovaries stopped growing. I found out by my doctors. Because I've got diabetes . . . really small hands and feet. It didn't worry me at all really. I mind my nieces and nephews lots of times. I wouldn't like a child. It's too much hassle. I can't cope with the little ones, I can't chase after them. Babysitting my nieces and nephews is enough. I like them and all that but they are really hard to look after. It's hard enough just being myself. I couldn't look after another person, especially a baby. Rob understands.

While Alicia cannot physically have children, it is clear that this is an issue that has been discussed in some detail between her and her partner.

Women who decided to go ahead with having a child, often in spite of family or societal opposition, often also showed a high degree of planning and decision-making.

Halldóra and her partner Kristján had been living together for some time. They had often talked about having a child 'but it was not on the agenda to have children right away', said Halldóra. They wanted to wait and see how well they could take care of themselves before they had a child. Halldóra was also afraid her epilepsy would make it difficult or impossible for her to have a child. Although her epilepsy was mostly under control she still had occasional fits. She also worried that her medication might harm the fetus. 'Because of this', Halldóra said, 'we were sometimes saying we might need to adopt a child'. She was using the birth-control pill when she unexpectedly became pregnant. She was three and a half months into the pregnacy when realised she was expecting a child.

This unplanned and unexpected pregnancy created mixed feelings. On the one hand, Halldóra and Kristján were happy and wanted to have the child. On the other hand, they worried about Halldóra's health. Halldóra consulted her family doctor and he told her there was no need for concern because there was nothing physically which hindered her in carrying and having the child, and the medication would not affect the fetus. Halldóra and Kristján thought about an abortion, 'But it was always "no". We could not destroy this life that had already began'. Halldóra decided to have the child.

For Halldóra and her partner, having a child was a serious undertaking. They had established safeguards to ensure that they could care for a child as well as themselves and had also carefully considered Halldóra's health. Confronted with her unexpected pregnancy, they weighed up the choices before deciding on the way which seemed best to them. What more can we ask of any prospective parents?

Conclusion

We have found this a difficult chapter to write. In part this is because the women's stories have an integrity and wholeness, which loses much of its power when they are fragmented and analysed. But there is a power too in the aggregated voices, which can be heard through the chapter. For many women with intellectual disabilities decision making about having a child is a serious and central issue in their lives. None of the women with whom we spoke had been through this process without struggle and pain. The issue for us in this chapter has not been whether or not the women who spoke to us would be 'good mothers'. Rather, it has been the way in which they have been constituted by society and by their families, and how this has impacted on decision-making for them.

We would have to conclude that the traditional discourse which prohibited women with intellectual disabilities from having children still remains dominant and that some of the reasons women give for their child-bearing decisions reflect an internalisation of this discourse. While other women may struggle to broaden definitions of motherhood and family, the women with intellectual disabilities with whom we spoke, are struggling to take a first step towards fulfilling their desire for children.

Note

1 The Icelandic study was funded by grants from the Icelandic Research Council and the University of Iceland's Research Fund. The Australian study, *Living Safer Sexual Lives* was funded by a grant from the Victorian Health Promotion Foundation. We thank the women with intellectual disabilities who spent time with us and spoke with us about motherhood and family life.

REFERENCES

Andron, L. and Tymchuk, A. (1987) 'Parents who are mentally retarded', in A. Craft (ed.) *Mental Handicap and Sexuality: Issues and Perspectives*, D. J. Costello, Tunbridge Wells.

Asch, A. and Fine, M. (1992) 'Beyond pedestals: revisiting the lives of women with disability', in M. Fine (ed.) *Disruptive Voices: The Possibilities of Feminist Research*, University of Michigan Press, USA.

Booth, T. and Booth, W. (1994) *Parenting Under Pressure: Mothers and Fathers with Learning Difficulties*, Open University Press, Milton Keynes.

Booth, T. and Booth, W. (1998) *Growing Up With Parents Who Have Learning Difficulties*, Routledge, London.

Brantlinger, E. (1995) *Sterilisation of People with Mental Disabilities: Issues, Perspectives, and Cases*, Auburn House, CT, USA.

Browne, S., Connors, D. and Stern, N. (eds.) (1985) *With the Power of Each Breath: A Disabled Women's Anthology*, Cleis Press, San Francisco, CA, USA.

Dowrick, S. and Grundberg, S. (1980) *Why Children?*, The Women's Press, London.

Feldman, M. (1986) 'Research on parenting by mentally retarded parents', *Psychiatric Clinics of North America*, 9(4): 777–96.

Feldman, M. (1994) 'Parenting education for parents with intellectual disabilities: a review of outcome studies', *Research in Developmental Disabilities*, 15(4): 299–332.

Gilligan, C. (1993) *In a Different Voice: Psychological Theory and Women's Development*, Harvard University Press, Cambridge, MA, USA.

Hammersley, M. and Atkinson, P. (1994) *Ethnography: Principles in Practice*, Tavistock, London.

Johnson, K. (1998a) *Deinstitutionalising Women: An Ethnographic Study of Institutional Closure*, Cambridge University Press, Melbourne, Australia.

Johnson, K. (1998b) 'Deinstitutionalisation: the management of rights', *Disability & Society*, 13(3): 375–87.

Johnson, K., Hillier, L. and Harrison, L. (1999) *Living Safer Sexual Lives: People With Intellectual Disability and Sexuality*, paper presented at the Psychology and Law Conference, July 6–9 1999, Trinity College, Dublin.

Keith, L. (1994) *Mustn't Grumble: Writing By Disabled Women*, The Women's Press, London.

Keltner, B., Wise, L., and Taylor, G. (1999) 'Mothers with intellectual limitations and their 2-year-old children's developmental outcomes', *Journal of Intellectual & Developmental Disability*, 24(1): 45–57.

Llewellyn, G. (1993) 'Parents with intellectual disability: facts, fallacies and professional responsibilities', *Community Bulletin*, 17(1): 10–19.

Llewellyn, G. (1994) 'Generic family support services: are parents with learning disabilities catered for?', *Mental Handicap Research*, 7(1): 64–77.

Llewellyn, G. (1995) 'Relationships and social support: views of parents with mental retardation/intellectual disability', *Mental Retardation*, 33(6): 349–63.

McCarthy, M. (1999) *Sexuality and Women with Learning Disabilities*, Jessica Kingsley, London.

Melberg Schwier, K. (1994) *Couples with Intellectual Disabilities Talk about Living and Loving*, Woodbine House, Rockville, MD, USA.

Millear, A. with Johnson, K. (2000) 'Thirty-nine months under the Disability Discrimination Act, in R. Traustadóttir and K. Johnson (eds.), *Women with Intellectual Disabilities: Finding a Place in the World*, Jessica Kingsley, London.

Morris, J. (1991) *Pride Against Prejudice: Transforming Attitudes to Disability*, New Society, Philadelphia, PA, USA.

Oakley, A. (1980) *Becoming a Mother*, Schocken Books, New York, USA.

Pixa-Kettner, U. (1999) 'Follow-up study on parenting with intellectual disability in Germany', *Journal of Intellectual & Developmental Disability*, 24(1): 75–93.

Potts, M. and Fido, R. (1991) *A Fit Person To Be Removed: Personal Accounts Of Life In a Mental Deficiency Institution*, Northcote House, Plymouth.

Rich, A. (1979a) 'Motherhood in bondage', in A. Rich, *On Lies, Secrets, and Silence: Selected Prose 1966–1978*, W.W. Norton & Co., New York, USA.

Rich, A. (1979b) 'Motherhood: the contemporary emergency and the quantum leap', in A. Rich, *On Lies, Secrets, and Silence: Selected Prose 1966–1978*, W. W. Norton & Co., New York, USA.

Rose, N. (1979) 'The psychological complex: mental measurement and social administration', *Ideology and Consciousness*, 5: 5–68.

Scheerenberger, R. (1983) *A History of Mental Retardation*, Paul H. Brookes, Baltimore, USA.

Sigurjónsdóttir, H. and Traustadóttir, R. (2000) 'Motherhood, family and community life', in R. Traustadóttir and K. Johnson (eds.), *Women with Intellectual Disabilities: Finding a Place In The World*, Jessica Kingsley, London.

Slattery, J. with Johnson, K. (2000) 'Family, marriage, friends and work: this is my life'. In, R. Traustadóttir and K. Johnson (eds.), *Women with Intellectual Disabilities: Finding a Place In The World*, Jessica Kingsley, London.

Taylor, S. and Bogdan, R. (1998) *Introduction to Qualitative Research Methods: A Guidebook and Resource* (3rd revised edition), John Wiley and Sons, New York, USA.

Traustadóttir, R. and Sigurjónsdóttir, H. (1998) *Umdeildar fjölskyldur: Seinfærir/*

roskaheftir foreldrar og börn eirra [Contested Families: Parents with Intellectual Disabilities and their Children] Félagsvísindastofnun Háskóla Íslands, Reykjavík.

Trent, J. (1994) *Inventing the Feeble Mind: A History of Mental Retardation in the United States,* University of California Press, Berkeley, USA.

Walmsley, J. (2000) 'Caring: a place in the world?', in R. Traustadóttir and K. Johnson (eds.), *Women with Intellectual Disabilities: Finding a Place In The World,* Jessica Kingsley, London

Walmsley, J. and Downer J. (1997) 'Shouting the loudest: self advocacy, power and diversity', in P. Ramcharan, G. Roberts, G. Grant and J. Borland (eds.) *Empowerment in Everyday Life: Learning Disability,* Jessica Kingsley, London.

Wates, M. and Jade, R. (eds.) (1999) *Bigger Than the Sky: Disabled Women On Parenting,* The Women's Press, London.

18 Ageing with disability in Japan

Miho Iwakuma

The world is rapidly 'greying' due to an increasingly ageing population. From ancient times, humans have dreamed of longevity and eternal youth. Thanks to medical advancements, life expectancy has drastically increased, and one half of our wishes are almost granted. Now, we are no longer satisfied with merely living longer, we expect to stay healthy and independent too. The rapid growth of an ageing population has resulted in much general interest in ageing, and there is now an abundance of research pertaining to ageing and disability. As one might expect, this is because a perfect correlation exists between population age and the number of people with impairments (Coni *et al.* 1992).

Ageing takes places in cultural milieus. Different cultures, with different traditions and customs, mirror various ageing realities (Hashimoto 1993; Sennet and Czarniecki 1991). Although the 'greying' phenomenon can be seen in many developed nations, Japanese society is facing a tougher challenge, because population ageing here is coupled with decreasing birth rates and an increasing number of nuclear families (Hashimoto 1993). In fact, life expectancy for the Japanese, especially for women, is the longest in the world at 83.1 years (Freed 1990) and many elderly Japanese have disabilities.

Although the population of Japanese with impairments constitutes 4.8 per cent of the total population, ageing has become a prominent topic (Sori-fu 1998). A national poll, taken by the Japanese government, illustrates a sharp generational divide (Sori-fu 1998). In the last forty years, the number of Japanese with impairments per thousand has doubled, while the number of those aged under 50 has actually decreased. By 1996, 67 per cent of all Japanese with physical impairments were over 60. Consequently, ageing issues cannot be discussed fully without considering disability, and vice versa.

In the post-war era, more and more disabled people have survived into old age. Due to prolonged life expectancy, the significant population of disabled Second World War veterans, the large number of polio survivors from the 1940s and 1950s, and many other reasons, the phenomenon of ageing with disability has become more visible only in the last 15 to 20 years (Zarb and Oliver 1993). For example, in the USA, about 24 per cent of persons with spinal cord injury have now survived for more than twenty years, and 20 per cent of these people are now older than 61 (Menter 1993). They face a new challenge – of ageism in addition to 'ableism'.

So far, however, interest in ageing and disability has focused on age-related impairments; that is, impairment as a consequence of ageing or the effect of impairment on the ageing process. The other side of the 'disability and ageing' equation, ageing with disability, has rarely been discussed or studied (*see* Zarb and Oliver 1993). Both groups of people have similar needs in later life: fewer stairs in buildings, kerb cuts on the pavements, and accessible public transportation (Quinn 1998). More-over, many disabled adults will increasingly 'blend in' as they age, for example people with visual impairments in elderly residential homes, where most people have some difficulty with sight (Hey 1987). As Simon (1988: 218) argues (in relation to never-married disabled women), 'unlike other key rites of passage . . . disability in old age is all-inclusive. No group is left out'.

However, the paths leading to ageing by disabled and non-disabled adults are different. In short, despite a great interest in ageing in Japan, the USA and elsewhere, research on the ageing of disabled people is severely limited. Until the Second World War, people who were severely injured had little hope of survival. This fact was especially true for individuals who incurred high lesions on the spinal cord (Menter 1993). The war created, for the first time in human history, a 'body' of paralysed people (Kemp and Krause 1999; Crewe 1990). Since then, medical and mechanical innovations have helped people not only survive but also to live longer and healthier lives. Currently, it is estimated that individuals with spinal cord injury (hereafter, referred to as SCI) live an average of thirty to forty years after the injury (Samsa, G. *et al.* 1993; Whiteneck *et al.* 1992). In the past fifty years, post-SCI life expectancy of people has increased by 2,000 per cent (Whiteneck *et al.* 1992) while the increase in life expectancy for the non-disabled popula-tion is only 30 per cent (Kemp and Krause 1999). Consequently, and not surprisingly, people with disabilities themselves have become more interested in ageing issues.

Undoubtedly, the fast ageing rate of Japanese society contributes to the large portion of elderly disabled people. However, the aged-with-disability population remains largely invisible, as they merge with the population of those with age-related impairments (Simon 1988). A study by Ando *et al.* (1992) took a rare look at the situation of aged/

ageing Japanese with SCI, suggesting that there were approximately 66,000 Japanese people with SCI and that more than half were older than 50. As in Western countries, traffic accidents (e.g. motorbike injuries) are the leading cause of SCI among young people. However, contrary to popular perception, and unlike the West, in Japan more than half of people with SCI acquire the injury after the age of 50 (Ando *et al.* 1992).

In this chapter, I investigate the previously under-researched topic of ageing with disability in Japan. In particular, I will attempt to explain what it is like to be Japanese with impairments (particularly spinal cord injuries) and to age in Japanese culture.

The study

I interviewed more than thirty Japanese people with physical impairments, in Japan. The participants were recruited at a local rehabilitation hospital, recreation centre, and through a network of personal connections. Most of the participants have paralyses due to spinal cord injuries and use wheelchairs, while others are amputees, but can walk. Their ages vary from 17 to older than 70. There was, however, a gender imbalance. Only three were women. This discrepancy reflects the population of people with SCI in general. Indeed, more than 70 per cent of people with SCI are men (Quinn 1998).

After obtaining the permission of the participants to take part in the study, I made appointments to interview them. Most of the interviews were conducted on a one-to-one basis. However, I sometimes decided to hold small group interviews (not more than three people) where some of the individuals were the newly disabled. I felt strongly that listening to others and sharing stories of disability would be beneficial to those who felt uncertainty for the future. As Deegan (1991: 53) asserts, ' . . . very often a disabled person who is only a few "steps" ahead of another person can be more effective than one whose achievements seem overly impressive and distanced'. All the interviews were tape-recorded, and transcribed.

I used a phenomenological method in analysing the interviews. Phenomenology is both philosophy and method. French phenomenologist, Merleau-Ponty (1962: vii) explains:

Phenomenology is the study of essences; and according to it, all problems amount to finding definitions of essences . . . but phenomenology is also a philosophy which puts essences back to existence, and does not expect to arrive at an understanding of man and the world from any starting point other than that of their "facticity". It is a transcendental philosophy which places in abeyance the assertions arising out of the natural attitude, the better to understand them; but it is also a philosophy for which the world is always 'already there' before reflection begins – as an inalienable presence; and all its efforts are concentrated upon re-achieving a direct and primitive contact with the world, and endowing that contact with a philosophical status. It is the search for a philosophy which shall be a 'rigorous science', but it also offers an account of space, time, and the world as we 'live' them. It tries to give a direct description of our experience as it is . . .

Toombs (1992, p. xi) calls phenomenology an 'essentially reflective enterprise' and illustrates its purpose as letting 'what is given appear as pure phenomenon (the thing-as-meant) and to work to describe the invariant features of such phenomena'. Phenomenological method is widely employed not only in various social science areas, but also in paramedical fields, such as nursing (Carpenter 1995). My own approach followed analytical steps developed by Colaizzi (1978). The procedure can be summarised as follows:

- description of the phenomena of interest by the researcher
- collection of subjects' descriptions of the phenomena
- reading all the subjects' descriptions of the phenomena
- returning to the original transcripts and extracting significant statements
- trying to spell out the meaning of each significant statement
- organising the aggregate formalised meanings into clusters of themes
- writing an exhaustive description
- returning to the subjects for validation of the descriptions
- if new data are revealed, incorporating them into an exhaustive description.

The remaining sections of this chapter address six recurring themes on ageing, revealed through the analysis of the interview transcripts within this approach.

Time has stopped since the accident

Most of the participants acquired their impairments through accidents (e.g. traffic or sports accidents). Sudden disabling incidents vividly divided their lives into pre-injury and post-injury times. I twice interviewed a young man with quadriplegia who acquired his impairment at the age of 20. The interviews took place in the first and second years after the accident. In the first year, I heard that he was so fearful of being seen by others that he never went outside his home, even to the porch. When he was exercising at the rehabilitation hospital, he fainted several times. He was quiet, pale, and still struggling to manage his 'new' body. In the second year, he was attending a vocational/rehabilitation school in a different prefecture. He had lost pounds by smoking, met other youths with similar impairments, and was learning how to put a wheelchair into a car, the last step to gaining 'jiritsu' (independence). During the interview he said, 'Time has stopped since I was 20. I forgot another birthday came around. A birthday card sent to the hospital reminded me that a year had passed'.

Another participant who has had quadriplegia for more than ten years also felt that 'I can't think of the future when I become 60. It feels like time has stopped since I was 39 (since the accident)'. As these statements illustrate, becoming disabled not only alters our physical state, but may also alter our conception of time and life course progression.

How much will I be able to move around?

All the participants in the study were 'healthy' enough to come to the local hospital or recreation centre to play sports, or to study at the vocational school. This was true for both the young and the old. Yet many expressed a vague concern for the future. The most common expression was 'How much will I be able to move around in the future?', which seemed to assume greater physical restriction with age. A male amputee, and competitive wheelchair basketball player, said:

I can foresee that ageing will cause some problems on my legs. Although now I am walking with ease, basically I rely on a prosthesis to walk . . . When I'm hopping around without it (prosthesis), I sometimes wonder if I can still do this when I become 50 or 70.

However, many participants eased their concern when they saw older people with impairments. A man with quadriplegia commented:

I sometimes wonder how much I'll be able to move around when aged. I sense that the age of 50 is still OK by seeing others. Seeing seniors with disabilities can give me some idea about what I will become in future.

In Japan, disabled people are still rarely seen in public places or in the mass media. The local rehabilitation hospital is one of the few places where disabled people see older individuals with impairments. Another participant stated that:

When I went to the rehab. hospital, I saw a man in his 60s. But he was quite active, pushing a chair, putting the chair into a car, and driving it. Besides, he was at the hospital to play tennis. Seeing that older man in wheelchair convinced me that I'll be fine when I become his age.

Those participants who played sports seemed to have more opportunities to see older individuals with impairments as role models with whom they could identify. For example, one of the participants played wheelchair tennis, she was one of the best players in Japan. Like others, she expressed uncertainty, but 'not a terror', for the future. She too witnessed an older disabled woman who still played wheelchair tennis, and felt that 'I'd be fine 'till her age'. From these statements, it seems that intergenerational contacts between younger and older disabled people may contribute to reducing anxiety, and to presenting a more realistic picture of the future.

We age differently than the non-disabled

As stated earlier, most non-disabled people develop age-related impairments in later life, and thus become a part of the disabled population. Most adults, with and without impairments, eventually become part of the same cohort of elderly disabled people. However, many of the participants perceived that they would age differently from their non-disabled counterparts: 'I sense our ageing process is not the same as the non-disableds'. Another participant agreed that there was a fundamental difference in the ageing process between disabled people and non-disabled people, although he could not pinpoint what it was. One of the participants, a male amputee who had been a representative of the Japanese wheelchair basketball team, articulated the difference as follows:

Ageing with disability and acquiring disability as a result of ageing are completely different. (This is because) people who acquired disability in younger years would have a whole life ahead of them (and therefore would) be able to think more positively, and be given more opportunities to fulfil their wishes in life.

This kind of comment echoes with the next theme, that disabled people may be better prepared for ageing.

We are better prepared for it (ageing)

Ageing is often accompanied by increasing physical difficulties and, in a sense, becoming old is a gradual expansion of one's 'disabledness'. During the interviews, I asked a question about ageing with disability and encountering disability with old age. In this context, many of the participants mentioned their 'readiness' for ageing compared to the non-disabled population. For my part, I also feel that becoming disabled in younger years is easier in terms of ageing than the double jeopardy of becoming disabled when older. As they age, non-disabled people begin to experience the difficulties that we encounter daily. As one of the participants commented:

(I have) no fear of ageing . . . The non-disabled don't know how to live with physical difficulties or disability, whereas we already know it. Non-disabled people need to learn how to get around physical barriers (when they age), which makes them worried. But we, who are already in wheelchairs, have experienced those barriers and know how to deal with them. The non-disabled must be fearful of ageing (because) what they worry about most is being in a wheelchair.

In line with this comment, some of the participants implied that disabled people not only age differently from non-disabled people, but that they also age better. For example, one man with paraplegia was convinced that:

(People with disabilities) age differently. I think people like us with disabilities and being involved with society can have a better later life than the non-disabled would. [researcher: Because you do sports?] Doing sports is one thing. But I feel the disabled appreciate meeting others better than the non-disabled. I always think I'll be able to have a happier golden age than the non-disabled.

Concerns for the family

About half of the participants were married. Some had married after acquiring their impairments. Spouses were often the primary caregivers. Few of the families used any kind of public assistance, such as case-workers or visiting nurses, despite providing around-the-clock care. This is because the disability phenomenon in Japan, including care giving, is regarded as a private matter rather than a social matter, although there have been changes to this view in recent years. When I asked people about ageing, many expressed concerns for the family first, rather than for themselves.

I think the physical deterioration of the disabled goes faster than the non-disabled's. Besides, the caregiver (my wife) ages with me. I worry for the time when I can no longer lift myself up. By that time, my wife won't have strength to help me. So, I decided to train myself so that at least I can support my weight 'til I die.

Another man, whose impairment was the most severe among the participants in the study, was most concerned for his wife. He has used an electric wheelchair with a joystick since the accident, (in which his daughter had died). He could not eat, bathe, or change his clothes by himself. Everywhere he went, so did his wife and he clearly asserted that his fate was dependent upon her. He said, 'As a caregiver ages, I will become less mobile and active since there are very few things I can do by myself. I literally cannot live without my wife'.

I once witnessed another man with quadriplegia, carried on his wife's tiny back when transferring to a car or entering his home. He told me that before the accident, he had been a 'typical' Japanese artisan, who hardly spoke to his wife. After the accident, however, he and his wife started to communicate more often and better. When I interviewed the husband in the kitchen at his home, his wife was cooking in the same room. He answered the questions with deep, and sincere, appreciation – while also reflecting the gender expectations that exist in Japanese society:

The only wish I have is my wife won't go before me. That's it . . . I heard regular institutions never have a person like me with a bladder path. Doctors don't want to be responsible for any mishaps. So, the families are providing difficult care . . . I hope I can stay at home as long as possible, being taken care by my wife. Both of our kids are boys and it will be too much for their wives. When my wife went back to her family in the I- prefecture for 2 weeks, we decided to have a home-helper during the period. But she was useless (compared to my wife), although she said she was very experienced in nursing the severely disabled people.

Felt no fear of ageing

Before conducting the interviews, I had expected that most of the participants would have a strong concern or fear about ageing. To my surprise, however, I repeatedly heard the opposite. Many of the participants had gone through experiences at death's door, especially during the acute stage of acquiring their impairment. After these experiences and upheavals, many expressed the view that 'ageing is nothing'. Some mentioned themes like, 'the second life' or 'giving up *to hope*' (I will clarify this term later). One man told me that he had begun to think about ageing when he had met older people with impairments and heard their stories. However, even he, with the most severe impairments, did not express any fear of ageing.

I don't feel any fear particularly. We'll deal with it when something comes up. When my wife no longer can take care of me, we'll ask for a paid caregiver. And if hiring someone becomes impossible, I wouldn't mind going to some institution. So, I have no fear. I have already made up my mind.

When I asked him whether he felt no fear because he already experienced the inconveniences that non-disabled people would encounter when they age, he said:

Exactly [laugh]. (Without waiting for ageing,) I'm surrounded by so many difficulties already. I can't do anything. I can't even scratch myself. But I'm already used to this physical state. I can understand why people usually fear ageing because they are fearful of losing physical independence. But for my case, the only thing I have control over is my mouth. So, I already know what it is like to be old and less mobile. It can't get worse than this [laugh].

He added that he was unlikely to experience any physical deterioration because he hardly moved anyway. Another participant with severe quadriplegia also used the 'it can't get worse than this' theme. Another had been challenged twice, by cancer and by the accident in which he acquired his impairment. He felt that he had been given an extra gift to live after these incidents.

I had had gastric cancer before I became the disabled. A doctor told my family that I'd live only six more months. They told me what the doctor said, and I agonised a lot and gave up . . . So, I once gave up living. (This is why) the accident didn't devastate me that much. I gave up to hope, do my best. I was injured during that period. Although I sunk for a while (when injured), I came back soon because I had made up my mind.

Another man expressed his feeling:

I don't have any fear of ageing. I was told twice that I wouldn't make it. When I was injured and carried to the K hospital, they did nothing to me because they thought I would die soon anyway. But an orthopaedic doctor looked at me and said, 'It's his neck. We can save his life' . . . So, I feel no fear of ageing. The second time was when I had an operation on my bladder. 'You won't make it', the doctor told me at the bedside . . . Others say they are fearful of dying, but I have a so-what attitude. I'm ready for it . . . I have already encountered the toughest challenges. No worry. No regrets even if I have to go tomorrow.

Conclusions

Today, Japan leads the world in ageing. Life expectancy of the Japanese, especially that of Japanese women, is the longest in the world. Disabled people are also living longer than ever as medical technologies advance. However, the overwhelming number of aged non-disabled people largely overshadows this population. In this chapter, I have tried to uncover this 'hidden' ageing population by asking how Japanese people with physical impairments perceive ageing, and to what extent acquiring an impairment affects their ageing experiences.

Without doubt, acquiring impairment has turned these participants' lives around. For some, disability has changed their sense of temporality. Charmaz (1997: 4) demonstrates that experiencing chronic illness can drastically alter one's self and perception about the flow of time. She contends that, '. . . meanings are imbedded in experiences of time . . . both meanings of illness and self take root in subjectively experienced duration of time . . .', because, 'living with serious illness and disability can catapult people into a separate reality – with its own rules, rhythm, and tempo. Time changes – drastically'. Time is no longer an ironclad objective entity, but can 'drag on' or 'fly' depending upon the condition of the self.

Some participants, especially those with severe impairments, expressed a strong sense of unity with their spouses as they talked about ageing issues. This was not surprising, as they relied heavily on their help. Interestingly, many participants felt that their ageing path differed from their non-disabled peers because of their 'disabledness'. While many mentioned a 'readiness' for ageing, others pointed to their attentiveness to the body. Most of the participants were people with paralyses, and had become very conscious of their physical state since acquiring their impairments. This was perhaps because they had had to learn how to pick up subtle bodily signals (e.g. bowel movement or a rise of body temperature). Some had developed a custom of observing the whole body everyday, using a mirror to detect the slightest sign of a bedsore, or any kind of abnormality. This may account for the embodied way in which they also spoke about ageing.

Many of the participants felt that disabled people are better equipped for later life *because of their disability experiences*. Most surprisingly, many, even those with the most severe impairments, felt no fear of ageing. Frequently they uttered 'kakugo ga dekiteiru' ('I already made up my mind'), 'hiraki naotteru' ('[I have] so-what attitude') or 'akirame ga tuita' ('I gave up *to hope*') as they talked about ageing with disability. This last expression seems to be contradictory and benefits from some explanation.

Deegan (1991: 50) asserts that the recovery process is 'marked by an ever-deepening acceptance of our limitations . . . in accepting what we cannot do or be, we begin to discover who we can be and what we can do'. The participants who commented in this way seemed to be adjusting to disability by giving up what they used to be and what they were able to do. By letting the pre-injury time go, they started to see a new life with hope.

Such statements were grounded in confidence and pride that they had survived the traumatic experiences of acquiring impairment. As one participant summed up, 'nothing in the world scares me anymore'. The participants had different immediate experiences of the lived-world (or *Lebenswelt* in phenomenology) from that of non-disabled people, in terms of their perceptions toward ageing and ageing phenomena. Acquiring disability has provided a new 'horizon' from which to view the surrounding world. Many participants perceived that being disabled positively affected the ageing process. Finally, this study is important because it has listened to the rarely heard voices of disabled people.

REFERENCES

Ando, T., Hasegawa, Y., Mizuochi, K. and Hayashi, T. (1992) 'Korei sekizui-sonshosha' [Aged people with spinal cord injuries] *Rehabilitation Kenkyu*, 73: 9–14.

Carpenter, D. R. (1995) 'Phenomenological research approach', in H. J. Streubert & D. R. Carpenter (eds.), *Qualitative Research in Nursing*,: J. B. Lippincott Company, Philadelphia PA, USA.

Charmaz, K. (1997) *Good Days, Bad Days*, Rutgers University Press, New Brunswick, NJ, USA.

Colaizzi, P. (1978) 'Psychological research as the phenomenologist views it', in R. Vails and M. King (eds.) *Existential Phenomenological Alternatives for Psychology*, Oxford University Press, New York, USA.

Coni, N., Davidson, W. and Webster, S. (1992) *Ageing: The Facts*, Oxford University Press, Oxford.

Crewe, N. M. (1990). 'Ageing and severe physical disability: patterns of change and implications for service', *International Disability Studies*, 13: 158–61.

Deegan, P. E. (1991) 'Recovery: the lived experience of rehabilitation', in R. P. Marinelli and A. E. Dell Orto (eds.) *The Psychological and Social Impact of Disability*, Spring Publishing, New York, USA.

Freed, A. O. (1990) 'How Japanese families cope with fragile elderly', *Journal of Gerontological Social Work*, 15: 39–56.

Hashimoto, A. (1993) 'Family relations in later life: a cross-cultural perspectives', *Generations*, 17: 24–6.

Hey, S. C. (1987) 'Severe visual impairment, aging, and stigma: an investigation of the relationship between impairment and stigma in later life', in S. C. Hey, G. Kiger and J. Seidel (eds.), *Impaired and Disabled People in Society: Structure, Processes and the Individual*, The Society for Disability Studies/ Willamette University, Salem, OR, USA.

Kemp, B. J. and Krause, J. S. (1999) 'Depression and life satisfaction among people ageing with post-polio and spinal cord injury', *Disability and Rehabilitation*, 21: 241–9.

Menter, R. R. (1993) 'Issues of ageing with spinal cord injury', in G. G. Whiteneck, S. W. Charlifue, K. A. Gerhart, D. P. Lammertse, S. Manley, R. R. Menter and K. R. Seedroff (eds.) *Ageing With Spinal Cord Injury*, Demos Publication, New York, USA.

Merleau-Ponty, M. (1962) *Phenomenology of Perception* [C. Smith, trans.], Humanities Press, New York, USA.

Quinn, P. (1998) *Understanding Disability: A Lifespan Approach*, Sage, Thousand Oaks, CA, USA.

Samsa, G. P., Patrick, C. H. and Feussner, J. R. (1993) 'Long-term survival of veterans with traumatic spinal cord injury', *Archives of Neurology*, 50: 909–15.

Sori-fu (1998) *Shogaisha hakusho* [A people with disabilities white paper] Okurasho Press, Tokyo, Japan.

Sennett, D. (ed.). (1991) *Vital Signs: International Stories on Ageing*, Graywolf Press, Saint Paul, MA, USA.

Simon, B. L. (1988) 'Never-married old women and disability: a majority experience', in M. Fine and A. Asch (eds.) *Women With Disabilities: Essays in Psychology, Culture, and Politics*, Temple University Press, Philadelphia, PA, USA.

Toombs, S. K. (1992) *The Meaning of Illness*, Kluwer, Dordrecht, Netherlands.

Whiteneck, G. Charlifue, S., Frankel, H., Fraser, M., Gardner, P., Gerhart, K., Krishnam, R., Menter, R., Nuseibeh, I. and Short, J. (1992) 'Mortality, morbidity and psychological outcomes of persons with spinal cord injured more than 20 years ago', *Paraplegia*, 30: 617–30.

Zarb, G. and Oliver, M. (1993) *Ageing With a Disability: What Do They Expect After All These Years?*, University of Greenwich, London.

19   Ageing with intellectual disabilities; discovering disability with old age: same or different?

Nancy Breitenbach

It has become a truism to say that people are growing older. Nevertheless it is worthwhile to repeat the information: life expectancy has increased substantially in the past fifty years. Worldwide, the average longevity of men has increased by fourteen years since 1955, while women have gained eighteen years. Today, in industrialised countries, men commonly reach their mid-70s and women their 80s. Many of these older people have impairments: in Europe, for example, approximately 70 per cent of the disabled population are now over 60 years old.

People with life-long disabilities are enjoying longer lives too. Those for whom increased life expectancy is particularly spectacular are people with intellectual disabilities (Hogg *et al.* 1988; Janicki and Seltzer 1991; Janicki and Breitenbach 2000). This trend is illustrated in Table 19.1, which includes life expectancy figures drawn from a variety of sources.

Who could doubt that these added years are an advantage? For people regarded as 'slow learners', longer lives should mean greater opportunities for constructive training and life experience, more time to achieve self-determination. However this apparently positive development is also placing people with intellectual disabilities in increasing competition with other populations, for shrinking resources, and is bringing some fundamental issues to the fore. In essence, we need to ask whether

Table 19.1. *Evolution of average life expectancy (in years, men/women)*

Date	World average	Average in France	Average for Down's Syndrome	Average for all people with ID
1929–30			9	20/22
1947			13.5	
1955	48			
1996–97			60/64	70/74
2000	62/66	75/82		

older people with life-long disabilities and those who acquire them later in life have anything in common? It is a surprising question since, in many countries, the two groups are regarded as quite different from one another.

Forever young, old before their time

For centuries people with intellectual disabilities have been considered as eternal children, not only because of labelling based on their level of 'cognitive maturity', but because no one ever noticed them reaching old age. A great many did not live beyond early childhood (even today, only a fraction of African children born with an intellectual disability reach the age of five years). If some blended into the general population as low-grade manual labourers, most survivors lived out their lives unseen behind the opaque walls of their parents' homes, or those of institutions. Today their ability to live longer lives is widely acknowledged and new questions arise: at what age do people with intellectual disabilities become 'old'? Then again, at what point in time does *anyone* begin to age?

If one believes the advertisements published by the cosmetics industry, young women can be marked by the signs of age before they have even started their careers. On the other hand, if one reads the literature produced by the grey panthers, life 'begins' at 60. Part of the solution to the paradox lies in the fact that 'ageing' is relative. People who remain perfectly fit for many years may still feel young, but will nevertheless be considered old compared to others.

How do we become aware of our age as it increases? Besides a cognitive ability to master abstract notions such as number and time, realisation of age depends on access to mirrored images of the self. An obvious example is the glassy surface we encounter every morning, as we prepare our bodies for others to look at. The reflection under the harsh light in the lavatory is cruelly honest: one can see each morning the price paid for the day before. However, this intimate mirror does not provide a word for the transformations incurred. The naming comes when we affront the gaze of others, who inform us that what is happening is called 'ageing'. They will also probably infer that this ageing is not a positive development. The message is reinforced by the media which value youth and beauty, telling us to run to the chemist's to purchase colours and creams, to the gym to sweat and swim, in order to hold back the process.

A third mirror balances out the second, providing more positive feedback on our social progress. We are aware of a coherent cycle of events, telling us that we are moving forward in time: the beginning and the end of our education, entry into professional life, commitment to a sexual partner, the arrival and raising of children, various forms of social or financial advancement, grandchildren, retirement . . . This social calendar has a certain sequence to it (retirement does not, after all, occur at the age of 25, no matter how much we would like things to happen that way). Everyone knows that a certain age suits each step along the way, and the more the cycle advances, the older one gets. There will be losses as well as gains in this social curve, but the overall image is one of lifetime fulfilment.

We need to ask how people with intellectual disabilities obtain access to the same kinds of feedback. Do all people recognise and understand the meaning of the signs in the lavatory mirror? Do companions (not to speak of passers-by in the street) look at people with intellectual disabilities frankly, and inform them that they bear the signs of time? What access do they have to the life experiences that tell us we are moving on and that there is an end to all things?

Unfortunately, the perception of people with intellectual disability as immature, no matter what their age, persists in many minds and in everyday language. Families, even professionals who are years younger than the clientele they meet every day, continue to imagine them as not quite grown up . . . yet. So, even those who reach respectable ages are rarely perceived as 'old'. When their true age is finally acknowledged, it comes as a surprise.

Paradoxically, there is a popular conception that people with intellectual disabilities age prematurely. This idea is quite persistent, despite research that demonstrates more and more consistently how only a minority evolve in this way. One wonders why such images stick in people's minds. Is it an echo of the mortality rates of the past? Is it a reminder that people with intellectual disability have seldom gotten their fair share, covering a call for compensation? Or does the idea fulfil some more sinister wish?

As they grow older, people with intellectual disabilities are likely to incur a number of age-related illnesses or impairments, just as do other older people. As a result, despite the fact that many issues related to their old age (as well as to their disability) are of a social nature, much of the published literature is devoted to health and illness issues. This medical model applied to later life is consistent with approaches to ageing more generally. For more than a century now, physicians and biologists have studied everything that can deteriorate in the course of ageing (more so than what holds strong). Innumerable remedies have been prescribed to slow the process. Some, like cataract surgery, hip prostheses and various pharmaceuticals, significantly improve quality of life; others, like cosmetic surgery, are designed essentially to help the patient respond to social pressures. Few would argue with the advantages of modern medicine. It is important to remember, however, that as the medical professions control the field of gerontology, increased life expectancy may signify the return in force of their model to the field of disability.

Different profiles, separate paths

In the past, people with intellectual disabilities could be found in general, catchall institutions (in workhouses with the poor and the indigent; in long-stay hospitals beside the mentally ill and the demented elderly). Now these various groups are set on separate paths, through the distinctions of targeted service design. Contemporary support services for younger people with disabilities were established to rehabilitate (i.e. to bring disabled adults into the work force) whereas social security measures for older people were conceived to prevent poverty when workers' professional lives had ended.

Approaches to provision across the generations vary. In countries where institutions for people with intellectual disabilities have been downsized, to bring this population back into the community, large retirement communities and congregate care for the dependent elderly may still remain the norm. The opposite may equally well occur: families may be encouraged to abandon their disabled children to the state, yet be expected to care for their elders at home.

The social imagery of disability and old age differs in many ways. So long as elderly persons were a rarity, their white hair and wrinkles communicated a message of wisdom, acquired through experience and resilience. One had to be smart and tough to survive that long. This still applies in some cultures today. Contemporary industrialised society, however, has little tolerance for old age. The same bodily signs are now taken to mean that one's knowledge is out of date and that one is probably retired (i.e. drawing on society's resources rather than contributing to them). Ageing is seen as counter-productive, a malady, which should be delayed for as long as possible. Today, those identified as 'people with disabilities' have a future, in that they are perceived as still being capable of progress. 'Elderly people' do not have a future, since they appear only to decline. Because once old age has set in, it is 'too late'.

According to Henri-Jacques Stiker (1999), 'The disabled . . . offend, because they threaten the image we have of our tidy little identities as

Table 19.2. *The parallel myths of disability and old age*

Disabled people	Older people
It is abnormal to be disabled.	It is abnormal to be old.
Disabled people share the same experiences.	Older people are all the same.
Disabled people are marginalised.	Older people are inevitably lonely.
Disabled people are sexless.	Older people have no sexual desire.
Disabled people all age prematurely.	Older people all age the same way.
Disabled people are fragile.	Older people are frail.
Disabled people contribute nothing.	Older people have nothing left to contribute.
Disabled people cost money.	Older people are an economic burden on society.
Disabled people live on the edge of vulnerability.	Older people are one step away from mortality.

people in possession of their faculties, as useful, profit-bringing workers . . .'. Old age too threatens this image and negative imagery of old age is widespread. During the International Year of Older Persons (1999), the World Health Organization (1999) distributed a colourful document summing up the myths regarding people aged 60 or more, as follows:
- most older people live in developed countries
- older people are all the same
- men and women age the same way
- older people are frail
- older people have nothing to contribute
- older people are an economic burden on society.

Each of these myths is easily challenged by the facts, yet such myths persist. Consequently, when people with intellectual disabilities grow older, they may find that the devalued social image that they have borne all their lives is compounded by the devalued social images of old age. Aligning the myths associated with disability and old age shows how easy it is to accumulate negative images (*see* Table 19.2).

The risk of 'double jeopardy' is not simply theoretical (Walker *et al.* 1996). A recent study by Walker and Walker (1998) showed how ingrained ideas about older people can have direct effects on the way that service providers respond to clients' needs. The authors describe how two common conceptions (a) that physical and mental decline are 'normal' as people grow older and (b) that older people 'normally' withdraw from social life, influenced service provision. Specifically:

- Staff tended to anticipate the decline of their older clients, neglecting to identify any problems they associated with the ageing process, despite the fact that remedies could be provided, at least to improve the person's comfort;
- Staff assumed that the stimulation of existing abilities was useless, since sooner or later such capacities were bound to disappear;
- Staff reduced opportunities for social interaction and activity, under the assumption that the older people were no longer interested;
- Staff lost their motivation for work, assuming that no progress was possible for the older people and that even progress made in the past was doomed to evaporate.

The implication is that abandonment becomes a very real prospect, and must be counteracted in advance.

Roots and offshoots

Despite the fact that many older people have age-related impairments, they do not necessarily perceive themselves as 'disabled'. Late-life impairments are considered as add-ons; that is, they are not deemed to influence the fundamental identity of an 'older' person even though they may determine the person's quality of life.

In contrast, people with life-long impairments are more likely to be 'disability-rooted' (Turnbull and Turnbull 1999). Beyond the practical consequences of their impairment, perceptions of and reactions to it are more central to their existence, often having determined the paths taken in their lives. In other words, the distinction between disability and old age is both experiential and culturally induced. It matters little that older people's physical or mental impairments may be similar. What matters is how long disability has been part of a person's life, and the effect that this has had on their life style. Thus, people with impairments who grow old, and older people who have acquired impairments, generally perceive themselves as being very different from one another.

The acknowledgement of life experience and identity, as distinct from simply impaired function, is implicit in 'advantageous' social systems where age is a determining factor. For example, the concept of Developmental Disability in the United States entitles people to certain federal supports as long as their impairment was incurred before the age of 21 (supports for impairment and disability acquired thereafter depend on the individual's insurance coverage). In France, a major debate has been going on for more than ten years concerning the right of people with disabilities to have continued access to disability supports after the age of 60, rather than shifting into supports for older people (this age ceiling was inscribed in the social legislation twenty-five years ago, when few expected people with disabilities to live that long).

Differential identity can also be observed in everyday practice. Despite similar needs on a functional level, people with life-long and late-life impairments are considered incompatible. Employees in a day centre designed specifically for older people with intellectual disabilities and/or challenging behaviour may find the idea of also serving elderly people whose minds are impaired, inconceivable. A recreational group for retired people may respond to inquiries saying that it is not the place for people with disabilities (despite the fact that a great many of its members have sensory or mobility impairments). Blind spots such as these reinforce the assumption that shared services cannot work, that the needs of people with and without the disability label are so different that they cannot share the same space, much less get along together. 'Need' is confused with 'self-image'.

Yet, when older people, with and without disability experiences, have the opportunity to get beyond the labels (whether these are collectively- or self-imposed), many realise that they do not necessarily have to remain separate, like oil and vinegar. This has been shown in French studies concerning the placement of older people with mental disabilities in retirement homes for the elderly. Observers of ten settings, in which an average of ten per cent of the 596 residents had a life-long intellectual and/or psychological impairment, noticed that the labels with which people had arrived were dropped at the door of the retirement home: what counted was their ability to function within that context and to behave in a socially acceptable manner. This is not to say that joint placement is an ideal. It merely demonstrates that compatibility and conviviality are not inconceivable (Breitenbach 1997).

Pressures and positive effects

The niche occupied by the rather particular theme of intellectual disability and old age has changed. Several years ago it was a special sector, within the already special domain of intellectual disability: a handful of people among the 60 million people with intellectual disabilities around the world. Gradually, this handful of people has been displaced into the larger field of gerontology, where their needs are now competing for attention with the 580 million people who are 60 or older (a figure which is expected to increase by some 75 per cent in the next twenty years). The demography of an ageing world brings economic pressures, and a shift towards more functional models. Given that there is only so much money to go around, and that the needs are so great, why should states invest so heavily in people with life-long disabilities, and so little in the many older people with age-related impairments? How will society cope with this steadily growing population? This is particularly worrisome in the case of those, more numerous each day, who develop Alzheimer-type dementia (a disease that affects 20 per cent of people aged 80 or more and has long-term effects, not only on the individual but also on the support systems).

As a result of greater life expectancy for persons with intellectual disabilities, new decisions will have to be made: if they have depended all their lives on family caregivers, who will care for them when those caregivers are gone? Who will help them to cope with personal loss and bereavement, and how will this be done? Where and how will they be housed? In the long run, what types and degree of care/support will be necessary for their well being? Who will supervise their financial affairs (this last being a totally new issue, since until recently few people with intellectual disabilities had any personal property to watch over).

Despite the anxiety caused by these new developments, some things are changing for the better. Until recently, researchers and policy-makers tended to settle affairs concerning people with intellectual disabilities in dialogue with parents and professionals. Elderly people, especially those whose mental faculties are considered to be impaired, have often found themselves similarly disempowered. The person at the centre of concern was most often the passive 'object' of others' bene-volence. Developments in the self-advocacy and consumerist move-ments have begun to challenge this.

Coincident with the self-advocacy movement (if indeed it is a gratui-tous coincidence?), the new longevity of people with intellectual disabil-ities is producing a shift in the decision-making triangle. The extra years of experience and training that are now possible have helped people with intellectual disability to gain maturity. Self-advocacy is encouraging them to speak for themselves. Increasingly, all the parties are in a position to give their opinion on life opportunities and ageing issues.

Old age for people with intellectual disabilities offers a golden oppor-tunity to change social images. They are increasingly seen as adults with potential, persons with time before them to learn the skills they need, years enough to grow grey hair and to take on the image of maturity that goes with silvered temples.

REFERENCES

Breitenbach, N. (1997) 'Placement in ordinary retirement homes of older people with mental handicaps: issues and realities', unpublished paper.

Breitenbach, N. (1999) *Une Saison de Plus: Handicap Mental et Vieillissements*, Desclée de Brouwer, Paris, France.

Hogg, J., Moss, S. and Cooke, D. (1988) *Ageing and Mental Handicap*, Croom Helm, London.

Janicki, M. and Seltzer, M. (eds.) (1991) *Ageing and Developmental Disabilities: Challenges For the 1990s*, American Association on Mental Retardation, Washington DC, USA.

Janicki, M. and Breitenbach, N. (2000) *Ageing and Intellectual Disabilities – Improving Longevity and Promoting Healthy Ageing*, IASSID & Inclusion International, for the World Health Organisation, Geneva, Switzerland.

Stiker, H.-J. (1999) 'Using historical anthropology to *think* disability', in B. Holzer, A. Vreede and G. Weigt (eds.), *Disability In Different Cultures: Reflections of Local Concepts*, Transcript Verlag, Bielefeld, Germany.

Turnbull, R. and Turnbull, A. (1999) 'Family support: retrospective and prospective', in M. Wehmeyer and J. Patton (eds.), *Mental Retardation in the Year 2000 and Beyond*, ProEd, Austin, TX, USA.

Walker, A., Walker, C. and Ryan, T. (1996) 'Older people with learning difficulties leaving institutional care – a case of double jeopardy', *Ageing & Society*, 16: 1–26.

Walker, A. and Walker, C. (1998) 'Normalisation and "normal" ageing: the social construction of dependency among older people with learning difficulties', *Disability & Society*, 13(1): 125–42.

World Health Organisation (1999) *Ageing: Exploding the Myths*, WHO Ageing and Health Programme, Geneva, Switzerland.

20   Epilogue

Mark Priestley

Life can be a complex, often messy, business and people's life experiences do not fit neatly into academic disciplines or theoretical models. The life experiences represented in this book are diverse, yet disability is not simply about diversity. It is also about commonality – not a commonality of embodied experiences but a commonality of purpose, in the struggle for a more inclusive society. In these final remarks, I will draw on a number of themes arising from the preceding chapters. In particular, I will argue that a life course approach can be useful in revealing more clearly the relationship between lived experience and the broader socio-economic context, and that it enriches the development of disability studies. In so doing, I also hope to raise a number of questions.

Reviewing the book as a whole, I am struck both by its strengths and its weaknesses. Clearly, it would not have been possible to offer a comprehensive or 'representative' account in a single volume such as this. However, the chapters do present a very wide range of life course experiences and issues, in different countries, across different generations, and from different perspectives – personal, political and theoretical. The stories, and the issues they raise, blur the boundaries of public and private, of the personal and the political. They raise questions not only about disability, age and generation, but also about class and caste, gender, race and ethnicity.

There will, of course, be under-represented voices in every collection and this book is no exception. Offering a cross-national perspective on disability was an important objective for me. I wanted to provide a flavour of the various ways in which people encountered disabling barriers in different societies. As Rachel Hurst (1999: 25) points out:

There is no country in the world where disabled people's rights are not violated. The discrimination, oppression, violence and abuse faced by disabled people does not respect national boundaries, national wealth or national poverty.

In this context, I was pleased to be able to include contributions from such a wide range of cultural contexts. There are perspectives from thirteen different countries, across five continents (although there is no specific contribution from South or Central America). The chapters include issues relevant to people with a wide range of impairments, including people with physical, sensory and cognitive impairments (although I am conscious that there is no chapter written directly by anyone claiming the label of learning difficulties). There are voices representing the experiences of childhood, adulthood and old age (although there is no chapter written directly by children). Taken as a whole, and in the context of other cross-cultural works (e.g. Ingstad and Whyte 1995; Doe 1998; Stone 1999; Traustadóttir and Johnson 2000) these voices provide some important insights into the nature and processes of disablement in a changing world.

Trajectories, turning points and resources

It is common to conceive of lives over time as a linear progression that has both purpose and direction – a course to be steered, a pathway to be travelled, a story to be told. Linear models raise questions about over-simplification, and the potential for multiple narratives, but they can be useful in focusing our attention on trajectories and outcomes. Trajectories suggest both direction and velocity and these are useful analogies. There are many examples in this book of the kinds of forces that change the direction of people's lives, and those that impede or accelerate the pace of change. There is still much work to be done in this area: mapping the life course pathways that disabled people follow and the narratives that they use to chart their life experience. As Devva Kasnitz points out (in chapter six) such maps can be empowering, not only for the cartographer but also for those who travel after them.

As noted at the outset, the patterns of our lives are influenced by many factors (ranging from the global socio-economic context to unique aspects of personal biography). The chapters in this book illustrate an array of biographical influences: impairment, personality, family, advocacy, meetings with other disabled people, discovering the social model, experiences of discrimination, encounters with disabling barriers, and social, political and technological developments in a changing world. Taken as a collection, the chapters illustrate the significance of time and place in shaping people's lives. In this sense, the experience of disability reveals itself as situated within networks of personal relationships and social relations of power.

The recognition that disability is situated within, and contingent upon, social factors lends weight to a social model analysis, demonstrating how the principal factors shaping disabling experiences reside not within the body but within the wider society. However, this is not to deny that disability also involves embodied experiences and expressions of agency – far from it. The chapters in this book illustrate clearly how people's life narratives may sometimes be dominated by bodily discourse, and how this can become disabling. They illustrate how people within disabling societies have acted as agents of considerable social change, and suggest the social conditions that may have facilitated that process.

Thinking about life course trajectories also helps us to think about the different kinds of resources, or capital, that people draw upon during their lives. Thus, in chapter five, Emma Stone argues that the concepts of 'personhood' and 'life capital' are useful in explaining the life chances of disabled people in different cultural contexts. In chapter four, Gregor Wolbring pursues a similar theme, examining the value attributed to disabled lives (and by implication the resources that may or may not be invested in their survival). In order to make sense of the perceived worth of people's lives, and the disabling or enabling forces that influence their life course pathways, it is useful to think carefully about different kinds of capital.

Bourdieu (1979) distinguishes three forms of capital, forming the basis for social status and stratification: economic capital (income-producing wealth), social capital (the networks of contact that reflect a person's place in the social order); and cultural capital (the ways in which manners and styles of behaviour, dress and talk also accord social status). In many ways both disability and generation are about differential access to just such resources. Differential access to capital, and differential social investment in people's lives, raises many useful questions about the way that disabling societies work.

In a global context, it is clear that disabled people are considerably marginalised from access to economic capital and the benefits of its exploitation. Indeed, as Anita Ghai demonstrates, in chapter three, access even to a subsistence level income is by no means guaranteed for disabled people in much of the world. In chapter sixteen, Majid Turmusani points out that access to a source of income (predominantly through paid employment) is a priority issue for disabled people, especially in societies without established systems for the provision of cash welfare benefits to those out of work. As a consequence, disabled people are more likely to be amongst the poorest of the poor throughout the world. When we add to this the recognition that children and, in many societies, older people are similarly disadvantaged we begin to see the economic interrelationship between disability and generational location.

Access to social capital is also important. Indeed, the World Bank is currently investing considerable resources in its measurement (on the assumption that social capital is a prerequisite for economic prosperity). Social capital provides both the connections that bind us together and the gulfs that divide us – status is so often a consequence of what and more importantly, who we know. The sources of social capital include families, communities, commercial firms, civil society, the public sector, ethnicity and gender (each contributing resources of connectivity and social integration). Differential access to social networks of information and support can be a critical factor in shaping people's life course pathways. In light of the chapters in this book, we might ask some important questions. How does disabled people's access to sources of social capital affect life chances and life course pathways? How does this access vary across different generations and generational cohorts? How far is the disabled people's movement creating new sources of social capital, on which disabled people are able to draw, thereby increasing life choices and chances?

Finally, we might also speculate about the role of cultural capital in people's lives. This is not simply about life 'style' or 'manners'. It is about the cultural construction of age and impairment (we might for example draw on Bourdieu's 1977 notion of 'habitus' to problematise the notion of 'age appropriateness'). In this sense, the aesthetics of impairment and generation carry with them considerable signifiers of social status, predominantly negative social status (Thompson 1996, Turner and Stanley 1989). Such signifiers are of course culturally and historically situated. However, in a globalising world, cultural messages are more easily interpreted across national boundaries. We need to ask how the development of the international disabled people's movement is challenging negative representations of disabled people, and how far the promotion of a new, more empowering, aesthetic of disability culture offers disabled people access to new forms of cultural capital.

The individual and society

As is common in social inquiry, disability studies continues to grapple with the relationship between individual lived experience and macro-social analysis, between agency and structure, between embodied corporeality and objective social positioning, between difference and commonality. This book is no exception, and such debates are prominent both within and between the individual chapters. It is an interesting exercise to interrogate each of the chapters with this balancing act in mind, and to ask why certain themes are more or less prominent at different times. As Hubbard (2000: para 11.4) notes, 'Life histories have the potential to reveal how people interpret and understand social structures and encourages an exploration of how social structures are perceived by individuals at key turning point moments in their lives'. My own reading of the chapters suggests to me that a life course approach, and narrative life history methods, can indeed tell us a great deal about the way in which agency and structure interact.

The development of a social model of disability has emphasised both structure and agency. It has been characterised by a focused attention on the identification and removal of disabling barriers, and on the creation of enabling environments. In this sense it deals in fairly equal measure with the analysis of structures and environmental factors, on the one hand, and the agency of disabled people and their allies in changing those structures, on the other. In this sense, disability studies has mirrored the preoccupation of much social science with debating the opportunities and constraints on human agency that are created by social structure and positioning. Within this debate, recent postmodern sociology has generated a tendency to pit fluid, contextual notions of individual lived experiences against fixed and rigid notions of social structure. Yet the chapters in this book illustrate two counter-tendencies to this construction.

First, disabled people's life choices and life chances can be very fixed and limited, by comparison with non-disabled people, within particular social conditions. As Anita Ghai (chapter three) and Kelley Johnson *et al.* (chapter seventeen) show, gender, generation and poverty play a significant part here. Disabled people have been, in general terms, much less free to reinvent themselves or to manage their own lives. Second, societies can and do change. Developments in technology, production and political economy impact dramatically upon different generational cohorts. As Ruth Morgan (chapter eight), Kaido Kikkas (chapter ten) and Elena Iarskia-Smirnova (chapter nine) illustrate, population movements, war, political upheaval, cultural development and so on can be critical factors in shaping disabled people's life experiences and life course pathways.

Individual and collective agency have been recurrent themes in this book. The individual life stories illustrate the significance that people often attribute to personality and will power in reclaiming control over their lives. The role of parents and significant others in struggling for change at the micro level is also prominent. Alongside this, there is the contribution of disabled people's collective agency, in communities and in the wider disability movement. The contradictions of structural change in societies often manifest themselves in competing cultural discourses, representations and claims (as Sarah Irwin points out, in chapter two). Thus, the development of the international disabled people's movement (emphasised in chapter six by Devva Kasnitz) shows how the individual and collective agency of disabled people can bring about real change in societies, and in individual people's lives.

Within the social context, our bodies also change over the course of our lives. The physical and functional concomitants of growth, maturation and ageing are always with us. Indeed, the corporeality of 'impairment' is something of a human universal (Zola 1989). Consequently, the individual-society debate in disability studies is most evident in discussions about the importance that should be attributed to experiences of impairment (*see* Thomas 2000). As I hope this book shows, this may be a false debate. However, the way in which we, and others, interpret these changes is one of the key ways in which we mark the passage of generational transition. In the interaction of body and society, our identities and sense of self also change, in ways that are highly contextual and situated, yet also enduring (as Devorah Kalekin-Fishman illustrates in chapter twelve).

It is important to remember that individual life experiences are just that (whether they be experiences of embodiment or of disabling barriers). Their significance for social science and political action is in providing an analytical lens, through which we can view broader social structures and envisage strategies for change. Using a life course approach forces us to go beyond the snapshots of isolated experiences and to consider these across whole lifetimes and between generational cohorts, focusing our attention on the factors that can make a difference.

A life course approach?

The idea of looking at disability and generation is not in itself new. For example, Hockey and James (1993) examine the relationship between dependency and the life course, focusing on the common experiences of young children and older people, making reference to the emerging disability literature. Arber and Evandrou (1993) also address some of these themes in relation to older people, although they do not make an explicit link with disability issues, or with younger people.

As I hope this book shows, using a life course approach offers a unique way to make links between the individual lived experience of disability and the macro-social context in which disabled lives are played out. The use of life story narratives helps us to understand how lives are embedded within societies, and influenced by periods of social change. Using narrative, oral histories and autobiography can help to reveal 'lost' stories of disability, redressing the historical absence of marginalised groups, including people with the label of learning difficulties, and women in particular (as Kelley Johnson *et al.* demonstrate in chapter seventeen). In appropriate contexts, people may also be able to empower themselves, and others, through the telling of life stories in their own voices.

A life course approach highlights the relationship between discrimination on the basis of both perceived impairment and discrimination on the basis of perceived generational location. In this way, disability and generation have been mutually constructed as parallel categories in relation to citizenship, autonomy and personhood. They have been widely employed by both policy makers and cultural communities as parallel categories in the definition of competence and personhood. The cultural standards by which we judge social status and human capital in the modern world, are drawn from idealised notions of an 'independent adulthood'. By comparison, the domains of childhood, old age and disability are easily devalued (Priestley 2000).

Many more young disabled people are surviving into adulthood and old age, yet we know relatively little about their experiences of ageing. At the same time, more and more older people are living with impairments acquired later in life. Consequently, we need to consider the intersecting life course pathways of disabled people who 'become older' and older people who 'become disabled'. Recent international debates around disability and old age provide excellent opportunities to challenge the imagery of both groups as dependent. We need to ask what ageing means to disabled adults and what disability means to older people. How do people's choices and rights change as they make transitions between these groups?

Sociology itself has tended to reify generational status into certain ideal types – particularly in the notions of 'childhood' and 'old age'. Implicitly, within modern Western societies at least, such categories are premised upon a very particular construction of 'adulthood', which occupies the centre ground, or apex, of life course progression. The social construction of adulthood, with its gendered connotations of autonomy and independence, lies at the heart of our understanding of life course progression. The cultural markers of adult status are well known (e.g. having a home of one's own, exercising financial autonomy, forming relationships of choice, sustaining successful paid work and parenthood).

The construction of an idealised adulthood, and the policing of its boundaries, is achieved in large part through the development of social policies. Increasingly, this policy making process is taking place between states and across national borders (for example, within supra-national bodies like the European Union or the United Nations). The wide-spread language of generational rights in the international policy arena seems reassuring. However, the rhetoric masks some important under-lying debates about the nature of competency and interdependence at all stages of the life course. In this way, normative concepts of age appropriateness (or generational location) have been employed as the yardstick by which to measure disabled people's human rights.

The challenge of the disabled people's movement is to reclaim and redefine the concept of an ordinary life, and of normality in life course progression. As Ratzka (1997) argues:

Independent Living means that we demand the same choices and control in our every-day lives that our non-disabled brothers and sisters, neighbors and friends take for granted. We want to grow up in our families, go to the neighborhood school, use the same bus as our neighbors, work in jobs that are in line with our education and abilities, start families of our own. Just as everybody else, we need to be in charge of our lives, think and speak for ourselves. To this end we need to support and learn from each other, organise ourselves and work for political changes that lead to legal protection of our human and civil rights.

In this context disability studies has a significant contribution to make in problematising the 'normal' life course, and in revealing the social framework that defines its boundaries. Using a life course approach can help to raise the voices of those often excluded from these debates (particularly children and older people). As I hope this book shows, the vision of an enabling society must also be a society for all ages.

REFERENCES

Arber, S. and Evandrou, M. (eds.) (1993) *Ageing, Independence and the Life Course*, Jessica Kingsley, London.

Bourdieu, P. (1977) *Outline of Theory of Practice*, Cambridge University Press.

Bourdieu, P. (1979) *La Distinction: critique sociale du jugement*, Minuit, Paris, France.

Doe, T. (1998) *Cultural Variations of Independent Living: An International Review*, World Institute on Disability, Oakland, CA, USA (unpublished).

Hockey, J. and James, A. (1993) *Growing Up and Growing Older: Ageing and Dependency In The Life Course*, Sage, London.

Hubbard, G. (2000) 'The usefulness of indepth life history inyouth transitions', *Sociological Research Online*, 4(4): *http://www.socresonline.org.uk/4/4/hubbard.html*

Hurst, R. (1999) 'Disabled people's organisations and development: strategies for change', in E. Stone (ed.) *Disability and Development: Learning From Action and Research In The Majority World*, The Disability Press, Leeds.

Ingstad, B., and Whyte, S. (eds.) (1995) *Disability and Culture*, University of California Press, Berkeley CA, USA.

Priestley, M. (2000) 'Adults only: disability, social policy and the life course', *Journal of Social Policy*, 29(3): 421–39.

Ratzka, A. (1997) *Independent Living and Our Organisations*, paper presented to the 'Our Common World' conference, organised by Disability Rights Advocates Hungary, Siofok, May 9–11 1997.

Stone, E. (ed.) (1999) *Disability and Development: Learning From Action and Research on Disability in The Majority World*, Disability Press, Leeds.

Thomas, C. (2000) *Female Forms: Experiencing and Understanding Disability*, Open University Press, Milton Keynes.

Thompson, R. (ed.) (1996) *Freakery: Cultural Spectacles of the Extraordinary Body*, New York University Press, USA.

Traustadóttir, R. and Johnson, K. (eds.) (2000) *Women with Intellectual Disabilities: Finding a Place in the World*, Jessica Kingsley, London.

Turner, B. and Stanley, B. (1989) 'Ageing, status politics and sociological theory', *British Journal of Sociology*, 40(4): 588–606.

Zola, I. (1989) 'Towards a necessary universalizing of disability policy', *Millbank Memorial Quarterly*, 67(2): 401–28.

Index

abortion: for impairment 39–40, 41; for intellectually disabled 213, 214; sex selection vs. disability 40–6
acceptance of disability 81, 85–6
adulthood 246–7; employment and 192, 196–200; transitions to 192–3; *see also* youth transitions
African Decade of Disabled People 7
ageing 35, 219–23, 236–7, 246; age-related impairment 220, 224, 234, 235–6; attitudes to 223–8; of intellectually disabled 233–4, 237–8; normal/abnormal 145
agency 136–8, 170–1, 244–5
albinism 79–83, 97–9
Ando, T. 220–1
anti-discrimination legislation 5, 200
Association of Blind Asians 87
Australia: childbearing for intellectually disabled women 210–15; traumatic brain injury 181–2

Barnes, C. 22, 126, 128
Bauman, Z. 147
beliefs about disablement 233; in India 31; in South Africa 97, 98, 157–8; in USSR 106, 113–14
bioethics, exclusion of disabled people from debate 44–5
biography 102
blind women, in Uganda 58
body/mind: as capital 58–60, 61; and difference 54–5, 61; and personhood 55–8, 61
Borneo, personhood and impairment 57–8
brain injury, in young adulthood 179–89
Brazil, independent living 10

capital/ism 20–1, 242, 243; state-social constructions 58–9, 61
caring 172
Centre for Independent Living 11
cerebral palsy 55

Chambers, R. 52
charity approach 158, 165
Charmaz, K. 227
Child-to-Child 161
childhood 172–4, 175; disability as 27, 173–4, 232; *see also* disabled children
children's rights 53, 159–61, 174, 175
China, body/mind as capital 59–60
choices for women 207–9
citizenship 19, 174, 175
claiming *see* social claiming
class 138, 141
cognitive impairment 179, 181
collective agency 244–5
community 36; deaf people and 126–7, 128; integration into 182, 183, 186, 187, 188
Community Based Rehabilitation 35–6, 159, 164
Council of Europe, Convention on Human Rights and Biomedicine 40
Craib, I. 133
cultural capital 243
cultural differences in production of disability 21, 23, 53–60

Danish Council of Organisations of Disabled People 5
Deaf Federation of South Africa 96
Deaf Transitions 125–6, 127, 128, 132
deaf people 125–6; education for 94, 95; identity of 130–1; in Soweto 93–6
dependence 27, 36, 171–3, 198, 202; claiming and 23; of elderly disabled 35; and independence 19, 20, 21–2, 23
deprivation trap 52–3
disability; research on 89–90; talking about 86–7
disability movement 22–3
disabled children: education 103, 106, 115, 116–17, 121; exclusion of 30–1; in India 30–3; in South Africa 151–65; sport and identity for 109–10

Disabled Children's Action Group (South Africa) 152, 161
disabled people: attitudes to ageing 223–8; elderly and 234–7, 146; in India 30–5; in Japan 219–28; *see also* young disabled people
Disabled People South Africa 7, 96
Disabled People's International 6,9
disabling barriers 4, 5, 51, 56, 61, 128, 157
discourses of human services 186–8
discrimination 41–2, 97; in employment 99; institutional 41–2, 56

economic capital 30, 242
economic needs 193–4, 202
economic policies 160–1
education 87, 141–2; access to 9, 32, 156; in Estonia 116–17, 121; in India 32–3, 81–3; mainstream 98–9; in South Africa 156, 157–8, 164; in USSR 103, 106, 115, 116–17
elderly, and disabled people, perceptions of 234–7, 246
employment 8–9, 18–19, 121–2, 192; access to 193, 196–200, 202; exclusion from 19, 33; in India 33; for young disabled 168
empowerment 90, 186
equality rights movement 46
Estonia: disabled people in since independence 120–2; education in 115–17; Sterilisation Law 1936 116
Estonian Union of Disabled People's Organisations 120
ethnicity 138–9, 141
eugenics 38, 39–49, 206
European Economic Community, disability issues 5–6
European Network for Independent Living 11
euthanasia 44, 47
event history analysis 68–9, 70–4
exclusion 30–1, 44, 155; attitudes leading to 156–8; from work 192–3, 195–6, 202

family 79–80, 171, 225–6; of deaf people 127–8; disabled children and 31–2, 161
fate 36
financial dependence/independence 198, 202
Fish, J. 168–9
Fletcher, J. 41
France: disability supports for elderly 236–7; selective abortion 39–40
friendship, for young adults with brain injury 179, 180, 181

friendship interventions 182–8

gender 139; and disability in India 30, 31, 34
generation 16–17, 245–7
genetic disease: prenatal screening 38–9, 47; selective abortion 41, 43
globalisation 26
God 91–2
Greenberg, Aaron 42

Harre, R. 147
health services, access to 156
hearing impairment *see* deaf people
Hershey, L. 45
higher education 118, 198–9
Hinduism 27
Hockey, J. 18, 245
homosexuality 42–3
Honneth, A. 22
human rights movement 6; eugenics and 46–7

Iceland, childbearing for intellectually disabled women 209–10, 211–15
identity 80, 105, 131, 146–7, 193; life stories and 89, 90; negative 27–8, 33; role of resistance 104; work and 192, 196
Ife, J. 186–7
impairment 51, 52; personhood and 56, 57–8; poverty and 52–3, 61
impairment effects 129, 130, 131
independence 19, 20, 21–2, 168, 198, 199; practical 23, 172
independent living 10–11, 50
India 26, 79–85; colour prejudice 80–1; disabled children 30–5; elderly disabled 35; meaning of disability 27–8, 35; poverty and disability 28–30
individual, and society 143–5, 147
individualisation 133, 169, 170
inequality, life course as structure of 18–20
information, availability of 164–5
Integrated Child Development Scheme 30–1
integration 32, 76, 116–17
intellectual disabilities, women with 206, 207–9; decision-making on childbearing 213–15; exclusion from mothering 206, 207, 211–12
inter-agency collaboration 169
interests 21, 22, 24
International Covenant on Economic, Social and Culture Rights 193
International Day of Disabled Persons 5

International Labour Organization 8–9, 196
International Network on Bioethics and Disability 45
international policy agenda 4–6
International Year of Disabled Persons 4, 5
Israel: abnormality in 143; Holocaust survivors 143, 144; wounded soldiers 143–4

James, A. 18, 245
James, W. 147
Japan, ageing of disabled people 219–28
Jones, G. 171–2
Jordan 194; access to employment 197–200; higher education 198–9; Law for the Welfare of Disabled People 200; supported employment schemes 201–2

karate 199
Knutsson, K. E. 174

leadership in disability movements 67–8, 69–76, 94, 96, 97
life chances 11, 244
life course: impairment and 57; personhood and 57–8
life course approach 15, 16–18, 68–9, 70, 245–7; researching 123–5, 131–2, 133
life expectancy 11, 219, 220, 227, 231
life stories 89–90, 244

McGinty, J. 168–9
Mairs, N. 106, 110
majority world: access to employment 195–6, 200–2, 242; disability and survival 4, 50–62; needs of disabled people 193, 194, 199, 202
Malinga, J. 50
Mandela, Nelson 152
marginalisation 18–19, 31, 164, 175
marriage 34–5
materialist accounts of disability 20–1
Mayer, K. 68
Mead, G. H. 147
medical model of disability 43–4, 47, 186, 201
mobilisation 108, 109
mobility 199
Montero, F. 8
moral feelings 22
motherhood 206, 207, 209; exclusion from 211–13

needs of disabled people 193, 194, 199, 202

Nepal, cerebral palsy in 55
Nicaragua 8
Nkeli, J. 93
normality/abnormality 136, 138, 141, 143, 144–5, 146

Oliver, M. 22, 123

Pan-African Federation of the Disabled 7
participation in decision-making 144–5, 200
Peattie, 22
peer contact 71, 76, 77; disabled children 161, 173
personal relationships 197–8
personhood 55–8
Persons with Disabilities Act 1995 (India) 28
phenomenology 221–2
polio 108–9, 140, 145
political changes, and life events 91, 93, 95–6, 98
political involvement 199–200, 203
positioning theory 147
poverty 9–10, 194; link with disability 28–30, 52–3, 61, 155, 194–6; in South Africa 153–5
prenatal screening 38–9, 41, 42, 43, 45–6, 47
Priestley, M. 19
public life, visibility of disabled people 75, 76
punishment, impairment as 27, 157

quotas, 33, 200

rehabilitation and disability services 186–8
Rein, 22
religious practice 82–3, 118–19, 139
resistance 104, 110
resources, access to 154–6
Rich, A. 206, 207
rights movements 36, 46, 74, 169; *see also* children's rights
Russia, sporting activities for disabled children 108, 109–10

self, agency and 136–8
self-advocacy 238
self-determination 126
self-employment 201
Self-Help Associations of Paraplegics in Soweto 7
self-organisation 6–7
sex, protection against selective abortion 40–4

sexuality 34, 106, 182, 197–8
sheltered employment 201
sight 81, 83, 85–7
sign language 130
social arrangements, lifecourse perspective
    17, 18, 19
social change 17, 50, 53, 61
social claiming 15–16, 20–4
social model of disability 5, 43–4, 47, 48,
    51, 186, 244
social networks 180, 181–6
socialisation 128, 129
society 53–4, 105; individual and 147,
    243–5
Solihull Declaration 45
South Africa 7; Constitution 153, 159–60;
    disability policies 153–4; disabled
    children 151–65; identity and disability
    90–9; Integrated National Disability
    Strategy 154, 159
South African National Council of the
    Deaf 95, 96
special schools 98, 164; in Estonia 115–16;
    in USSR 114, 116
spinal cord injury 220, 221, 222–8
state 91; attitudes to disability 99
sterilisation 116, 208, 209, 212
Stone, D. 21
story-telling 125
structure/structuralism 9, 18, 170, 244
survival, disability and 51–60, 61

technology 38–48, 110
Thomas, C. 129
time, sense of 223, 227–8
Toombs, S. K. 222
transitional literature 168–70
traumatic brain injury 179–89
Tuma, N. 68
Turner, B. 19

Uganda 58

unemployed, marginalisation of 18–19
unemployment *see* employment
UNESCO World Conference on Sciences
    44
United Nations 4–5, 9; Convention on the
    Rights of the Child 153–4, 158, 160,
    175; Copenhagen Declaration on Social
    Development 10; Declaration on the
    Rights of Disabled Persons 4; *Rules on the
    Equalisation of Opportunities for Disabled
    Persons* 5, 120
USSR: attitude to disabled people 113–14;
    education for disabled children 106, 114,
    115–16; facilities for disabled children
    103–6, 108, 109, 115

van Langenhove, L. 147
visual impairment 81, 83, 85–7
voluntary sector 28
vulnerability 156

Walker, A. 235
Walker, C. 235
war, effect on disabled peopled 7–8
Warnock Report 167, 168
Watson, James 42
Weiner, S. 127–8
welfare 20, 21–2, 202
Wendell, S. 23
Wertz, D. 41
Williamson, B. 40
women 84, 85, 139; poverty of in India
    29–30; and prenatal screening 41, 45–6
work/welfare 20, 21–2; *see also*
    employment
World Health Organization, Draft
    Guidelines for Bioethics 40
World Institute on Disability 67

young disabled people 33, 34, 104–5;
    transition to adulthood 167–76
youth transitions 16, 170–4, 175